Sociological Insight

Classic Readings and Contemporary Issues

Edited by
Jerry Kloby
Laszlo Marcus
County College of Morris

Kendall Hunt
publishing company

Cover image © Shutterstock, Inc.

www.kendallhunt.com
Send all inquiries to:
4050 Westmark Drive
Dubuque, IA 52004-1840

Printed in the United States of America
10 9 8 7 6 5 4 3 2

Contents

Part 1

Introduction:
The Sociological Vision

Article 1

Sociology and Democracy

Joel M. Charon

> *... The theme of democracy stands out. One might, in truth, argue that the study*
> *of sociology is the study of issues relevant to understanding democratic society.*

In the final analysis, it may be true that ignorance is bliss. It may be true that people should be left alone with the myths they happen to pick up in interaction with one another. It may be true that a liberal arts education that does not have immediate practical value is worthless.

Sociology and a Liberal Arts Education

I do not believe any of these ideas, but I wonder about them a lot. One can more easily make a case for mathematics, foreign languages, writing, speech, psychology, and economics on the level of practical use. "The student needs to know these if he or she is to get along in life," the argument goes. It is far more difficult to make a case for sociology on the basis of practical use-unless, of course, by *practical use* one means *thinking about and understanding the world*. If a college education is ultimately an attempt to encourage people to wonder, investigate, and carefully examine their lives, then sociology is one of the most important disciplines.

Note its purpose: To get students to examine an aspect of life carefully and systematically that most people only casually and occasionally think about. It is to get people to understand what culture is and to recognize that what they believe is largely a result of their culture. It is to get them to see that they are born into a society that has a long history, that they are ranked and given roles in that society, and that ultimately they are told who they are, what to think, and how to act. It is to get them to see that the institutions they follow and normally accept are not the only ways in which society can function-that there are always alternatives. It is to get them to realize that those whom they regard as sick, evil, or criminal are often simply different. It is to get them to see that those they hate are often a product of social circumstances that should be understood more carefully and objectively.

In short, the purpose of sociology is to get people to examine objectively their lives and their society. This process is uncomfortable and sometimes unpleasant. I keep asking myself, as I teach the insights of sociology, "Why not just leave those students alone?" And, quite frankly, I do not usually know how to, answer this question. We are socialized into society. Shouldn't we simply accept that which we are socialized to believe? Isn't it better for society if people believe myth? Isn't it better for people's happiness to let them be?

I usually come back to what many people profess to be one primary purpose of a university education: "liberal arts." To me, the liberal arts should be "liberating." A university education should be liberating: It should help the individual escape the bonds of his or her imprisonment by bringing an understanding of that prison. We should read literature, understand art, and study biology and sociology in order to break through what those who defend society want us to know to reach a plane from which we can see reality in a more careful and unbiased way. In the end, sociology probably has the greatest potential for liberation in the academic world: At its best, it causes individuals to confront their ideas, actions, and being. We are never the same once we bring sociology into our lives. Life is scrutinized. Truth becomes far more tentative.

Sociology and Democracy

The Meaning of Democracy

Liberation, as you probably realize, has something to do with democracy. Although democracy is clearly an ideal that Americans claim for themselves, it is not usually clearly defined or deeply explored.

Sociology, however, explores democracy, and it asks rarely examined questions about the possibility for democracy in this-or any-society. To many people, democracy simply means "majority rule," and we too often superficially claim that if people go to a voting booth, then democracy has been established and the majority does, in fact, rule. Democracy, however, is far more than majority rule, and majority rule is far more than the existence of voting booths.

Democracy is very difficult to achieve. No society can become perfectly democratic; few societies really make much progress in that direction. Alexis de Tocqueville, a great French social scientist who wrote *Democracy in America (1840)* after traveling throughout much of the United States in *1831*, believed that here was a thriving democracy, one with great future potential. Tocqueville pointed out many of our shortcomings-most important, the existence of slavery-but he believed that we probably had a more democratic future than any other society in the world. What Tocqueville did was examine the nature of our society-our structure, culture, and institutions-and then show what qualities of our society encouraged the development of democracy. For example, he identified our willingness to join voluntary associations that would impact government, strong local ties, and the little need we had for a central government. Although much has changed since Tocqueville wrote, his lasting importance was to remind us that democracy is a very difficult social state to achieve, that certain social conditions make it possible and certain patterns support its continued existence. It is also, he wrote, very easy to lose.

Democracy is difficult to define. When I try, I usually end up listing four qualities. These describe a whole society, not just the government in that society. Although everyone will not agree that these are the basic qualities of a democracy, I think they offer a good place to begin:

1. *A democratic society is one in which the individual is free in both thinking and action.* People are in control of their own lives. To the extent that a society encourages freedom, we can call it a democratic society.

2. *A democratic society is one in which the government is effectively limited.* Those who control government do not do what they choose to do. Voting, law, organizations of people, and constitutions effectively limit their power. To the extent that government is effectively limited, we call it a democratic society.

3. *A democratic society is one in which human differences are respected and protected.* There is a general agreement that no matter what the majority favors, certain rights are reserved for the individual and for minorities who are different from the majority. Diversity is respected and even encouraged. To the extent that diversity and individuality is respected and protected, we call it a democratic society.

4. *A democratic society is one in which all people have an equal opportunity to live a decent life.* That is, privilege is not inherited, people have equality before the law, in educational opportunity, in opportunity for material success, and in whatever is deemed to be important in society. To the extent that real equality of opportunity exists, we call it a democratic society.

These four qualities that make up the definition of democracy described here must be tentative descriptions, and people should debate their relative significance. Some will regard other qualities to be more important, and some will regard only one or two of these qualities as necessary. I am only trying here to list four qualities that make sense to me and that guide my own estimate of whether the United States and other societies are democratic.

If these qualities do capture what democracy means, however, it should be obvious by now that the questions and thinking [that sociologists investigate] ... are relevant to both the understanding of and the working toward a democratic society. Because sociology focuses on social organization, structure, culture, institutions, social order, social class, social power, social conflict, socialization, and social change, sociology *must continually examine issues that are relevant to understanding a democratic society.* And, on top of this, because *sociology critically examines people and their society, it encourages the kind of thinking that is necessary for people living in and working for a democratic society.* One might, in truth, argue that the study of sociology is the study of issues relevant to understanding democratic society.

Sociology: An Approach to Understanding Democratic Society

[Sociology deals] with the nature of the human being and the role of socialization and culture in what we all become. To ask questions about human nature is to ask simultaneous questions about the possibility for democratic society, a society built on qualities that are not often widespread in society: respect for individual differences, compromise, and concern over inequality and lack of freedom. The sociological approach to the human being makes no assumption of fixed qualities, but it has a strong tendency to see human beings as living within social conditions that are responsible for forming many of their most important qualities. A society tends to produce certain types of people and certain social conditions, encouraging one value or another, one set of morals or another, one way of doing things or another. Conformity, control of the human being, tyranny, and pursuit of purely selfish interests can be encouraged; but so, too, can freedom, respect for people's rights, limited government, and equality. *The possibilities for and the limits to a human being who can live democratically are part of what sociology investigates through its questions concerning culture, socialization, and human nature.*

Those who think about society must inevitably consider the central problem of social order: How much freedom and how much individuality can we allow and still maintain society...? Those who favor greater freedom will occasionally wonder: How can there really be meaningful freedom in any society? As long as society exists, how much freedom can we encourage without destroying the underlying order? Are there limits? If so, how can we discover them? What are the costs, if any, of having a democratic society? Those who fear disorder and the collapse of society might ask: How much does the individual owe to society? Such questions are extremely difficult to answer, but they are investigated with the discipline of sociology, and they push the serious student to search for a delicate balance between order and freedom. Too often, people are willing to sell out freedom in the name of order; too often, people claim so much freedom that they do not seem to care about the continuation of society. The sociologist studies these problems and causes the student to reflect again and again on this dilemma inherent in all societies, especially those that claim to be part of the democratic tradition. There can be no freedom without society, Emile Durkheim reminds us, because a basic agreement over rules must precede the exercise of freedom. *But the problem is, How many rules? How much freedom? There is no more basic question for those who favor democracy, and there is no question more central to the discipline of sociology.*

The question of social order also leads us to the questions of what constitutes a nation and what constitutes a society.... These issues may not seem at first to have much relevance to democracy, but they surely do. It is easy for those who profess democracy to favor majority rule. It is much more difficult for any nation to develop institutions that respect the rights of all societies within its borders. A nation is a political state that rules over one-or more-societies. If it is democratic, the nation does not simply rule these societies but responds to their needs and rights, from true political representation to a decent standard of living. If it is democratic, the question the nation faces is *not* "How can we mold that society to be like the dominant society?" but "How can we create an order in which many societies can exist?" If it is democratic, the nation must balance the needs of each society's push for independence with the need for maintaining social order. *The whole meaning of what it is to be a society, as well as the associated problems of order and independence, are central sociological-and democratic-concerns.*

It is the question of control by social forces over the human being that places sociology squarely within the concerns of democracy. Much of sociology questions the possibility for substantial freedom. Democracy teaches that human beings should and can think for themselves. Much of the purpose of sociology, however, is to show us that our thinking is created by our social life; that, although we may claim that our ideas are our own, they really result from our cultures, from our positions in social structure, and from powerful and wealthy people.... Even to claim that "we are a democracy" can simply be part of an ideology, an exaggeration we accept because we are victims of various social forces. Our actions, too, result from a host of social forces that few of us understand or appreciate: institutions, opportunities, class, roles, social controlsto name only some-that quietly work on the individual, pushing him or her in directions not freely chosen.... Sociology seems to make democracy an almost impossible dream, and to some extent, the more sociology one knows, the more difficult **democracy seems.** *Indeed, sociology tends to simply uncover more and more ways in which human beings are shaped and controlled. This, in itself, makes sociology very relevant for understanding the limits of democracy. It causes one to seriously wonder whether human beings can be free in any sense.*

As I said earlier in this chapter, however, sociology *as a part o a liberal education is an attempt to liberate the individual from many of these controls. The first step in liberation is understanding; It is* really impossible to think for oneself or to act according to free choice unless one understands the various ways in which we are controlled. For example, it is only when I begin to see that my ideas of what it means to be a "man" have been formed through-a careful and calculated process throughout society that I can begin to act in the way I choose. Only when I begin to understand how powerful advertising has become in developing my personal tastes as well as my personal values can I begin to step back and direct my own life. And even then, an important sociological question continuously teases the thoughtful person: Can society exist if people are truly liberated? If people question everything, can there still be the unity necessary for order?

The study of social inequality-probably the central concern within all sociology-is, of course, an issue of primary importance to understanding the possibility for a democratic society.... It seems that it is the nature of society to be unequal. Many forces create and perpetuate inequality. Indeed, even in our groups and our formal organizations, great inequalities are the rule. Why? Why does it happen? And what are its implications for democracy? If society is characterized by great inequalities of wealth and power, then how can free thought and free action prevail among the population? If a society-in name, a democracy-has a small elite that dominates the decision making, what difference does going to the polls make? If large numbers of people must expend all their energy to barely survive because of their poverty, where is their freedom, their opportunity to influence the direction of society, their right to improve their lives? If society is characterized by racist and sexist institutions, how is democracy possible for those who are victims? *More than any other perspective, sociology makes us aware of many problems standing in the way of a democratic society, not the least of which are social, economic, and political inequality.*

This focus on social inequality will cause many individuals to look beyond the political arena to understand democracy. A democratic society requires not only limited government but also a limited military, a limited upper class, limited corporations, and limited interest groups. Limited government may bring freedom to the individual, but it also may simply create more unlimited power for economic elites in society, which is often an even more ruthless tyranny over individual freedom. *Sociology, be cause its subject is society, broadens our concerns, investigates the individual not only in relation to political institutions but also in relation to many other sources of power that can and do limit real democracy and control much of what we think and do.*

The democratic spirit cares about the welfare of all people. It respects life, values individual rights, encourages quality of life, and seeks justice for all. Sociology studies social problems.... Many people live lives of misery, characterized by poverty, crime, bad jobs, exploitation, lack of self-worth, stress, repressive institutions, violent conflict, inadequate socialization, and alienation of various kinds. These are more than problems caused by human biology or human genes; these are more than problems caused by the free choices of individual actors. Something social has generally caused misery to occur. *Although it is impossible for sociology-or a democratic society-to rid the world of such problems, it is part of the spirit of both to understand them, to suggest and to carry out ways to deal with them.* Democracy is shallow and cold if large numbers of people continue to live lives of misery.

… Ethnocentrism, although perhaps inevitable and even necessary to some extent, is a way of looking at one's own culture and others in a manner antagonistic to a basic principle of democracy: respect for human diversity and individuality. To claim that our culture is superior to others is to treat other cultures without respect, to reject them for what they are, to believe that everyone must be like us. Such ideas encourage violent conflict and war and justify discrimination, segregation, and exploitation. Sociology challenges us to be careful with ethnocentrism. We must understand what it is, what its causes are, and how it functions. An understanding of ethnocentrism will challenge us to ask: "When are my judgments of others simply cultural and when are they based on some more defensible standards (such as democratic standards)?" "When are my judgments narrow and intolerant; when are they more careful and thought out?" Even then, an understanding of ethnocentrism will not allow us to judge people who are different without seriously questioning our judgments. *Sociology and democracy are perspectives that push us to understand human differences and to be careful in condemning those differences.*

[Sociology also examines] social change and the power of the individual. This discussion, too, challenges many of our taken-for-granted "truths" concerning democracy. The sociologist's faith in the individual as an agent of change is not great. Democracy is truly an illusion if it means that the individual has an important say in the direction of society. But if sociology teaches us anything about change that has relevance for democracy, it is that intentionally created change is possible only through a power base. If a democracy is going to be more than a description in a book, people who desire change in society-ideally, toward more freedom, limited government, equality of opportunity, and respect for individual rights-must work together and act from a power base, recognizing that the existing political institutions are usually fixed against them. And before we go off armed with certainty, we should remember that our certainty was probably also socially produced and that, through our efforts, we may bring change we never intended and may even lose whatever democracy we now have. Social change is complex, depends on social power, and is difficult to bring about in a way we would like. *The sociologist will examine the possibility for intentional social change in a democratic society and will be motivated to isolate the many barriers each society establishes to real social change.*

Summary and Conclusion

Democracy exists at different levels. For some, it is a simplistic, shallow idea. For others, however, it is a complex and challenging idea to investigate and a reality worthwhile to create. If it is going to be more than a shallow idea, however, people should understand the nature of all society, the nature of power, ethnocentrism, inequality, change, and all the other concepts discussed and investigated in sociology. Whereas other disciplines may study issues relevant to understanding democracy and encourage people to think democratically, in a very basic sense, this study is the heart of sociology.

… Democracy means that one must understand reality not by accepting authority but by careful, thoughtful investigation. It is through evidence, not bias, that one should understand. It is through open debate, not a closed belief system that one should try to understand. *The principles of science and democracy are similar. There is no greater test of those principles than the discipline of sociology: an attempt to apply scientific principles to that for which we are all taught to feel a special reverence.*

Because it is a critical perspective that attempts to question what people have internalized from their cultures, sociology is a threat to those people who claim to know the truth. It punctures myth and asks questions that many of us would rather not hear. To see the world sociologically is to wonder about all things human. To see the world sociologically is to see events in a much larger context than the immediate situation, to think of individual events in relation to the larger present, to the past, and to the future. To see the world sociologically is to be suspicious of what those in power do (in our society and in our groups), and it is constantly to ask questions about what is and what can be.

The sociologist wonders about society and asks questions that get at the heart of many of our most sacred ideas. Perhaps this is why it seems so threatening to "those who know"; and perhaps this is why it is so exciting to those who take it seriously.

Article 2

The Land of Opportunity

James Loewen

igh school students have eyes, ears, and television sets (all too many have their own TV sets), so they know a lot about relative privilege in America. They measure their family's social position against that of other families, and their community's position against other communities. Middle-class students, especially, know little about how the American class structure works, however, and nothing at all about how it has changed over time. These students do not leave high school merely ignorant of the workings of the class structure; they come out as terrible sociologists. "Why are people poor?" I have asked first-year college students. Or, if their own class position is one of relative privilege, "Why is your family well off?" The answers I've received, to characterize them charitably, are half-formed and naive. The students blame the poor for not being successful. They have no understanding of the ways that opportunity is not equal in America and no notion that social structure pushes people around, influencing the ideas they hold and the lives they fashion.

High school history textbooks can take some of the credit for this state of affairs. Some textbooks cover certain high points of labor history, such as the 1894 Pullman strike near Chicago that President Cleveland broke with federal troops,[1] or the 1911 Triangle Shirtwaist fire that killed 146 women in New York City,[2] but the most recent event mentioned in most books is the Taft-Hartley Act of fifty years ago.[3] No book mentions the Hormel meat-packers'

---

[1] The trouble started when George M. Pullman, owner of the Pullman Palace Car Company, refused even to discuss his employees' grievances (for example, deep wage cuts) with them. The workers' cause was taken up by the American Railway Union, which started a boycott against all Pullman train cars. Because Pullman cars were used on nearly every train running, the boycott brought the entire U.S. rail system to a standstill. President Cleveland called in federal troops to break the strike (Cleveland justified his intervention by claiming that the boycott was interfering with the U.S. mail).—Ed.
[2] The fire broke out on Saturday, March 25. Smoke was first seen on the eighth floor of the building where some 500 people—mostly female—were working. Escape was nearly impossible because the owners of the factory had locked the doors in order to keep their employees at work. Many women and girls jumped to their deaths from the windows of the building rather than face death in fire.—Ed.
[3] The Taft-Hartley Act of 1947 placed serious restrictions on union activities, including the requirement that union leaders swear under oath that they weren't communists.—Ed.

---

strike in the mid-1980s or the air traffic controllers' strike broken by President Reagan. Nor do textbooks describe any continuing issues facing labor, such as the growth of multi-national corporations and their exporting of jobs overseas. With such omissions, textbooks authors can construe labor history as something that happened long ago, like slavery, and that, like slavery, was corrected long ago. It logically follows that unions appear anachronistic. The idea that they might be necessary in order for workers to have a voice in the workplace goes unstated.

Textbooks' treatments of events in labor history are never anchored in any analysis of social class. This amounts to delivering the footnotes instead of the lecture! Six of the dozen high school American history textbooks I examined contain no index listing at all for "social class," "social stratification," "class structure," "income distribution," "inequality," or any conceivably related topic. Not one book lists "upper class," "working class," or "lower class." Two of the textbooks list "middle class," but only to assure students that America is a middle-class country. "Except for slaves, most of the colonists were members of the 'middling ranks,'" says *Land of Promise*, and nails home the point that we are a middle-class country by asking students to "Describe three 'middle-class' values that united free Americans of all classes." Several of the textbooks note the explosion of middle-class suburbs after World War II. Talking about the middle class is hardly equivalent to discussing social stratification, however; in fact, as Gregory Mantsios (1988) has pointed out, "such references appear to be acceptable precisely because they mute class differences."

Stressing how middle-class we all are is particularly problematic today, because the proportion of households earning between 75 percent and 125 percent of the median income has fallen steadily since 1967. The Reagan-Bush administrations accelerated this shrinkage of the middle class, and most families who left its ranks fell rather than rose. This is the kind of historical trend one would think history books would take as appropriate subject matter, but only four of the twelve books in my sample provide any analysis of social stratification in the United States. Even these fragmentary analyses are set mostly in colonial America. *Land of Promise* lives up to its reassuring title by heading its discussion of social class "Social Mobility." "One great difference between colonial and European society was that the colonists had more social mobility," echoes *The American Tradition*. "In contrast with contemporary Europe, eighteenth-century America was a shining land of equality and opportunity—with the notorious exception of slavery," chimes in *The American Pageant*. Although *The Challenge of Freedom* identifies three social classes—upper, middle, and lower—among whites in colonial society, compared to Europe "there was greater *social mobility*."

Never mind that the most violent class conflicts in American history—Bacon's Rebellion and Shays's Rebellion[4]—took place in and just after colonial times. Textbooks still say that colonial society was relatively classless and marked by upward mobility. And things have gotten rosier since. "By 1815," *The Challenge of Freedom* assures us, two classes had withered away and "America was a country of middle class people and of middle class goals." This book returns repeatedly, at intervals of every fifty years or so, to the theme of how open opportunity is in America. "In the years after 1945, *social mobility*—movement from one social class to another—became more widespread in America," *Challenge* concludes. "This meant that people had a better chance to move upward in society." The stress on upward mobility is striking. There is almost nothing in any of these textbooks about class inequalities or barriers of any kind to social mobility. "What conditions made it possible for poor white immigrants to become richer in the colonies?" *Land of Promise* asks. "What conditions made/make it difficult?" goes unasked. Textbook authors thus present an America in which, as preachers were fond of saying in the nineteenth century, men start from "humble origins" and attain "the most elevated positions."

Social class is probably the single most important variable in society. From womb to tomb, it correlates with almost all other social characteristics of people that we can measure. Affluent expectant mothers are more likely to get prenatal care, receive current medical advice, and enjoy general health, fitness, and nutrition. Many poor and working-class mothers-to-be first contact the medical profession in the last month, sometimes the last hours, of their pregnancies. Rich babies come out healthier and weighing more than poor babies. The infants go home to very different situations. Poor babies are more likely to have high levels of poisonous lead in their environments and their bodies. Rich babies get more time and verbal interaction with their parents and higher quality day care when not with their parents. When they enter kindergarten, and through the twelve years that follow, rich children benefit from suburban schools that spend two to three times as much money per student as schools in inner cities or impoverished rural areas. Poor children are taught in classes that are often 50 percent larger than the classes of affluent children. Differences such as these help account for the higher school-dropout rate among poor children.

Even when poor children are fortunate enough to attend the same school as rich children, they encounter teachers who expect only children of affluent families to know the right answers. Social science research shows that teachers are often surprised and even

---

[4] Bacon's Rebellion (1676) involved a bloody dispute between settlers and colonial authorities. The settlers' complaints included the fact that the authorities were not providing protection against hostile Native Americans. Shays's Rebellion (1786–1787) resulted from the refusal of Massachusetts legislators to assist debt-ridden farmers who were facing foreclosures.—Ed.

distressed when poor children excel. Teachers and counselors believe they can predict who is "college material." Since many working-class children give off the wrong signals, even in first grade, they end up in the "general education" track in high school. "If you are the child of low-income parents, the chances are good that you will receive limited and often care-less attention from adults in your high school," in the words of Theodore Sizer's best-selling study of American high schools, *Horace's Compromise*. "If you are the child of upper-mid-dle-income parents, the chances are good that you will receive substantial and careful atten-tion" (quoted in Karp 1985, 73). Researcher Reba Page (1987) has provided vivid accounts of how high school American history courses use rote learning to turn off lower-class stu-dents. Thus schools have put into practice Woodrow Wilson's recommendation: "We want one class of persons to have a liberal education, and we want another class of persons, a very much larger class of necessity in every society, to forgo the privilege of a liberal education[5] and fit themselves to perform specific difficult manual tasks" (quoted in Lapham 1991).

As if this unequal home and school life were not enough, rich teenagers then enroll in the Princeton Review or other coaching sessions for the Scholastic Aptitude Test. Even without coaching, affluent children are advantaged because their background is similar to that of the test-makers, so they are comfortable with the vocabulary and subtle subcultural assumptions of the test. To no one's surprise, social class correlates strongly with SAT scores.

All these are among the reasons why social class predicts the rate of college attendance and the type of college chosen more effectively than does any other factor, including intel-lectual ability, however measured. After college, most affluent children get white-collar jobs, most working-class children get blue-collar jobs, and the class differences continue. As adults, rich people are more likely to have hired an attorney and to be a member of formal organizations that increase their civic power. Poor people are more likely to watch TV. Because affluent families can save some money while poor families must spend what they make, wealth differences are ten times larger than income differences. Therefore most poor and working-class families cannot accumulate the down payment required to buy a house, which in turn shuts them out from our most important tax shelter, the writeoff of home mortgage interest. Working-class parents cannot afford to live in elite subdivisions or hire high-quality day care, so the process of educational inequality replicates itself in the next generation. Finally, affluent Americans also have longer life expectancies than lower- and working-class people, the largest single cause of which is better access to health care. Echoing the results of Helen Keller's study of blindness, research has determined that poor health is not distributed randomly about the social structure but is concentrated in the

---

[5] "Liberal education," by definition, is education suited for the free (or liberated) citizen. The contrasting form of edu-cation is not "conservative education," but "vocational training."—Ed.

lower class. Social Security then becomes a huge transfer system, using monies contributed by all Americans to pay benefits disproportionately to longer-lived affluent Americans.

Ultimately, social class determines how people think about social class. When asked if poverty in America is the fault of the poor or the fault of the system, 57 percent of business leaders blamed the poor; just 9 percent blamed the system. Labor leaders showed sharply reversed choices: only 15 percent said the poor were at fault while 56 percent blamed the system. (Some replied "don't know" or chose a middle position.) The largest single difference between our two main political parties lies in how their members think about social class: 55 percent of Republicans blamed the poor for their poverty, while only 13 percent blamed the system for it; 68 percent of Democrats, on the other hand, blamed the system, while only 5 percent blamed the poor (Verba and Orren 1985,72–75).

Few of these statements are news, I know, which is why I have not documented most of them, but the majority of high school students do not know or understand these ideas. Moreover, the processes have changed over time, for the class structure in America today is not the same as it was in 1890, let alone in colonial America. Yet in *Land of Promise*, for example, social class goes unmentioned after 1670.

Many teachers compound the problem by avoiding talking about social class. Recent interviews with teachers "revealed that they had a much broader knowledge of the economy, both academically and experientially, than they admitted in class." Teachers "expressed fear that students might find out about the injustices and inadequacies of their economic and political institutions" (McNeil 1983,116)....

Historically, social class is intertwined with all kinds of events and processes in our past. Our governing system was established by rich men, following theories that emphasized government as a bulwark of the propertied class. Although rich himself, James Madison worried about social inequality and wrote *The Federalist* #10 to explain how the proposed government would not succumb to the influence of the affluent. Madison did not fully succeed, according to Edward Pessen, who examined the social-class backgrounds of all American presidents through Reagan. Pessen found that more than 40 percent hailed from the upper class, mostly from the upper fringes of that elite group, and another 15 percent originated in families located between the upper and upper-middle classes. More than 25 percent came from a solid upper-middle-class background, leaving just six presidents, or 15 percent, to come from the middle and lower-middle classes and just one, Andrew Johnson, representing any part of the lower class. For good reason, Pessen (1984) titled his book *The Log Cabin Myth*. While it was sad when the great ship *Titanic* went down, as the old song refrain goes, it was saddest for the lower classes: among women, only 4 of 143 first-class passengers were lost, while 15 of 93 second-class passengers drowned, along with 81 of 179 third-class women and girls. The crew ordered third-class passengers to remain below deck, holding some of them there at gunpoint (Hollingshead and Redlich 1958). More recently, social class played a major role in determining who fought in the Vietnam War: sons of the affluent won educational and medical deferments through most of the conflict (Baskir and Strauss 1986). Textbooks and teachers ignore all this.

Teachers may avoid social class out of a laudable desire not to embarrass their charges. If so, their concern is misguided. When my students from nonaffluent backgrounds learn about the class system, they find the experience liberating. Once they see the social processes that have helped keep their families poor, they can let go of their negative self-image about being poor. If to understand is to pardon, for working-class children to understand how stratification works is to pardon *themselves* and their families. Knowledge of the social-class system also reduces the tendency of Americans from other social classes to blame the victim for being poor. Pedagogically, stratification provides a gripping learning experience. Students are fascinated to discover how the upper class wields disproportionate power relating to everything from energy bills in Congress to zoning decisions in small towns.

Consider a white ninth-grade student taking American history in a predominantly middle-class town in Vermont. Her father tapes Sheet rock, earning an income that in slow construction seasons leaves the family quite poor. Her mother helps out by driving a school bus part-time, in addition to taking care of her two younger siblings. The girl lives with her family in a small house, a winterized former summer cabin, while most of her classmates live in large suburban homes. How is this girl to understand her poverty? Since history textbooks present the American past as 390 years of progress and portray our society as a land of opportunity in which folks get what they deserve and deserve what they get, the failures of working-class Americans to transcend their class origin inevitably get laid at their own doorsteps.

Within the white working-class community the girl will probably find few resources—teachers, church parishioners, family members—who can tell her of heroes or struggles among people of her background, for, except in pockets of continuing class conflict, the working class usually forgets its own history. More than any other group, white working-class students believe that they deserve their low status. A subculture of shame results. This negative self-image is foremost among what Richard Sennett and Jonathan Cobb have called "the hidden injuries of class" (1972). Several years ago, two students of mine provided a demonstration: they drove around Burlington, Vermont, in a big, nearly new, shiny black American car (probably a Lexus would be more appropriate today) and then in a battered ten-year-old subcompact. In each vehicle, when they reached a stoplight and it turned green, they waited until they were honked at before driving on. Motorists averaged less than seven seconds to honk at them in the subcompact, but in the luxury car the students enjoyed 13.2 seconds before anyone honked. Besides providing a good reason to buy a luxury car, this experiment shows how Americans unconsciously grant respect to the educated and successful. Since motorists of all social stations honked at the subcompact more readily, working-class drivers were in a sense disrespecting themselves while deferring to their betters. The biting quip "If you're so smart, why aren't you rich?" conveys the injury done to the self-image of the poor when the idea that America is a meritocracy goes unchallenged in school.

Part of the problem is that American history textbooks describe American education itself as meritocratic. A huge body of research confirms that education is dominated by the class structure and operates to replicate that structure in the next generation. Meanwhile, history textbooks blithely tell of such federal largesse to education as the Elementary and Secondary Education Act, passed under Pres. Lyndon Johnson. Not one textbook offers any data on or analysis of inequality within educational institutions. None mentions how school districts in low-income areas labor under financial constraints so shocking that Jonathan Kozol (1991) calls them "savage inequalities." No textbook ever suggests that students might research the history of their own school and the population it serves. The only two textbooks that relate education to the class system at all see it as a remedy! Schooling "was a key to upward mobility in postwar America," in the words of *The Challenge of Freedom*.

The tendency of teachers and textbooks to avoid social class as if it were a dirty little secret only reinforces the reluctance of working-class families to talk about it. Paul Cowan has told of interviewing the children of Italian immigrant workers involved in the famous 1912 Lawrence, Massachusetts, mill strike. He spoke with the daughter of one of the Lawrence workers who testified at a Washington congressional hearing investigating the strike. The worker, Camella Teoli, then thirteen years old, had been scalped by a cotton-twisting machine just before the strike and had been hospitalized for several months. Her testimony "became front-page news all over America." But Teoli's daughter, interviewed in 1976 after her mother's death, could not help Cowan. Her mother had told her nothing of the incident, nothing of her trip to Washington, nothing about her impact on America's conscience— even though almost every day, the daughter "had combed her mother's hair into a bun that disguised the bald spot" (Gutman 1987, 386–390). A professional of working-class origin told me a similar story about being ashamed of her uncle "for being a steelworker." A certain defensiveness is built into working-class culture; even its successful acts of working-class resistance, like the Lawrence strike, necessarily presuppose lower status and income, hence connote a certain inferiority. If the larger community is so good, as textbooks tell us it is, then celebrating or even passing on the memory of conflict with it seems somehow disloyal.

Textbooks do present immigrant history. Around the turn of the century immigrants dominated the American urban working class, even in cities as distant from seacoasts as Des Moines and Louisville. When more than 70 percent of the white population was native stock, less than 10 percent of the urban working class was (Gutman 1987, 386–390). But when textbooks tell the immigrant story, they emphasize Joseph Pulitzer, Andrew Carnegie, and their ilk—immigrants who made super-good. Several textbooks apply the phrases *rags to riches* or *land of opportunity* to the immigrant experience. Such legendary successes were achieved, to be sure, but they were the exceptions, not the rule. Ninety-five percent of the executives and financiers in America around the turn of the century came from upper-class or upper-middle-class backgrounds. Fewer than 3 percent started as poor immigrants or farm children. Throughout the nineteenth century, just 2 percent of American industrialists came from working-class origins (Miller 1962,326–328). By concentrating on the inspiring exceptions, textbooks present immigrant history as another heartening confirmation of America as the land of unparalleled opportunity.

Again and again, textbooks emphasize how America has differed from Europe in having less class stratification and more economic and social mobility. This is another aspect of the archetype of American exceptionalism: our society has been uniquely fair. It would never occur to historians in, say, France or Australia, to claim that their society was exceptionally equalitarian. Does this treatment of the United States prepare students for reality? It certainly does not accurately describe our country today, Social scientists have on many occasions compared the degree of economic equality in the United States with that in other industrial nations. Depending on the measure used, the United States has ranked sixth of six, seventh of seven, ninth of twelve, or fourteenth of fourteen (Verba and Orren 1985,10). In the United States the richest fifth of the population earns eleven times as much income as the poorest fifth, one of the highest ratios in the industrialized world; in Great Britain the ratio is seven to one, in Japan just four to one (Mantsios 1988, 59). In Japan the average chief executive officer in an automobile-manufacturing firm makes 20 times as much as the average worker in an automobile assembly plant; in the United States he (and it is not she) makes 192 times as much *(Harper's* 1990,19). The Jeffersonian conceit of a nation of independent farmers and merchants is also long gone: only one working American in thirteen is self-employed, compared to one in eight in Western Europe *(Harper's* 1993,19). Thus not only do we have far fewer independent entrepreneurs compared to two hundred years ago, we have fewer compared to Europe today.

Since textbooks claim that colonial America was radically less stratified than Europe, they should tell their readers when inequality set in. It surely was not a recent development. By 1910 the top 1 percent of the United States population received more than a third of all personal income, while the bottom fifth got less than one-eighth (Tyack and Hansot 1981). This level of inequality was on a par with that in Germany or Great Britain (Williamson and Lindert 1980). If textbooks acknowledged inequality, then they could describe the changes in our class structure over time, which would introduce their students to fascinating historical debate.

For example, some historians argue that wealth in colonial society was more equally distributed than it is today and that economic inequality increased during the presidency of Andrew Jackson—a period known, ironically, as the age of the common man. Others believe that the flowering of the large corporation in the late nineteenth century made the class structure more rigid. Walter Dean Burnham, has argued that the Republican presidential victory in 1896 (McKinley over Bryan) brought about a sweeping political realignment that changed "a fairly democratic regime into a rather broadly based oligarchy,"[6] so by the 1920s business controlled public policy (1965, 23–25). Clearly the gap between rich and poor, like the distance between blacks and whites, was greater at the end of the Progressive Era in 1920 than at its beginning around 1890 (Schwartz 1991, 94). The story is not all one of increasing stratification, for between the depression and the end of World War II income and wealth in America gradually became more equal. Distributions of income then remained reasonably constant until President Reagan took office in 1981, when inequality began to grow. Still other scholars think that little change has occurred since the Revolution. Lee Soltow (1989), for example, finds "surprising inequality of wealth and income" in America in 1798. At least for Boston, Stephan Themstrom (1973) concludes that inequalities in life chances owing to social class show an eerie continuity. All this is part of American history. But it is not part of American history as taught in high school.

To social scientists, the level of inequality is a portentous thing to know about a society. When we rank countries by this variable, we find Scandinavian nations at the top, the most equal, and agricultural societies like Colombia and India near the bottom. The policies of the Reagan and Bush administrations, which openly favored the rich, abetted a trend already in motion, causing inequality to increase measurably between 1981 and 1992. For the United States to move perceptibly toward Colombia in social inequality is a development of no small import (Danziger and Gottschalf 1993; Kohn 1990; Macrobert 1984). Surely high school students would be interested to learn that in 1950 physicians made two and a half times what unionized industrial workers made but now make six times as much. Surely they need to understand that top managers of clothing firms, who used to earn fifty times what their American employees made, now make 1,500 times what their Malaysian workers earn. Surely it is wrong for our history textbooks and teachers to withhold the historical information that might prompt and inform discussion of these trends.

Why might they commit such a blunder? First and foremost, publisher censorship of textbook authors. "You always run the risk, if you talk about social class, of being labeled Marxist," the editor for social studies and history at one of the biggest publishing houses

---

[6] *Oligarchy* means "rule by a few"—as opposed to *aristocracy*, which means, technically, "rule by the best few."—Ed.

told me. This editor communicates the taboo, formally or subtly, to every writer she works with, and she implied that most other editors do too.

Publisher pressure derives in part from textbook adoption boards and committees in states and school districts. These are subject in turn to pressure from organized groups and individuals who appear before them. Perhaps the most robust such lobby is Educational Research Analysts, led by Mel Gabler of Texas. Gabler's stable of right-wing critics regards even alleging that a textbook contains some class analysis as a devastating criticism. As one writer has put it, "Formulating issues in terms of class is unacceptable, perhaps even un-American" (Mantsios 1988). Fear of not winning adoption in Texas is a prime source of publisher angst, and might help explain why *Life and Liberty* limits its social-class analysis to colonial times in *England!* By contrast, "the colonies were places of great opportunity," even back then. Some Texans cannot easily be placated, however. Deborah L. Brezina, a Gabler ally, complained to the Texas textbook board that *Life and Liberty* describes America "as an unjust society," unfair to lower economic groups, and therefore should not be approved. Such pressure is hardly new. Harold Rugg's *Introduction to Problems of American Culture* and his popular history textbook, written during the depression, included some class analysis. In the early 1940s, according to Frances FitzGerald, the National Association of Manufacturers attacked Rugg's books, partly for this feature, and "brought to an end" social and economic analysis in American history textbooks (1979).

More often the influence of the upper class is less direct. The most potent rationale for class privilege in American history has been Social Darwinism,[7] an archetype that still has great power in American culture. The notion that people rise and fall in a survival of the fittest may not conform to the data on inter-generational mobility in the United States, but that has hardly caused the archetype to fade away from American education, particularly from American history classes (Tyack and Hansot 1981). Facts that do not fit with the archetype, such as the entire literature of social stratification, simply get left out....

But isn't it nice simply to believe that America is equal? Maybe the "land of opportunity" archetype is an empowering myth—maybe believing in it might even help make it come true. For if students *think* the sky is the limit, they may reach for the sky, while if they don't, they won't.

The analogy of gender points to the problem with this line of thought. How could high school girls understand their place in American history if their textbooks told them that, from colonial America to the present, women have had equal opportunity for upward mobility and political participation? How could they then explain why no woman has been

---

[7] For a discussion of this concept, see chapter 1 in *The Practical Skeptic: Cone Concepts in Sociology.*—Ed.

president? Girls would have to infer, perhaps unconsciously, that it has been their own gender's fault, a conclusion that is hardly empowering.

Textbooks do tell how women were denied the right to vote in many states until 1920 and faced other barriers to upward mobility. Textbooks also tell of barriers confronting racial minorities. The final question *Land of Promise* asks students following its "Social Mobility" section is "What social barriers prevented blacks, Indians, and women from competing on an equal basis with white male colonists?" After its passage extolling upward mobility, *The Challenge of Freedom* notes, "Not all people, however, enjoyed equal rights or an equal chance to improve their way of life," and goes on to address the issues of sexism and racism. But neither here nor anywhere else do *Promise* or *Challenge* (or most other textbooks) hint that opportunity might not be equal today for white Americans of the lower and working classes. Perhaps as a result, even business leaders and Republicans, the respondents statistically most likely to engage in what sociologists call "blaming the victim," blame the social system rather than African Americans for black poverty and blame the system rather than women for the latter's unequal achievement in the workplace. In sum, affluent Americans, like their textbooks, are willing to credit racial discrimination as the cause of poverty among blacks and Indians and sex discrimination as the cause of women's inequality but don't see class discrimination as the cause of poverty in general (Verba and Orren 1985, 72–75).

More than math or science, more even than American literature, courses in American history hold the promise of telling high school students how they and their parents, their communities, and their society came to be as they are. One way things are is unequal by social class. Although poor and working-class children usually cannot identify the cause of their alienation, history often turns them off because it justifies rather than explains the present. When these students react by dropping out, intellectually if not physically, their poor school performance helps convince them as well as their peers in the faster tracks that the system is meritocratic and that they themselves lack merit. In the end, the absence of social-class analysis in American history courses amounts to one more way that education in America is rigged against the working class.

References

Baskir, I., and W. Strauss. 1986. *Chance and Circumstance*. New York: Random House.

Bowles, S., and H. Gintis. 1976. *Schooling in Capitalist America*. New York: Basic Books.

Brezina, D. L. 1993. "Critique of *Life and Liberty*," distributed by Mel Gabler's Educational Research Analysts.

Burnham, W. D. 1965. "The Changing Shape of the American Political University." *American Political Science Review* 59: 23–25.

Danziger, S., and P. Gottschalf. 1993. *Uneven Tides.* New York: Sage.

FitzGerald, F. 1979. *America Revised.* New York: Vintage Books.

Gutman, H. 1987. *Power and Culture.* New York: Pantheon Books.

Harper's. 1990. "Index" (citing data from the United Automobile Workers; Chrysler Corp; "Notice of Annual Meeting of Stockholders"). April 1.

Harper's. 1993. "Index" (citing the Organization for Economic Cooperation and Development). January 19.

Hollingshead, A., and F. C. Redlich. 1958. *Social Class and Mental Illness.* New York: Wiley.

Karp, Walter. 1985. "Why Johnny Can't Think." *Harper's,* June, p. 73.

Kohn, A. 1990. *You Know What They Say....* New York: HarperCollins.

Kozol, J. 1991. *Savage Inequalities.* New York: Crown.

Lapham, Lewis. 1991. "Notebook." *Harper's,* July, p. 10.

Macrobert, A. 1984. "The Unfairness of It All." *Vermont Vanguard Press,* September 30, pp. 12–13.

Mantsios, Gregory. 1988. "Class in America: Myths and Realities." In Paula S. Rothenberg (ed.), *Racism and Sexism: An Integrated Study.* New York: St. Martin's Press.

McNeil, Linda. 1983. "Teaching and Classroom Control." In M. W. Apple and L. Weis (eds.), *Ideology and Practice in Schooling.* Philadelphia: Temple University Press.

Miller, W. 1962. "American Historians and the Business Elite." In W. Miller (ed.), *Men in Business.* New York: Harper & Row.

Page, Reba. 1987. *The Lower-track Students' View of Curriculum.* Washington, DC: American Education Research Association.

Pessen, E. 1984. *The Log Cabin Myth.* New Haven, CT: Yale University Press.

Schwartz, B. 1991. "The Reconstruction of Abraham Lincoln," in D. Middleton and D. Edwards (eds.), *Collective Remembering.* London: Sage.

Sennett, R., and J. Cobb. 1972. *The Hidden Injuries of Class.* New York: Knopf.

Soltow, L. 1989. *Distribution of Wealth and Income in the United States in 1798.* Pittsburgh: University of Pittsburgh Press.

Thernstrom, S. 1973. *The Other Bostonians.* Cambridge, MA: Harvard University Press.

Tyack, D., and E. Hansot. 1981. "Conflict and Consensus in American Public Education." *Daedalus* 110: 11–12.

Verba, S., and G. Orren. 1985. *Equality in America.* Cambridge, MA: Harvard University Press.

Williamson and Lindert. 1980. *American Inequality: A Macroeconomic History.* New York: Academic Press.

Article 3

The Role of the Behavioral Scientist in the Civil Rights Movement

Martin Luther King, Jr.

The Civil Rights Movement Needs the Help of Social Scientists

In the preface to their book, *Applied Sociology* (1965), S. M. Miller and Alvin Gouldner state: "It is the historic mission of the social sciences to enable mankind to take possession of society". It follows that for Negroes who substantially are excluded from society this science is needed even more desperately than for any other group in the population.

For social scientists, the opportunity to serve in a life-giving purpose is a humanist challenge of rare distinction. Negroes too are eager for a rendezvous with truth and discovery. We are aware that social scientists, unlike some of their colleagues in the physical sciences, have been spared the grim feelings of guilt that attended the invention of nuclear weapons of destruction. Social scientists, in the main, are fortunate to be able to extirpate evil, not to invent it.

If the Negro needs social sciences for direction and for self-understanding, the white society is in even more urgent need. White America needs to understand that it is poisoned to its soul by racism and the understanding needs to be carefully documented and consequently more difficult to reject. The present crisis arises because although it is historically imperative that our society take the next step to equality, we find ourselves psychologically and socially imprisoned. All too many white Americans are horrified not with conditions of Negro life but with the product of these conditions—the Negro himself.

White America is seeking to keep the walls of segregation substantially intact while the evolution of society and the Negro's desperation is causing them to crumble. The white majority, unprepared and unwilling to accept radical structural change, is resisting and producing chaos while complaining that if there were no chaos orderly change would come.

Negroes want the social scientist to address the white community and "tell it like it is". White America has an appalling lack of knowledge concerning the reality of Negro life. One reason some advances were made in the South during the past decade was the discovery by northern whites of the brutal facts of southern segregated life. It was the Negro who educated the nation by dramatizing the evils through nonviolent protest. The social scientist played little or no role in disclosing truth. The Negro action movement with raw courage did it virtually alone. When the majority of the country could not live with the extremes of brutality they witnessed, political remedies were enacted and customs were altered.

These partial advances were, however, limited principally to the South and progress did not automatically spread throughout the nation. There was also little depth to the changes. White America stopped murder, but that is not the same thing as ordaining brotherhood; nor is the ending of lynch rule the same thing as inaugurating justice.

After some years of Negro-white unity and partial successes, white America shifted gears and went into reverse. Negroes, alive with hope and enthusiasm, ran into sharply stiffened white resistance at all levels and bitter tensions broke out in sporadic episodes of violence. New lines of hostility were drawn and the era of good feeling disappeared.

The decade of 1955 to 1965, with its constructive elements, misled us. Everyone, activists and social scientists, underestimated the amount of violence and rage Negroes were suppressing and the amount of bigotry the white majority was disguising.

Science should have been employed more fully to warn us that the Negro, after 350 years of handicaps, mired in an intricate network of contemporary barriers, could not be ushered into equality by tentative and superficial changes.

Mass nonviolent protests, a social invention of Negroes, were effective in Montgomery, Birmingham and Selma in forcing national legislation which served to change Negro life sufficiently to curb explosions. But when changes were confined to the South alone, the North, in the absence of change, began to seethe.

The freedom movement did not adapt its tactics to the different and unique northern urban conditions. It failed to see that nonviolent marches in the South were forms of rebellion. When Negroes took over the streets and shops, southern society shook to its roots. Negroes could contain their rage when they found the means to force relatively radical changes in their environment.

In the North, on the other hand, street demonstrations were not even a mild expression of militancy. The turmoil of cities absorbs demonstrations as merely transitory drama which is ordinary in city life. Without a more effective tactic for upsetting the status quo, the power structure could maintain its intransigence and hostility. Into the vacuum of inaction, violence and riots flowed and a new period opened.

Urban Riots ...

Urban riots must now be recognized as durable social phenomena. They may be deplored, but they are there and should be understood. Urban riots are a special form of violence. They are not insurrections. The rioters are not seeking to seize territory or to attain control of institutions. They are mainly intended to shock the white community. They are a distorted form of social protest. The looting which is their principal feature serves many functions. It enables the most enraged and deprived Negro to take hold of consumer goods with the ease the white man does by using his purse. Often the Negro does not even want what he takes; he wants the experience of taking. But most of all, alienated from society and knowing that this society cherishes property above people, he is shocking it by abusing property rights. There are thus elements of emotional catharsis in the violent act. This may explain why most cities in which riots have occurred have not had a repetition, even though the causative conditions remain. It is also noteworthy that the amount of physical harm done to white people other than police is infinitesimal and in Detroit whites and Negroes looted in unity.

A profound judgment of today's riots was expressed by Victor Hugo a century ago. He said, "If a soul is left in darkness, sins will be committed. The guilty one is not he who commits the sin, but he who causes the darkness".

The policy makers of the white society have caused the darkness; they create discrimination; they structured slums; and they perpetuate unemployment, ignorance and poverty. It is incontestable and deplorable that Negroes have committed crimes; but they are derivative crimes. They are born of the greater crimes of the white society. When we ask Negroes to abide by the law, let us also demand that the white man abide by law in the ghettos. Day-in and day-out he violates welfare laws to deprive the poor of their meager allotments; he flagrantly violates building codes and regulations; his police make a mockery of law; and he violates laws on equal employment and education and the provisions for civic services. The slums are the handiwork of a vicious system of the white society; Negroes live in them but do not make them any more than a prisoner makes a prison. Let us say boldly that if the total violations of law by the white man in the slums over the years were calculated and compared with the law-breaking of a few days of riots, the hardened criminal would be the white man. These are often difficult things to say but I have come to see more and more that it is necessary to utter the truth in order to deal with the great problems that we face in our society.

Vietnam War ...

There is another cause of riots that is too important to mention casually—the war in Vietnam. Here again, we are dealing with a controversial issue. But I am convinced that the war in Vietnam has played havoc with our domestic destinies. The bombs that fall in Vietnam explode at home. It does not take much to see what great damage this war has done to the image of our nation. It has left our country politically and morally isolated in the world, where our only friends happen to be puppet nations like Taiwan, Thailand and South Korea. The major allies in the world that have been with us in war and peace are not with us in this war. As a result we find ourselves socially and politically isolated.

The war in Vietnam has torn up the Geneva Accord. It has seriously impaired the United Nations. It has exacerbated the hatreds between continents, and worse still, between races. It has frustrated our development at home by telling our under-privileged citizens that we place insatiable military demands above their most critical needs. It has greatly contributed to the forces of reaction in America, and strengthened the military-industrial complex, against which even President Eisenhower solemnly warned us. It has practically destroyed Vietnam, and left thousands of American and Vietnamese youth maimed and mutilated. And it has exposed the whole world to the risk of nuclear warfare.

As I looked at what this war was doing to our nation, and to the domestic situation and to the Civil Rights movement, I found it necessary to speak vigorously out against it. My speaking out against the war has not gone without criticisms. There are those who tell me that I should stick with civil rights, and stay in my place. I can only respond that I have fought too hard and long to end segregated public accommodations to segregate my own moral concerns. It is my deep conviction that justice is indivisible, that injustice anywhere is a threat to justice everywhere. For those who tell me I am hurting the Civil Rights move-ment, and ask, "Don't you think that in order to be respected, and in order to regain sup-port, you must stop talking against the war". I can only say that I am not a concensus leader. I do not seek to determine what is right and wrong by taking a Gallop Poll to determine majority opinion. And it is again my deep conviction that ultimately a genuine leader is not a searcher for concensus, but a molder of concensus. On some positions cowardice asks the question, "Is it safe"?! Expediency asks the question, "It it politic"? Vanity asks the question, "Is it popular"? But, conscience must ask the question, "Is it right"? And there comes a time when one must take a stand that is neither safe, nor politic, nor popular. But one must take it because it is right. And that is where I find myself today.

Moreover, I am convinced, even if war continues, that a genuine massive act of concern will do more to quell riots than the most massive deployment of troops.

Unemployment ...

The unemployment of Negro youth ranges up to 40 per cent in some slums. The riots are almost entirely youth events—the age range of participants is from 13 to 25. What hypoc-risy it is to talk of saving the new generation—to make it the generation of hope—while consigning it to unemployment and provoking it to violent alternatives.

When our nation was bankrupt in the 30's we created an agency to provide jobs to all at their existing level of skill. In our overwhelming affluence today what excuse is there for not setting up a national agency for full employment immediately?

The other program which would give reality to hope and opportunity would be the demolition of the slums to be replaced by decent housing built by residents of the ghettos.

These programs are not only eminently sound and vitally needed, but they have the support of an overwhelming majority of the nation—white and Negro. The Harris Poll on August 21, 1967, disclosed that an astounding 69 per cent of the country support a works program to provide employment to all and an equally astonishing 65 per cent approve a program to tear down the slums.

There is a program and there is heavy majority support for it. Yet, the administration and Congress tinker with trivial proposals to limit costs in an extravagant gamble with disaster.

The President has lamented that he cannot persuade Congress. He can, if the will is there, go to the people, mobilize the people's support and thereby substantially increase his power to persuade Congress. Our most urgent task is to find the tactics that will move the government no matter how determined it is to resist.

Civil Disobedience ...

I believe we will have to find the militant middle between riots on the one hand and weak and timid supplication for justice on the other hand. That middle ground, I believe, is civil disobedience. It can be aggressive but nonviolent; it can dislocate but not destroy. The specific planning will take some study and analysis to avoid mistakes of the past when it was employed on too small a scale and sustained too briefly.

Civil disobedience can restore Negro-white unity. There have been some very important sane white voices even during the most desperate moments of the riots. One reason is that the urban crisis intersects the Negro crisis in the city. Many white decision makers may care little about saving Negroes, but they must care about saving their cities. The vast majority of production is created in cities; most white Americans live in them. The suburbs to which they flee cannot exist detached from cities. Hence powerful white elements have goals that merge with ours.

The Role for the Social Scientist

Now there are many roles for social scientists in meeting these problems. Kenneth Clark has said that Negroes are moved by a suicide instinct in riots and Negroes know there is a tragic truth in this observation. Social scientists should also disclose the suicide instinct that governs the administration and Congress in their total failure to respond constructively.

What other areas are there for social scientists to assist the civil rights movement? There are many, but I would like to suggest three because they have an urgent quality.

Social science may be able to search out some answers to the problem of Negro leadership. E. Franklin Frazier, in his profound work, *Black Bourgeoisie*, laid painfully bare the tendency of the upwardly mobile Negro to separate from his community, divorce himself from responsibility to it, while failing to gain acceptance into the white community. There has been significant improvements from the days Frazier researched, but anyone knowledgeable about Negro life knows its middle class is not yet bearing its weight. Every riot has carried strong overtone of hostility of lower class Negroes toward the affluent Negro and vice versa. No contemporary study of scientific depth has totally studied this problem. Social science should be able to suggest mechanisms to create a wholesome black unity and a sense of peoplehood while the process of integration proceeds.

As one example of this gap in research, there are no studies, to my knowledge, to explain adequately the absence of Negro trade union leadership. Eighty-five per cent of Negroes are working people. Some 2,000,000 are in trade unions but in 50 years we have produced only one national leader—A. Philip Randolph.

Discrimination explains a great deal, but not everything. The picture is so dark even a few rays of light may signal a useful direction.

Political Action ...

The second area for scientific examination is political action. In the past two decades. Negroes have expended more effort in quest of the franchise than they have in all other campaigns combined. Demonstrations, sit-ins and marches, though more spectacular, are dwarfed by the enormous number of man-hours expended to register millions, particularly in the South. Negro organizations from extreme militant to conservative persuasion, Negro leaders who would not even talk to each other, all have been agreed on the key importance of voting. Stokely Carmichael said black power means the vote and Roy Wilkins, while saying black power means black death, also energetically sought the power of the ballot.

A recent major work by social scientists Matthew and Prothro concludes that "The concrete benefits to be derived from the franchise—under conditions that prevail in the South—have often been exaggerated", ... that voting is not the key that will unlock the door to racial equality because "the concrete measurable payoffs from Negro voting in the South will not be revolutionary" (1966).

James A. Wilson supports this view, arguing, "Because of the structure of American politics as well as the nature of the Negro community, Negro politics will accomplish only limited objectives" (1965).

If their conclusion can be supported, then the major effort Negroes have invested in the past twenty years has been in the wrong direction and the major pillar of their hope is a pillar of sand. My own instinct is that these views are essentially erroneous, but they must be seriously examined.

The need for a penetrating massive scientific study of this subject cannot be overstated. Lipsit in 1957 asserted that a limitation in focus in political sociology has resulted in a failure of much contemporary research to consider a number of significant theoretical questions. The time is short for social science to illuminate this critically important area. If the main thrust of Negro effort has been, and remains, substantially irrelevant, we may be facing an agonizing crisis of tactical theory.

The third area for study concerns psychological and ideological changes in Negroes. It is fashionable now to be pessimistic. Undeniably, the freedom movement has encountered setbacks. Yet I still believe there are significant aspects of progress.

Negroes today are experiencing an inner transformation that is liberating them from ideological dependence on the white majority. What has penetrated substantially all strata of Negro life is the revolutionary idea that the philosophy and morals of the dominant white society are not holy or sacred but in all too many respects are degenerate and profane.

Negroes have been oppressed for centuries not merely by bonds of economic and political servitude. The worst aspect of their oppression was their inability to question and defy the fundamental precepts of the larger society. Negroes have been loath in the past to hurl any fundamental challenges because they were coerced and conditioned into thinking within the context of the dominant white ideology. This is changing and new radical trends are appearing in Negro thought. I use radical in its broad sense to refer to reaching into roots.

Ten years of struggle have sensitized and opened the Negro's eyes to reaching. For the first time in their history, Negroes have become aware of the deeper causes for the crudity and cruelty that governed white society's responses to their needs. They discovered that their plight was not a consequence of superficial prejudice but was systemic.

The slashing blows of backlash and frontlash have hurt the Negro, but they have also awakened him and revealed the nature of the oppressor. To lose illusions is to gain truth. Negroes have grown wiser and more mature and they are hearing more clearly those who are raising fundamental questions about our society whether the critics be Negro or white. When this process of awareness and independence crystallizes, every rebuke, every evasion, become hammer blows on the wedge that splits the Negro from the larger society.

Social science is needed to explain where this development is going to take us. Are we moving away, not from integration, but from the society which made it a problem in the first place? How deep and at what rate of speed is this process occurring? These are some vital questions to be answered if we are to have a clear sense of our direction.

We know we haven't found the answers to all forms of social change. We know, however, that we did find some answers. We have achieved and we are confident. We also know we are confronted now with far greater complexities and we have not yet discovered all the theory we need.

And may I say together, we must solve the problems right here in America. As I have said time and time again. Negroes still have faith in America. Black people still have faith in a dream that we will all live together as brothers in this country of plenty one day.

But I was distressed when I read in the *New York Times* of August 31, 1967 that a sociologist from Michigan State University, the outgoing president of the American Sociological Society, stated in San Francisco that Negroes should be given a chance to find an all Negro community in South America: "that the valleys of the Andes Mountains would be an ideal place for American Negroes to build a second Israel." He further declared that "The United States Government should negotiate for a remote but fertile land in Equador, Peru or Bolivia for this relocation". I feel that it is rather absurd and appalling that a leading social scientist today would suggest to black people, that after all these years of suffering an exploitation as well as investment in the American dream, that we should turn around and run at this point in history. I say that we will not run! Professor Loomis even compared the relocation task of the Negro to the relocation task of the Jews in Israel. The Jews were made exiles. They did not choose to abandon Europe, they were driven out. Furthermore, Israel has a deep tradition, and Biblical roots for Jews. The Wailing Wall is a good example of these roots. They also had significant financial aid from the United States for the relocation and rebuilding effort. What tradition does the Andes, especially the valley of the Andes mountains, have for Negroes?

And I assert at this time that once again we must reaffirm our belief in building a democratic society, in which blacks and whites can live together as brothers, where we will all come to see that integration is not a problem, but an opportunity to particiate in the beauty of diversity.

The problem is deep. It is gigantic in extent, and chaotic in detail. And I do not believe that it will be solved until there is a kind of cosmic discontent enlarging in the bosoms of people of good will all over this nation.

There are certain technical words in every academic discipline which soon become stereotypes and even clichés. Every academic discipline has its technical nomenclature. You who are in the field of psychology have given us a great word. It is the word maladjusted. This word is probably used more than any other word in psychology. It is a good word; certainly it is good that in dealing with what the word implies you are declaring that destructive maladjustment should be destroyed. You are saying that all must seek the well-adjusted life in order to avoid neurotic and schizophrenic personalities.

But on the other hand, I am sure that we will recognize that there are some things in our society, some things in our world, to which we should never be adjusted. There are some things concerning which we must always be maladjusted if we are to be people of good will. We must never adjust ourselves to racial discrimination and racial segregation. We must never adjust ourselves to religious bigotry. We must never adjust ourselves to economic conditions that take necessities from the many to give luxuries to the few. We must never adjust ourselves to the madness of militarism, and the self-defeating effects of physical violence.

In a day when Sputniks, Explorers and Geminies are dashing through outer space, when guided ballistic missiles are carving highways of death through the stratosphere, no nation can finally win a war. It is no longer a choice between violence and nonviolence, it is either nonviolence or nonexistence. As President Kennedy declared, "Mankind must put an end to war, or war will put an end to mankind". And so the alternative to disarmament, the alternative to a suspension in the development and use of nuclear weapons, the alternative to strengthening the United Nations and eventually disarming the whole world, may well be a civilization plunged into the abyss of annihilation. Our earthly habitat will be transformed into an inferno that even Dante could not envision.

Creative Maladjustment …

Thus, it may well be that our world is in dire need of a new organization, The International Association for the Advancement of Creative Maladjustment. Men and women should be as maladjusted as the prophet Amos, who in the midst of the injustices of his day, could cry out in words that echo across the centuries, "Let justice roll down like waters and righteousness like a mighty stream"; or as maladjusted as Abraham Lincoln, who in the midst of his vacillations finally came to see that this nation could not survive half slave and half free; or as maladjusted as Thomas Jefferson, who in the midst of an age amazingly adjusted to slavery, could scratch across the pages of history, words lifted to cosmic proportions, "We hold these truths to be self evident, that all men are created equal. That they are endowed by their creator with certain inalienable rights. And that amoung these are life, liberty, and the pursuit of happiness". And though such creative maladjustment, we may be able to emerge from the bleak and desolate midnight of man's inhumanity to man, into the bright and glittering daybreak of freedom and justice.

I have not lost hope. I must confess that these have been very difficult days for me personally. And these have been difficult days for every civil rights leader, for every lover of justice and peace. They have been days of frustration—days when we could not quite see where we were going, and when we often felt that our works were in vain, days when we were tempted to end up in the valley of despair. But in spite of this, I still have faith in the future, and my politics will continue to be a politic of hope. Our goal is freedom. And I somehow still believe that in spite of the so-called white backlash, we are going to get there, because however untrue it is to its destiny, the goal of America is freedom.

Abused and scorned though we may be, our destiny as a people is tied up with the destiny of America. Before the Pilgrim fathers landed at Plymouth, we were here. Before Jefferson scratched across the pages of history the great words that I just quoted, we were here. Before the beautiful words of the "Star Spangled Banner" were written, we were here. For more than two centuries, our forebears laboured here without wages. They made Cotton King. They built the home of their masters in the midst of the most humiliating and oppressive conditions.

And yet out of a bottomless vitality, they continued to grow and develop. If the inexpressable cruelties of slavery could not stop us, the opposition that we now face will surely fail. We shall win our freedom because both the sacred heritage of our nation, and the eternal will of the almighty God, are embodied in our echoing demands.

And so I can still sing, although many have stopped singing it, "We shall overcome". We shall overcome because the arch of the moral universe is long, but it bends toward justice. We shall overcome because Carlysle is right, "No lie can live forever". We shall overcome because William Cullen Bryant is right, "Truth crushed to earth will rise again". We shall overcome because James Russell Lowell is right, "Truth forever on the scaffold, wrong forever on the throne, yet that scaffold sways a future". And so with this faith, we will be able to hew out of the mountain of despair a stone of hope. We will be able to transform the jangling discords of our nation into a beautiful symphony of brotherhood. This will be a great day. This will not be the day of the white man, it will not be the day of the black man, it will be the day of man as man.

References

Frazier, E. Franklin. *Black Bourgeoisie*. New York: McMillian, 1962.

Lipsit, Martin. Political Sociology. In *Sociology Today*. New York: Basic Books, 1959.

Matthews, Donald R. and Prothro, James W. *Negroes and the New Southern Politics*. New York: Harcourt Brace, 1966.

Miller, S. M. and Gouldner, A. *Applied Sociology*. New York: The Free Press, 1965.

New York Times. August 31, 1967.

Wilson, James A. The Negro in Politics. *Daedalus*, Fall, 1965.

Part 2

Doing Research and Analyzing Data

Article 4

Rise in Income Improves Children's Behavior

by Anahad O'connor

The notion that poverty and mental illness are intertwined is nothing new, as past research has demonstrated time and time again. But finding evidence that one begets the other has often proved difficult.

Now new research that coincided with the opening of an Indian casino may have come a step closer to identifying a link by suggesting that lifting children out of poverty can diminish some psychiatric symptoms, though others seem unaffected.

A study published in last week's issue of The Journal of the American Medical Association looked at children before and after their families rose above the poverty level. Rates of deviant and aggressive behaviors, the study noted, declined as incomes rose.

"This comes closer to pointing to a causal relationship than we can usually get," said Dr. E. Jane Costello, a psychiatric epidemiologist at Duke who was the lead author. "Moving families out of poverty led to a reduction in children's behavioral symptoms."

The study took place over eight years in rural North Carolina and tracked 1,420 children ages 9 to 13, 25 percent of them from a Cherokee reservation. Tests for psychiatric symptoms were given at the start of the study and repeated each year.

When the study began, 68 percent of the children were from families living below the federally defined poverty line. On average, the poorer children exhibited more behaviors associated with psychiatric problems than those who did not live in poverty. But midway through the study, the opening of a local casino offered researchers a chance to analyze the effects of quick rises in income.

Just over 14 percent of the American Indian children rose above the poverty level when the casino started distributing a percentage of its profits to tribal families. The payment, given to people over age 18 and put into a trust fund for those younger, has increased slightly each year, reaching about $6,000 per person by 2001.

"This is unique because it's a situation where everybody got the extra money," Dr. Costello said. "You can't take a bunch of babies and randomly assign them to grow up in comfort or poverty. So this is about as close to a natural experiment as you can get."

When the researchers conducted their tests soon after, they noticed that the rate of psychiatric symptoms among the children who had risen from poverty was dropping. As time went on, the children were less inclined to stubbornness, temper tantrums, stealing, bullying and vandalism—all symptoms of conduct and oppositional defiant disorders.

After four years, the rate of such behaviors had dropped to the same levels found among children whose families had never been poor. Children whose families broke the poverty threshold had a 40 percent decrease in behavioral symptoms. But the payments had no effect on children whose families had been unable to rise from poverty or on the children whose families had not been poor to begin with.

The researchers also found that symptoms of anxiety and depression, although more common in poor children, remained the same despite moving out of poverty.

The deciding factor appeared to be the amount of time parents had to supervise their children. Parents who moved out of poverty reported having more time to spend with their children. In the other groups, the amount of time the parents had on their hands was not much different.

"What this shows very nicely is that an economic shift can allow for more time and better parenting," said Dr. Nancy Adler, professor of medical psychology at the University of California at San Francisco.

In children, acting out is often a result of frustration that can stem from feeling ignored or not getting enough validation from the parents, said Dr. Arline Geronimus, a professor of public health at the University of Michigan.

As a result, behaviors associated with frustration would be the first to change when parents had more attention to devote to their children. "Anxiety and depression, on the other hand, are a little more extreme and might not be as susceptible to change," Dr. Geronimus added.

Recent research suggests that anxiety disorders and depression run in families and probably reflect a mix of genetic and environmental causes.

The study highlights the role that adult supervision may have on mental health in children, but another factor, Dr. Geronimus said, may be the psychological benefits that the casino payments produce.

The Indian families were much more likely to be poor than their non-Indian neighbors at the start of the study. After the payments, though, a higher proportion of Indian families moved out of poverty.

"There's the possibility that this improved the general outlook of the families—that the whole community has more than before," Dr. Geronimus said. "In addition to the material resources, there might have been some psychological benefits."

Those psychological benefits may also be a byproduct of the jobs that the casino has generated, said James Sanders, director of an adolescent drug and alcohol treatment center on the reservation.

"The jobs give people the chance to pull themselves up by their bootstraps and get out of poverty," said Mr. Sanders, whose son took part in the study. "That carries over into less juvenile crime, less domestic violence and an overall better living experience for the families."

But one question that lingers is why the economic change had a significant effect on only a small proportion of the children. All of the families that received the payment were given the same amount of money, but only 14 percent moved out of poverty while 53 percent remained poor.

The answer could be related to the number of siblings in each family. A $6,000 payment could be a huge help to a poor family with one child, for example, "but that money might not go as far for a family with multiple children," Dr. Adler said.

In 2002, the average poverty threshold for a family of three was $14,348.

Though some questions remain, the study ultimately suggests that poverty puts stress on families, which can increase the likelihood that children will develop behavioral problems. That, said Dr. Geronimus, speaks to the notion that welfare policy is heading in the wrong direction.

"Parents on welfare are increasingly required to work more and more hours while spending less time with their families," she said. "These findings suggest the opposite: parents value having more time to spend with their kids, not less, and their kids respond favorably to that."

Article 5

Science and Ethics: A Long History of Abuse

Jerry Kloby

Bad Science

Science has made tremendous contributions to understanding the world and making life better. But there is also science that is "bad," in several senses of the word. There's bad science in the sense that the research did not follow accepted procedures for minimizing bias, testing hypotheses, and making well-founded conclusions based on empirical evidence. And there is bad science in the sense that the research used subjects in a morally objectionable manner, sometimes inflicting serious and permanent harm to the people involved. What follows are several notorious examples of the latter. As you read about these, compare the scope of the problems involved to those involved in classic social/psychological experiments such as those run by Stanley Milgram and Philip Zimbardo,

Nazi Medical Research

Beginning in 1939, the Nazis began systematically killing patients in state mental hospitals with doctors playing critical roles by selecting patients and supervising their execution. Nazi doctors also decided which prisoners would be killed immediately and which would be used as forced labor in the concentrations camps.

In addition to assisting the Nazi policy of genocide, doctors also used the camps to conduct medical research. The experiments included exposing individuals to freezing cold and tremendous heat, forcing them to drink salt water to see how soon they would die, administering experimental poisons, and injecting dye into prisoners' eyes to try to change their eye color. They also used prisoners to practice surgical techniques.

The Tuskegee Syphilis Study

Begun in 1932 by the U.S. Public Health Service (PHS), the study's organizers wanted to know the consequences of untreated syphilis in African-American men. The devastating effects of syphilis in white men were well known. The research was based on the racist assumption that the disease might follow a different course for blacks.

Three hundred ninety nine poor and mostly illiterate black men from Macon County, Alabama, who were suffering from syphilis were recruited for the study. None of them were informed that they had the disease. Instead, researchers told them they were being treated for "bad blood." The men were told they would receive free treatment, transportation to the health clinics, free meals on examination day, and payment of burial expenses.

In the early 1940s penicillin was developed as an effective and simple treatment for syphilis. But throughout the entire study the men were never treated with penicillin and the researchers went to great lengths to keep them from getting treatment elsewhere.

Questions about the project were raised in the mid-1960s by Peter Bruxton, who worked for the PHS, and by Bill Jenkins, an epidemiologist working for the Centers for Disease Control. Bruxton raised his concerns again in 1968 after leaving the PHS. This time, fearing a public relations disaster, the PHS convened a panel to evaluate the study. They voted to continue it.

Buxton later mentioned the study to a reporter who broke the story in 1972 and the public response forced an end to the study. By then, at least 28 and maybe as many as one hundred of the subjects had died as a direct result of syphilis complications.[1]

The Willowbrook Hepatitis Study

At the Willowbrook State School, a New York State institution for mentally retarded children, two professors of pediatric medicine from New York University School of Medicine deliberately infected children with hepatitis beginning in 1956. The study was intended to follow the course of viral hepatitis, and to study the effectiveness of an agent for inoculating against the disease. Consent was obtained from parents, but the parents received only vague descriptions of the nature of the research and potential risks. In addition, there is evidence that parents were told their children would only be admitted to Willowbrook if they enrolled in the study. The ethical flaws in the study were not exposed until 1970 and widespread criticism occurred in 1972, which caused research to come to an end.[2]

Radiation Testing

In 1996 the Federal Government agreed to pay $4.8 million as compensation for injecting 12 people with radioactive materials in secret Cold War experiments. The settlement was part of efforts to make amends for many unethical experiments carried out by government doctors, scientists, and military officials from 1944 to 1974 on as many as 20,000 people. The financial settlement ended several court cases involving injections of uranium or plutonium

---

[1] Weitz, Rose. *The Sociology of Health, Illness, and Health Care: A Critical Approach*, Belmont, CA: Wadsworth Publishing
[2] Weitz, pp. 406-407

into 12 people in experiments in Rochester, NY, and elsewhere from 1945 to 1947. Most of the people were being treated for existing illnesses at hospitals when they became subjects of the radiation research that had nothing to do with their disorders.

Some estimate that about 7,500 military men and more than 200 civilian children received high doses of radium in the initial experiments in the 1940s and 1950s. More may have been subjected to later experiments. At Vanderbilt University, 820 pregnant women were given small doses of radioactive iron.[3]

Chemical and Biological Agents

In May of 2002, the Pentagon disclosed that ships and sailors had been sprayed with chemical and biological agents in Cold-War era tests that took place in international waters. Later, in October, the Pentagon acknowledged much wider testing of toxic weapons, including using chemical and live biological agents in tests on American soil as well as in Canada and Great Britain.[4]

Sixteen declassified documents describe how military exercised used VX and sarin nerve gases to test the vulnerability of American forces to unconventional attack. The reports detail tests conducted from 1962 to 1971 in Alaska, Hawaii, Maryland, and Florida.

Death and Darkness in the Amazon

In 2000, journalist Patrick Tierney, published a book, *Darkness in El Dorado*, that detailed how geneticist James Neel used a virulent measles vaccine to spark an epidemic among the Yanomami people of the Amazon region in South America in the 1960s. Thousands were infected and hundreds died as a result. The particular strain was a strong live virus, about which the World Health Organization had issued warnings. According to Tierney, Neel ordered his research team not to offer any medical assistance, insisting that they were there as scientists—only to observe. Neel's work was funded by the U.S. Atomic Energy Commission.[5] The AEC was interested in the Yanomami in order to get blood samples of remote people who were not likely to have been contaminated by radiation.

Buying Favorable Research Conclusions

A University of Massachusetts study showed no racial inequities in the location and operation of our nation's toxic and hazardous waste facilities. The findings were widely circulated

---

[3] Hilts, Philip J. 1996 "U.S. to Settle for $4.8 Million in Suits on Radiation Testing," *New York Times*, November 11.

[4] Shanker, Thom. 2002. "U.S. Troops Were Subjected to a Wider Toxic Testing," *New York Times*, October 9, 2006

[5] Tierney, Patrick, *Darkness in El Dorado*, 2000, W. W. Norton. See also, Wilford, John Noble and Simon Romero, 2000, "Book Seeks to Indict Anthropologists Who Studied Brazil Indians," *New York Times*, September 28; and Brown, Paul, 2000. "Scientist "Killed Amazon Indians to Test Race Theory," *Guardian* (London), September 23.

in industry circles. But the study was sponsored by the Institute of Chemical Waste Management, an industry trade group. The CWM gave a quarter of a million dollars to fund the study. Critics discovered that the study's research excluded many toxic waste sites including two of the largest ones that happened to be owned by WMX, one of the largest waste companies in the nation. One was located in a predominately black area of Alabama and one in a Latino community in California.

Cancer Research on Veterans

In January of 2005, at a federal courthouse in Albany, New York, Paul Kornak, 53, pleaded guilty to fraud, making false statements, and criminally negligent homicide, in the death of Air Force veteran James DiGeorgio.[6] Kornak had altered patient records, and posed as a doctor, in order to get veterans to participate in an experimental drug study at the Stratton Veterans Affairs Medical Center in Albany. Kornak was the Medical Center's research coordinator for four years. Scores of veteran were put at risk by Kornak's actions but allegations of carelessness, fraud, and patient abuse in the hospital's cancer research program predated Kornak's tenure and employees said the administrators dismissed their concerns and even harassed them for standing up for the veterans.

"Research violations were a way of life for ten years," said Jeffrey Fudin, one of the hospital's pharmacists. The Department of Veteran affairs found a "systemic weaknesses in the human research protections program, especially in studies funded by industry." Mr. Fudin started making his allegations in 1993 but his allegations were usually dismissed and Fudin eventually sued claiming harassment and reprisals for whistle-blowing. But it wasn't until 2002 that the F.D.A. sent an investigative team to Albany. The action came after Ilex, a cancer drug company that was doing research at the Albany hospital, found discrepancies in the paperwork that raised serious concerns. Ilex shut down its research and notified the F.D.A.

The F.D.A. team spent more than 50 days at the hospital and studied files of more than 50 research subjects, finding problems with almost every one.

According to *The New York Times*, problems such as these are a result of a boom in new drug development. Clinical research grew into a multibillion-dollar industry in the 1990s and has overwhelmed the systems developed to protect research subjects.

Ensuring Ethical Treatment of Research Subjects

At least 350 doctors committed medical crimes under the Nazi regime. The Nuremberg trials after World War II put many of the Nazis and 23 of the doctors on trial for war crimes.

---

[6] Sontag, Deborah, 2005. "Abuses Endangered Veterans in Cancer Drug Experiments," *New York Times*, February 6.

One of the byproducts of these trials was the **Nuremberg Code** that helped establish international guidelines for the ethical treatment of human research subjects. Among these are:

- The voluntary consent of the human subject is absolutely essential.

- The experiment should be such as to yield fruitful results for the good of society, unprocurable by other methods or means of study, and not random and unnecessary in nature.

- The experiment should be so conducted as to avoid all unnecessary physical and mental suffering and injury.

- During the course of the experiment, the human subject should be at liberty to bring the experiment to an end.[7]

The Wilson Memorandum

In 1953, Secretary of Defense Charles Wilson issued a memorandum almost identical to the Nuremberg Code and called for the informed consent of experiment volunteers. However, the government did not make it policy, instead, they classified it top secret.[8]

The 1974 National Research Act

The most far-reaching national law that guides contemporary scientific research is the National Research Act, which created the National Commission for the Protection of Human Subjects of Biomedical and Behavioral Research, which was charged to identify the basic ethical principles that should underlie the conduct of biomedical and behavioral research involving human subjects and to develop guidelines that should be followed to assure that such research is conducted in accordance with those principles.

The Commission drafted the *Belmont Report*, a foundational document in the promotion of ethics in human subjects research in the United States. Among the report's basic principles were respect for persons, beneficence, and justice. In practice, this means that subjects, to the degree that they are capable, must be given the opportunity to choose what shall or shall not happen to them. Human subjects should not be harmed, and research should maximize possible benefits and minimize possible harms.[9]

---

[7] Weitz, p. 403.

[8] Alcalay, Glenn, 1995. "Damage Control on Human Radiation Experiments," *Covet Action*, Spring.

[9] History of Research Ethics, University of Nevada, Las Vegas. http://research.unlv.edu/ORI-HSR/history-ethics.htm

Part 3

Culture and Socialization

Article 6

The Social Psychology of George Herbert Mead

Bernard N. Meltzer

A. Preliminary Remarks

While mead's system of Social Psychology is given its fullest exposition in *Mind, Self and Society*, each of three other books (as well as a few articles) rounds out the complete picture.

It should be pointed out at this juncture that Mead himself published no full-length systematic statement of his theory. All four of the books bearing his authorship are post-humously collected and edited works. They comprise a loose accumulation of his lecture notes, fragmentary manuscripts, and tentative drafts of unpublished essays. Since the chief aim of his editors has been completeness—rather than organization—the books consist, in considerable part, of alternative formulations, highly repetitive materials, and sketchily developed ideas.

Nevertheless, a brief description of these volumes is in order, since they constitute the major source-materials concerning Mead's social psychology.

Philosophy of the Present (1932) contains the Paul Carus Foundation lectures delivered by Mead in 1930, a year before his death. These lectures present a philosophy of history from the pragmatist's point of view. Moreover, this volume presents his ideas on the analogous developments of social experience and of scientific hypotheses.

Mind, Self and Society (1934) is chiefly a collection of lectures delivered to his classes in Social Psychology at the University of Chicago.

Movements of Thought in the 19th Century (1936) is largely a collection of lectures delivered to his classes in the History of Ideas.

Philosophy of the Act (1938), according to Paul Schilpp, represents a fairly *systematic* statement of the philosophy of pragmatism. This "systematic" statement I found (as did G. S. Lee) to be made up of essays and miscellaneous fragments, which are technical and repetitious, obscure and difficult.

From *The Social Psychology of George Herbert Mead* by Bernard N. Meltzer. Reprinted by permission of the Estate of Bernard N. Meltzer.

A final observation regarding the content of these books should be made: Mead's orientation is generally *philosophical*. Rather than marshalling his own empirical evidence, he uses the findings of various sciences and employs frequent apt and insightful illustrations from everyday life. These illustrations usually are not used to prove points, but rather to serve as data to be analyzed in terms of his scheme.

Before launching upon a presentation of Mead's social-psychological theories, it might be wise to explain his designation of his viewpoint as that of "Social Behaviorism." By this term Mead means to refer to the description of behavior at the distinctively human level. Thus, for social behaviorism, the basic datum is the social act. As we shall see, the study of social arts entails concern with the covert aspects of behavior. Further, the concept of the "social act" implies that human conduct and experience has a fundamental social dimension—that the social context is an inescapable element in distinctively human actions.

Like Watsonian radial behaviorism, Mead's social behaviorism starts with the observable actions of individuals; but *unlike* the former, social behaviorism conceives behavior in broad enough terms to include *covert* activity. This inclusion is deemed necessary to understanding the distinctive character of human conduct, which Mead considers a qualitatively different emergent from infrahuman behavior. Watson's behaviorism, on the other hand, reduces human behavior to the very same mechanisms as are found on the infrahuman level. As a corollary, Watson sees the social dimension of human behavior as merely a sort of external influence upon the individual. Mead, by contrast, views generically human behavior as *social* behavior, human acts as *social* acts. For Mead, both the content and the very existence of distinctively human behavior are accountable only on a social basis. (These distinctions should become more clear in the course of this report.)

It can readily be inferred from this brief explanation of Mead's usage of the term "social behaviorism" that, before we can explore the nature and function of the mind—which Mead considers a uniquely human attribute—supporting theories of society, and of self—another uniquely human attribute—require elaboration. Hence, the natural, logical order of Mead's thinking seems to have been society, self, and mind—rather than "Mind, Self, and Society."

B. Content of Mead's Social Psychology

1. Society

According to Mead, all group life is essentially a matter of cooperative behavior. Mead makes a distinction, however, between infrahuman society and human society. Insects—whose society most closely approximates the complexity of human social life—act together in certain ways because of their biological makeup. Thus, their cooperative behavior is physiologically determined. This is shown by many facts, among which is the fact of the fixity, the stability, of the relationships of insect-society members to one another. Insects, according to the evidence, go on for countless generations without any difference in their patterns of association. This picture of infrahuman society remains essentially valid as one ascends the scale of animal life, until we arrive at the human level.

In the case of human association, the situation is fundamentally different. Human cooperation is not brought about by mere physiological factors. The very diversity of the patterns of human group life makes it quite clear that human cooperative life cannot be explained in the same terms as the cooperative life of insects and the lower animals. The fact that human patterns are not stabilized and cannot be explained in biological terms led Mead to seek another basis of explanation of human association. Such cooperation can only be brought about by some process wherein: (a) each acting individual ascertains the *intention* of the acts of others, and then (b) makes his own response on the basis of that intention. What this means is that, in order for human beings to cooperate, there must be present some sort of mechanism whereby each acting individual: (a) can come to understand the lines of action of others, and (b) can guide his own behavior to fit in with those lines of action. Human behavior is not a matter of responding directly to the activities of others. Rather, it involves responding to the *intentions* of others, i.e., to the future, intended behavior of others—not merely to their present actions.

We can better understand the character of this distinctively human mode of interaction between individuals by contrasting it with the infrahuman "conversation of gestures." For example when a mother hen clucks, her chicks will respond by running to her. This does not imply however, that the hen clucks *in order* to guide the chicks, i.e., with the *intention* of guiding them. Clucking is a natural sign or signal—rather than a significant (meaningful) symbol—as it is not meaningful to the hen. That is, the hen (according to Mead) does not take the role, or viewpoint, of the chicks toward its own gesture and respond to it, in imagination, as they do. The hen does not envision the response of the chicks to her clucking. Thus, hens and chicks do not share the same experience.

Let us take another illustration by Mead: Two hostile dogs, in the pre-fight stage, may go through elaborate conversation of gestures (snarling, growling, baring fangs, walking stiffleggedly around one another, etc.). The dogs are adjusting themselves to one another by responding to one another's gestures. (A gesture is that portion of an act which represents the entire act; it is the initial, overt phase of the act, which epitomizes it, e.g., shaking one's fist at someone.) Now, in the case of the dogs the response to a gesture is dictated by preestablished tendencies to respond in certain ways. Each gesture leads to a direct, immediate, automatic, and unreflecting response by the recipient of the gesture (the other dog).

Neither dog responds to the *intention* of the gestures. Further, each dog does not make his gestures with the intent of eliciting certain responses in the other dog. Thus, animal interaction is devoid of conscious, deliberate meaning.

To summarize: Gestures, at the nonhuman or nonlinguistic level, do not carry the connotation of conscious meaning or intent, but serve merely as cues for the appropriate responses of others. Gestural communication takes place immediately, without any interruption of the act, without the mediation of a definition or meaning. Each organism adjusts "instinctively" to the other, it does not stop and figure out which response it will give. Its behavior is, largely, a series of direct automatic responses to stimuli.

Human beings, on the other hand, respond to one another on the basis of intentions or meanings of gestures. This renders the gesture *symbolic*, i.e., the gesture becomes a symbol to be interpreted; it becomes something which, in the imaginations of the participants, stands for the entire act.

Thus, individual A begins to act, i.e., makes a gesture: for example, he draws back an arm. Individual B (who perceives the gesture) completes, or fills in, the act in his imagination; i.e., B imaginatively projects the gesture into the future: "He will strike me." In other words, B perceives what the gesture stands for, thus getting its meaning. In contrast to the direct responses of the chicks and the dogs, the human being inserts an interpretation between the gesture of another and his response to it. Human behavior involves responses to *interpreted* stimuli.[1]

We see, then, that people respond to one another on the basis of imaginative activity. In order to engage in concerted behavior, however, each participating individual must be able to attach the same meaning to the same gesture. Unless interacting individuals interpret gestures similarly, unless they fill out the imagined portion in the same way, there can be no cooperative action. This is another way of saying what has by now become a truism in sociology and social psychology: Human society rests upon a basis of *consensus*, i.e., the sharing of meanings in the form of common understandings and expectations.

In the case of the human being, each person has the ability to respond to his own gestures; and thus, it is possible to have the same meaning for the gestures as other persons. (For example: As I say "chair," I present to myself the same image as to my hearer;

---

[1] The foregoing distinctions can also be expressed in terms of the differences between "signs," or "signals," and symbols. A sign stands for something else because of the fact that it is present at approximately the same time and place with that "something else." A symbol, on the other hand, stands for something else because its users have agreed to let it stand for that "something else." Thus, signs are directly and intrinsically linked with present or proximate situations; while symbols, having arbitrary and conventional, rather than intrinsic, meanings, transcend the immediate situation. (We shall return to this important point in our discussion of "mind.") Only symbols, of course, involve interpretation, self-stimulation and shared meaning.

moreover, the same image as when someone else says "chair.") This ability to stimulate oneself as one stimulates another, and to respond to oneself as another does, Mead ascribes largely to man's vocal-auditory mechanism. (The ability to hear oneself implies at least the potentiality for responding to oneself.) When a gesture has a shared, common meaning, when it is—in other words—a *linguistic* element, we can designate it as a "significant symbol." (Take the words, "Open the window": the pattern of action symbolized by these words must be in the mind of the speaker as well as the listener. Each must respond, in imagination, to the words in the same way. The speaker must have an image of the listener responding to his words by opening the window, and the listener must have an image of his opening the window.)

The imaginative completion of an act—which Mead calls "meaning" and which represents mental activity—necessarily takes place through *role-taking*. To complete imaginatively the total act which a gesture stands for, the individual must put himself in the position of the other person, must identify with him. The earliest beginnings of role-taking occur when an already established act of another individual is stopped short of completion, thereby requiring the observing individual to fill in, or complete, the activity imaginatively. (For example, a crying infant may have an image of its mother coming to stop its crying.)

As Mead points out, then, the relation of human beings to one another arises from the developed ability of the human being to respond to his own gestures. This ability enables different human beings to respond in the same way to the same gesture, thereby sharing one another's experience.

This latter point is of great importance. Behavior is viewed as "social" not simply when it is a response to others, but rather when it has incorporated in it the behavior of others. The human being responds to himself as other persons respond to him, and in so doing he imaginatively shares the conduct of others. That is, in imagining their response he shares that response.[2]

2. Self

To state that the human being can respond to his own gestures necessarily implies that he possesses a *self*. In referring to the human being as having a self, Mead simply means that such an individual may act socially toward himself, just as toward others. He may praise, blame, or encourage himself; he may become disgusted with himself, may seek to

---

[2] To anyone who has taken even one course in sociology it is probably superfluous to stress the importance of symbols, particularly language, in the acquisition of all other elements of culture. The process of socialization is essentially a process of symbolic interaction.

punish himself, and so forth. Thus, the human being may become the object of his own actions. The self is formed in the same way as other objects—through the "definitions" made by others.

The mechanism whereby the individual becomes able to view himself as an object is that of role-taking, involving the process of communication, especially by vocal gestures or speech. (Such communication necessarily involves role-taking.) It is only by taking the role of others that the individual can come to see himself as an object. The standpoint of others provides a platform for getting outside oneself and thus viewing oneself. The development of the self is concurrent with the development of the ability to take roles.

The crucial importance of language in this process must be underscored. It is through language (significant symbols) that the child acquires the meanings and definitions of those around him. By learning the symbols of his groups, he comes to internalize their definitions of events or things, including their definitions of his own conduct.

It is quite evident that, rather than assuming the existence of selves and explaining society thereby, Mead starts out from the prior existence of society as the context within which selves arise. This view contrasts with the nominalistic position of the social contract theorists and of various individualistic psychologies.

Genesis of the Self. The relationship between role-playing and various stages in the development of the self is described below:

1. *Preparatory Stage* (not explicitly named by Mead, but inferable from various fragmentary essays). This stage is one of meaningless imitation by the infant (for example, "reading" the newspaper). The child does certain things that others near it do without any understanding of what he is doing. Such imitation, however, implies that the child is incipiently taking the roles of those around it, i.e., is on the verge of putting itself in the position of others and acting like them.

2. *Play Stage*. In this stage the actual playing of roles occurs. The child plays mother, teacher, storekeeper, postman, streetcar conductor, Mr. Jones, etc. What is of central importance in such play-acting is that it places the child in the position where it is able to act back toward itself in such roles as "mother" or "teacher." In this stage, then, the child first begins to form a self, that is, to direct activity toward itself— and it does so by taking the roles of others. This is clearly indicated by use of the third person in referring to oneself instead of the first person: "John wants …," "John is a bad boy."

    However, in this stage the young child's configuration of roles is unstable; the child passes from one role to another in unorganized, inconsistent fashion. He has, as yet, no unitary standpoint from which to view himself, and hence, he has no unified conception of himself. In other words, the child forms a number of separate and discrete objects of itself, depending on the roles in which it acts toward itself.

3. *Game Stage.* This is the "completing" stage of the self. In time, the child finds himself in situations wherein he must take a number of roles simultaneously. That is, he must respond to the expectations of several people at the same time. This sort of situation is exemplified by the game of baseball—to use Mead's own illustration. Each player must visualize the intentions and expectations of several other players. In such situations the child must take the roles of groups of individuals as over against particular roles. The child becomes enabled to do this by abstracting a "composite" role out of the concrete roles of particular persons. In the course of his association with others, then, he builds up a *generalized other*, a generalized role or standpoint from which he views himself and his behavior. This generalized other represents, then, the set of standpoints which are common to the group.

Having achieved this generalized standpoing, the individual can conduct himself in an organized, consistent manner. He can view himself from a consistent standpoint. This means, then, that the individual can transcend the local and present expectations and definitions with which he comes in contact. An illustration of this point would be the Englishman who "dresses for dinner" in the wilds of Africa. Thus, through having a generalized other, the individual becomes emancipated from the pressures of the pecularities of the immediate situation. He can act with a certain amount of consistency in a variety of situations because he acts in accordance with a generalized set of expectations and definitions that he has internalized.

The "I" and the "Me." The self is essentially a social process within the individual involving two analytically distinguishable phases: The "I" and the "Me."

The "I" is the impulsive tendency of the individual. It is the initial, spontaneous, unorganized aspect of human experience. Thus, it represents the undirected tendencies of the individual.

The "Me" represents the incorporated other within the individual. Thus, it comprises the organized set of attitudes and definitions, understandings and expectations—or simply meanings—common to the group. In any given situation the "Me" comprises the generalized other and, often, some particular other.

Every act begins in the form of an "I" and usually ends in the form of the "Me." For the "I" represents the initiation of the act prior to its coming under control of the definitions or expectations of others (the "Me"). The "I" thus gives *propulsion* while the "Me" gives *direction* to the act. Human behavior, then, can be viewed as a perpetual series of initiations of acts by the "I" and of acting-back-upon the act (that is, guidance of the act) by the "Me." The act is a resultant of this interplay.

The "I," being spontaneous and propulsive, offers the potentiality for new, creative activity. The "Me," being regulatory, disposes the individual to both goal-directed activity and conformity. In the operation of these aspects of the self, we have the basis for, on the one hand, social control and, on the other, novelty and innovation. We are thus provided with a basis for understanding the mutuality of the relationship between the individual and society.[3]

Implications of Selfhood. Some of the major implications of selfhood in human behavior are as follows:

1. The possession of a self makes of the individual a society in miniature. That is, he may engage in interaction with himself just as two or more different individuals might. In the course of this interaction, he can come to view himself in a new way, thereby bringing about changes in himself.

2. The ability to act toward oneself makes possible an inner experience which need not reach overt expression. That is, the individual, by virtue of having a self, is thereby endowed with the possibility of having a mental life: He can make indications to himself—which constitutes *mind*.

3. The individual with a self is thereby enabled to direct and control his behavior. Instead of being subject to all impulses and stimuli directly playing upon him, the individual can check, guide, and organize his behavior. He is, then, *not a mere* passive agent.

---

[3] At first glance, Mead's "I" and "Me" may appear to bear a close affinity with Freud's concepts of Id, Ego, and Superego. The resemblance is, for the most part, more apparent than real. While the Superego is held to be harshly frustrating and repressive of the instinctual, libidinous, and agressive Id, the "Me" is held to provide necessary direction—often of a *gratifying* nature—to the otherwise undirected impulses constituting the "I." Putting the matter in figurative terms: Freud views the Id and the Superego as locked in combat upon the battleground of the Ego; Mead sees the "I" and "Me" engaged in close collaboration. This difference in perspective may derive from different preoccupations: Freud was primarily concerned with tension, anxiety, and "abnormal" behavior; Mead was primarily concerned with behavior generically.

It is true, on the other hand, that the Id, Ego, and Superego—particularly as modified by such neoFreudians as Karen Horney, Erich Fromm, and H. S. Sullivan—converge at a few points with the "I" and "Me." This is especially evident in the emphasis of both the Superego and "Me" concepts upon the internalization of the norms of significant others through the process of identification, or role-taking.

Incidentally, it should be noted that both sets of concepts refer to processes of behavior, *not* to concrete entities or structures. See, also, the discussion of "mind" which follows.

All three of these implications of selfhood may be summarized by the statement that the self and the mind (mental activity) are twin emergents in the social process.

C. Summary

At several points in this report the reader must have been aware of the extremely close interwoven character of Mead's various concepts. In the discussions of society, or self, and of mind, certain ideas seemed to require frequent (and, perhaps, repetitious) statement. A brief summary of Mead's position may help to reveal more meaningfully the way in which his key concepts interlock and logically imply one another.

The human individual is born into a society characterized by *symbolic interaction*. The use of *significant symbols* by those around him enables him to pass from the conversation of gestures—which involves direct, unmeaningful response to the overt acts of others—to the occasional *taking of the roles* of others. This role-taking, enables him to share the perspectives of others. Concurrent with role-taking, the *self* develops, i.e., the capacity to act toward oneself. Action toward oneself comes to take the form of viewing oneself from the standpoint, or perspective, of the *generalized other* (the composite representative of others, of society, within the individual), which implies defining one's behavior in terms of the expectations of others. In the process of such viewing of oneself, the individual must carry on symbolic interaction with himself, involving an internal conversation between his impulsive aspect (the "I") and the incorporated perspectives of others (the "Me"). The *mind*, or mental activity, is present in behavior whenever such symbolic interaction goes on—whether the individual is merely "thinking" (in the everyday sense of the word) or is also interacting with another individual. (In both cases the individual must indicate things to himself.) Mental activity necessarily involves *meanings*, which usually attach to and define, *objects*. The meaning of an object or event is simply an image of the pattern of action which defines the object or event. That is, the completion in one's imagination of an act, or the mental picture of the actions and experiences symbolized by an object, defines the act or the object. In the unit of study that Mead calls "the act," all of the foregoing processes are usually entailed. The concluding point to be made in this summary is the same as the point with which I began: Mead's concept intertwine and mutually imply one another. To drive home this important point, I must emphasize that human society (characterized by symbolic interaction) both precedes the rise of individual selves and minds, and is maintained by the rise of individual selves and minds. This means, then, that symbolic interaction is both the medium for the development of human beings and the process by which human beings associate as human beings.

Finally, it should be clearly evident by now that any distinctively human act necessarily involves: symbolic interaction, role-taking, meaning, mind, and self. Where one of these concepts is involved, the others are, also, necessarily involved. Here we see, unmistakably, the organic unity of Mead's position.

Article 7

The Metropolis and Mental Life

Georg Simmel

The deepest problems of modern life derive from the claim of the individual to preserve the autonomy and individuality of his existence in the face of overwhelming social forces, of historical heritage, of external culture, and of the technique of life. The fight with nature which primitive man has to wage for his *bodily* existence attains in this modern form its latest transformation. The eighteenth century called upon man to free himself of all the historical bonds in the state and in religion, in morals, and in economics. Man's nature, originally good and common to all, should develop unhampered. In addition to more liberty, the nineteenth century demanded the functional specialization of man and his work; this specialization makes one individual incomparable to another, and each of them indispensable to the highest possible extent. However, this specialization makes each man the more directly dependent upon the supplementary activities of all others. Nietzsche sees the full development of the individual conditioned by the most ruthless struggle of individuals; socialism believes in the suppression of all competition for the same reason. Be that as it may, in all these positions the same basic motive is at work: the person resists to being leveled down and worn out by a social-technological mechanism. An inquiry into the inner meaning of specifically modern life and its products, into the soul of the cultural body, so to speak, must seek to solve the equation which structures like the metropolis set up between the individual and the super-individual contents of life. Such an inquiry must answer the question of how the personality accommodates itself in the adjustments to external forces. This will be my task today.

The psychological basis of the metropolitan type of individuality consists in the *intensification of nervous stimulation* which results from the swift and uninterrupted change of outer and inner stimuli. Man is a differentiating creature. His mind is stimulated by the difference between a momentary impression and the one which preceded it. Lasting impressions, impressions which differ only slightly from one another, impressions which take a regular and habitual course and show regular and habitual contrasts—all these use up, so to speak, less consciousness than does the rapid crowding of changing images, the sharp discontinuity in the grasp of a single glance, and the unexpectedness of onrushing impressions. These are the psychological conditions which the metropolis creates. With each crossing of the street, with the tempo and multiplicity of economic, occupational and social life, the city sets up a deep contrast with small town and rural life with reference to the sensory foundations of psychic life. The metropolis exacts from man as a discriminating creature a different amount of consciousness than does rural life. Here the rhythm of life and sensory mental imagery flows more slowly, more habitually, and more evenly. Precisely in this connection the sophisticated character of metropolitan psychic life becomes understandable—as over against small-town life which rests more upon deeply felt and emotional relationships. These latter are rooted in the more unconscious layers of the psyche and grow most readily in the steady rhythm of uninterrupted habituations. The intellect, however, has its locus in the transparent, conscious, higher layers of the psyche; it is the most adaptable of our inner forces. In order to accommodate to change and to the contrast of phenomena, the intellect does not require any shocks and inner upheavals; it is only through such upheavals that the more conservative mind could accommodate to the metropolitan rhythm of events. Thus the metropolitan type of man—which, of course, exists in a thousand individual variants—develops an organ protecting him against the threatening currents and discrepancies of his external environment which would uproot him. He reacts with his head instead of his heart....

There is perhaps no psychic phenomenon which has been so unconditionally reserved to the metropolis as has the blasé attitude. The blasé attitude results first from the rapidly changing and closely compressed contrasting stimulations of the nerves. From this, the enhancement of metropolitan intellectuality, also, seems originally to stem. Therefore, stupid people who are not intellectually alive in the first place usually are not exactly blasé. A life in boundless pursuit of pleasure makes one blasé because it agitates the nerves to their strongest reactivity for such a long time that they finally cease to react at all. In the same way, through the rapidity and contradictoriness of their changes, more harmless impressions force such violent responses, tearing the nerves so brutally hither and thither that their last reserves of strength are spent; and if one remains in the same milieu they have no time to gather new strength. An incapacity thus emerges to react to new sensations with the appropriate energy. This constitutes that blasé attitude which, in fact, every metropolitan child shows when compared with children of quieter and less changeable milieus....

This reserve with its overtone of hidden aversion appears in turn as the form or the cloak of a more general mental phenomenon of the metropolis: it grants to the individual a kind and an amount of personal freedom which has no analogy whatsoever under other conditions. The metropolis goes back to one of the large developmental tendencies of social life as such, to one of the few tendencies for which an approximately universal formula can be discovered. The earliest phase of social formations found in historical as well as in contemporary social structures is this: a relatively small circle firmly closed against neighboring, strange, or in some way antagonistic circles. However, this circle is closely coherent and allows its individual members only a narrow field for the development of unique qualities and free, self-responsible movements. Political and kinship groups, parties and religious associations begin in this way. The self-preservation of very young associations requires the establishment of strict boundaries and a centripetal unity. Therefore they cannot allow the individual freedom and unique inner and outer development. From this stage social development proceeds at once in two different, yet corresponding, directions. To the extent to which the group grows—numerically, spatially, in significance and in content of life—to the same degree the group's direct, inner unity loosens, and the rigidity of the original demarcation against others is softened through mutual relations and connections. At the same time, the individual gains freedom of movement, far beyond the first jealous delimitation. The individual also gains a specific individuality to which the division of labor in the enlarged group gives both occasion and necessity.

The most profound reason, however, why the metropolis conduces to the urge for the most individual personal existence—no matter whether justified and successful—appears to me to be the following: the development of modern culture is characterized by the preponderance of what one may call the "objective spirit" over the "subjective spirit." This is to say, in language as well as in law, in the technique of production as well as in art, in science as well as in the objects of the domestic environment, there is embodied a sum of spirit. The individual in his intellectual development follows the growth of this spirit very imperfectly and at an ever increasing distance. If, for instance, we view the immense culture which for the last hundred years has been embodied in things and in knowledge, in institutions and in comforts, and if we compare all this with the cultural progress of the individual during the same period—at least in high status groups—a frightful disproportion in growth between the two becomes evident. Indeed, at some points we notice a retrogression in the culture of the individual with reference to spirituality, delicacy, and idealism. This discrepancy results essentially from the growing division of labor. For the division of labor demands from the individual an ever more one-sided accomplishment, and the greatest advance in a one-sided pursuit only too frequently means dearth to the personality of the individual. In any case, he can cope less and less with the overgrowth of objective culture. The individual is reduced to a negligible quantity, perhaps less in his consciousness than in his practice and in the totality of his obscure emotional states that are derived from this practice. The individual has become a mere cog in an enormous organization of things and powers which tear from his hands all progress, spirituality, and value in order to transform them from their subjective form into the form of a purely objective life. It needs merely to be pointed out that the metropolis is the genuine arena of this culture which outgrows all personal life. Here in buildings and educational institutions, in the wonders and comforts of space-conquering technology, in the formations of community life, and in the visible institutions of the state, is offered such an overwhelming fullness of crystallized and impersonalized spirit that the personality, so to speak, cannot maintain itself under its impact. On the one hand, life is made infinitely easy for the personality in that stimulations, interests, uses of time and consciousness are offered to it from all sides. They carry the person as if in a stream, and one needs hardly to swim for oneself. On the other hand, however, life is composed more and more of these impersonal contents and offerings which tend to displace the genuine personal colorations and incomparabilities. This results in the individual's summoning the utmost in uniqueness and particularization, in order to preserve his most personal core. He has to exaggerate this personal element in order to remain audible even to himself.

Article 8

Habits of the Heart: Religion in American Life

Robert N. Bellah, Richard Madsen, William M. Sullivan, Ann Swidler, and Steven M. Tipton

R eligion is one of the most important of the many ways in which Americans "get involved" in the life of their community and society. Americans give more money and donate more time to religious bodies and religiously associated organizations than to all other voluntary associations put together. Some 40 percent of Americans attend religious services at least once a week (a much greater number than would be found in Western Europe or even Canada) and religious membership is around 60 percent of the total population.

In our research, we were interested in religion not in isolation but as part of the texture of private and public life in the United States. Although we seldom asked specifically about religion, time and again in our conversations, religion emerged as important to the people we were interviewing, as the national statistics just quoted would lead one to expect.

For some, religion is primarily a private matter having to do with family and local congregation. For others, it is private in one sense but also a primary vehicle for the expression of national and even global concerns. Though Americans overwhelmingly accept the doctrine of the separation of church and state, most of them believe, as they always have, that religion has an important role to play in the public realm.

. . .

The Local Congregation [—Involvement and Independence]

We may begin a closer examination of how religion operates in the lives of those to whom we talked by looking at the local congregation, which traditionally has a certain priority. The local church is a community of worship that contains within itself, in small, so to speak, the features of the larger church, and in some Protestant traditions can exist autonomously.

The church as a community of worship is an adaptation of the Jewish synagogue. Both Jews and Christians view their communities as existing in a covenant relationship with God, and the Sabbath worship around which religious life centers is a celebration of that covenant. Worship calls to mind the story of the relationship of the community with God: how God brought his chosen people out of Egypt or gave his only begotten son for the salvation of mankind. Worship also reiterates the obligations that the community has undertaken, including the biblical insistence on justice and righteousness, and on love of God and neighbor, as well as the promises God has made that make it possible for the community to hope for the future. Though worship has its special times and places, especially on the Sabbath in the house of the Lord, it functions as a model or pattern for the whole of life. Through reminding the people of their relationship to God, it establishes patterns of character and virtue that should operate in economic and political life as well as in the context of worship. The community maintains itself as a community of memory, and the various religious traditions have somewhat different memories.

The very freedom, openness, and pluralism of American religious life makes this traditional pattern hard for Americans to understand. For one thing, the traditional pattern assumes a certain priority of the religious community over the individual. The community exists before the individual is born and will continue after his or her death. The relationship of the individual to God is ultimately personal, but it is mediated by the whole pattern of community life. There is a givenness about the community and the tradition. They are not normally a matter of individual choice.

For Americans, the traditional relationship between the individual and the religious community is to some degree reversed. On the basis of our interviews, we are not surprised to learn that a 1978 Gallup poll found that 80 percent of Americans agreed that "an individual should arrive at his or her own religious beliefs independent of any churches synagogues." From the traditional point of view, this is a strange statement—it is precisely within church or synagogue that one comes to one's religious beliefs—but to many Americans it is the Gallup finding that is normal.

Nan Pfautz, raised in a strict Baptist church, is now an active member of a Presbyterian congregation near San Jose. Her church membership gives her a sense of community involvement, of engagement with issues at once social and moral. She speaks of her "commitment" to the church, so that being a member means being willing to give time, money, and care to the community it embodies and to its wider purposes. Yet, like many Americans, she feels that her personal relationship to God transcends her involvement in any particular church. Indeed, she speaks with humorous disdain of "churchy people" such as those who condemn others for violations of external norms. She says, "I believe I have a commitment to God which is beyond church. I felt my relationship with God was O.K. when I wasn't with the church."

For Nan, the church's value is primarily an ethical one. "Church to me is a community, and it's an organization that I belong to. They do an awful lot of good." Her obligations to the church come from the fact that she has chosen to join it, and "just like any organization that you belong to, it shouldn't be just to have another piece of paper in your wallet." As with the Kiwanis or any other organization, "you have a responsibility to do something or don't be there," to devote time and money, and especially to "care about the people." It is this caring community, above all, that the church represents. "I really love my church and what they have done for me, and what they do for other people, and the community that's there." Conceived as an association of loving individuals, the church acquires its value from "the caring about people. What I like about my church is its community."

…

In talking to Art Townsend, the pastor of Nan's church, we found views quite consonant with hers. Art is not unaware of the church as a community of memory, though he is as apt to tell a story from the Maharishi or a Zen Buddhist text as from the New Testament. But what excites him are the individuals themselves: "The church is really a part of me and I am a part of the church, and my shift professionally has gone from 'how can I please them and make them like me so that I can keep my job and get a promotion' to 'how can I love them, how can I help these beautiful, special people to experience how absolutely wonderful they are.'" It is the self—both his and those of others—that must be the source of all religious meaning. In Art's optimistic vision, human beings need to learn to "lighten up" as "one of the steps to enlightenment." His job in turn is to "help them take the scales from their eyes and experience and see their magnificence." Difficulties between people are misunderstandings among selves who are ultimately in harmony. If a couple who are angry or disappointed or bored with each other really share their feelings, "you get into a deeper level, and what happens is that feelings draw together, and you actually, literally feel the feeling the same way the other person feels it. And when you do, there is a shift, there is a zing, and it is like the two become one."

For Art Townsend, God becomes the guarantee of what he has "experienced in my life, that there is nothing that happens to me that is not for the fulfillment of my higher self." His cheery mysticism eliminates any real possibility of sin, evil, or damnation, since "if I thought God were such a being that he would waste a human soul on the basis of its mistakes, that would be a little limiting." In consonance with this primarily expressive individualist ethos, Art's philosophy is remarkably upbeat. Tragedy and sacrifice are not what they seem. "Problems become the playground of consciousness" and are to be welcomed as opportunities for growth.

Such a view can justify high levels of social activism, and Art Townsend's church engages in a wide variety of activities, volunteering as a congregation to care for Vietnamese refugee families, supporting broader understanding of the homosexual minority, and visiting the sick or distressed in the congregation. A member such as Nan Pfautz carries her sense of responsibility further, participating through the church in a range of activities from environmental protection to fighting multinational corporations marketing infant formula in the Third World. But it is clear for her, as for Art Townsend, that the ultimate meaning of the church is an expressive-individualist one. Its value is as a loving community in which individuals can experience the joy of belonging. As the church secretary says, "Certainly all the things that we do involve caring about people in a loving manner, at least I hope that we do." She puts it succinctly when she says, "For the most part, I think this community is a safe place for a lot of people."

Art Townsend's Presbyterian church would be viewed as theologically liberal. A look at a nearby conservative church brings out many differences but also many similarities. Pastor Larry Beckett describes his church as independent, conservative, and evangelical, and as neither liberal nor fundamentalist. At first glance, this conservative evangelical church is more clearly a community of memory than Art Townsend's. Larry Beckett indicates that its central beliefs are the divinity of Christ and the authority of scripture. A great deal of time is given to the study and exposition of scripture. Larry even gave a brief course on New Testament Greek so that the original text would be to some degree available to the congregation. While Larry insists that the great commandment to love God and one's neighbor is the essence of biblical teaching, his church tries to follow the specific commandments as much as possible It is, for example, strongly against divorce because of Jesus' injunction (Matt. 19:6) against putting asunder what God has joined together. The firm insistence on belief in God and in the divinity of Christ, the importance of Christ as a model for how to act, and the attempt to apply specific biblical injunctions as far as possible provide the members of this church with a structure of external authority that might make the members of Art Townsend's congregation uneasy. Not so different socially and occupationally from the nearby Presbyterian church, and subject to many of the same insecurities and tensions, the members of this evangelical church have found a faith that is secure and unchanging. As Larry Beckett says, "God doesn't change. The values don't change. Jesus Christ doesn't change. In fact, the Bible says He is the same yesterday, today, and forever. Everything in life is always changing, but God doesn't change."

…

For Larry Beckett and the members of his congregation, biblical Christianity provides an alternative to the utilitarian individualist values of this world. But that alternative, appealing precisely because it is "real clear," does not go very far in helping them understand their connection to the world or the society in which they live. The Bible provides unambiguous moral answers about "the essential issues—love, obedience, faith, hope," so that "killing or, say, murdering is never right. Or adultery. A relationship outside of your marriage is never right. The Bible says that real simple." To "follow the Scriptures and the words of Jesus" provides a clear, but narrow, morality centered on family and personal life. One must personally, as an individual, resist temptation and put the good of others ahead of one's own. Christian love applies to one-to-one relationships—I may not cheat my neighbor, or exploit him, or sell him something I know he can't afford. But outside this sphere of personal morality, the evangelical church has little to say about wider social commitments. Indeed, the sect draws together those who have found a personal relationship to Christ into a special loving community, and while it urgently seeks to have everyone make the same commitment, it separates its members off from attachment to the wider society. Morality becomes personal, not social; private, not public.

Both Larry Beckett's conservative church and Art Townsend's liberal one stress stable, loving relationships, in which the intention to care outweighs the flux of momentary feelings, as the ideal pattern in marriage, family, and work relationships. Thus both attempt to counter the more exploitative tendencies of utilitarian individualism. But in both cases, their sense of religious community has trouble moving beyond an individualistic morality. In Art Townsend's faith, a distinctively religious vision has been absorbed into the categories of contemporary psychology. No autonomous standard of good and evil survives outside the needs of individual psyches for growth. Community and attachment come not from the demands of a tradition, but from the empathetic sharing of feelings among therapeutically attuned selves.

Larry Beckett's evangelical church, in contrast, maintains a vision of the concrete moral commitments that bind church members. But the bonds of loyalty, help, and responsibility remain oriented to the exclusive sect of those who are "real" Christians. Direct reliance on the Bible provides a second language with which to resist the temptations of the "world," but the almost exclusive concentration on the Bible, especially the New Testament, with no larger memory of how Christians have coped with the world historically, diminishes the capacity of their second language to deal adequately with current social reality. There is even a tendency visible in many evangelical circles to thin the biblical language of sin and redemption to an idea of Jesus as the friend who helps us find happiness and self-fulfillment. The emphasis on love, so evident within the community, is not shared with the world, except through missionary outreach.

There are thousands of local churches in the United States, representing an enormous range of variation in doctrine and worship. Yet most define themselves as communities of personal support. A recent study suggests that what Catholics look for does not differ from the concerns of the various types of Protestants we have been discussing. When asked the direction the church should take in future years, the two things that a national sample of Catholics most asked for were "personal and accessible priests" and "warmer, more personal parishes." The salience of these needs for personal intimacy in American religious life suggests why the local church, like other voluntary communities, indeed like the contemporary family, is so fragile, requires so much energy to keep it going, and has so faint a hold on commitment when such needs are not met.

Religious Individualism

Religious individualism, evident in these examples of church religion, goes very deep in the United States. Even in seventeenth-century Massachusetts, a personal experience of salvation was a prerequisite for acceptance as a church member. It is true that when Anne Hutchinson began to draw her own theological conclusions from her religious experiences and teach them to others, conclusions that differed from those of the established ministry, she was tried and banished from Massachusetts. But through the peculiarly American phenomenon of revivalism, the emphasis on personal experience would eventually override all efforts at church discipline. Already in the eighteenth century, it was possible for individuals to find the form of religion that best suited their inclinations. By the nineteenth century, religious bodies had to compete in a consumers' market and grew or declined in terms of changing patterns of individual religious taste. But religious individualism in the United States could not be contained within the churches, however diverse they were. We have noted the presence of individuals who found their own way in religion even in the eighteenth century. Thomas Jefferson said, "I am a sect myself," and Thomas Paine, "My mind is my church." Many of the most influential figures in nineteenth-century American culture could find a home in none of the existing religious bodies, though they were attracted to the religious teachings of several traditions. One thinks of Ralph Waldo Emerson, Henry David Thoreau, and Walt Whitman.

Many of these nineteenth-century figures were attracted to a vague pantheistic mysticism that tended to identify the divine with a higher self. In recent times, what had been a pattern confined to the cultural elite has spread to significant sections of the educated middle class. Tim Eichelberger, a young Campaign for Economic Democracy activist in Southern California, is typical of many religious individualists when he says, "I feel religious in a way. I have no denomination or anything like that." In 1971, when he was seventeen, he became interested in Buddhism. What attracted him was the capacity of Buddhism to allow him to "transcend" his situation: "I was always into change and growth and changing what you were sort of born into and I was always interested in not having that control me. I wanted to define my own self." His religious interest involved the practice of yoga and a serious interest in leading a nonviolent life. "I was into this religious purity and I worked the earth around me to be pure, nonviolence, nonconflict Harmony. Harmony with the earth. Man living in harmony with the earth; men living in harmony with each other." His certainty about nonviolence eventually broke down when he had to acknowledge his rage after being rejected in a love relationship. Coming to terms with his anger made him see that struggle is a part of life, Eventually, he found that involvement in CED gave an expression to his ideals as well as his understanding of life as a struggle. His political concern with helping people attain "self-respect, self-determination, self-realization" continues his older religious concern to define his own self. But neither his religion nor his politics transcend an individualism in which "self-realization" is the highest aspiration.

That radical religious individualism can find its own institutional form is suggested by the story of Cassie Cromwell, a suburban San Diego volunteer a generation older than Eichelberger, who came to her own religious views in adolescence when she joined the Unitarian church. She sums up her beliefs succinctly: "I am a pantheist. I believe in the 'holiness' of the earth and all other living things. We are a product of this life system and are inextricably linked to all parts of it. By treating other living things disrespectfully, we are disrespectful of ourselves. Our very survival depends on the air 'god,' the water, sun, etc." Not surprisingly, she has been especially concerned with working for ecological causes. Like Eichelberger, she began with a berugn view of life an then had to modify it. "I used to believe that man was basically good," her statement of her philosophy continues. "I didn't believe in evil. I still don't know what evil is but see greed, ignorance, insensitivity to other people and other living things, and irresponsibility." Unlike most of those to whom we talked, Cassie is willing to make value judgments about religion and is openly critical of Christianity. She believes that "the Christian idea of the superiority of man makes it so difficult to have a proper concern for the environment. Because only man has a soul, everything on the earth can be killed and transformed for the benefit of man. That's not right."

Commoner among religious individualists than criticism of religious beliefs is criticism of institutional religion, or the church as such. "Hypocrisy" is one of the most frequent charges against organized religion. Churchgoers do not practice what they preach. Either they are not loving enough or they do not practice the moral injunctions they espouse. As one person said, "It's not religion or the church you go to that's going to save you." Rather it is your "personal relationship" with God. Christ will" come into your heart" if you ask, without any church at all.

In the cases of Tim Eichelberger and Cassie Cromwell, we can see how mystical beliefs can provide an opening for involvement in the world. Nonetheless, the links are tenuous and to some extent fortuitous. Both had to modify their more cosmic flights in order to take account of evil and aggression and work for the causes they believe in. The CED provides a focus for Eichelberger's activities, as the ecology movement does for Cassie. But their fundamental views were formed outside those contexts and their relation to the respective groups, even Cassie's long standing connection with the Unitarians, remains one of convenience. As social ideals, neither "self-realization" nor the "life system" provide practical guidance. Indeed, although both Tim and Cassie value "harmony with the earth," they lack a notion of nature from which any clear social norms could be derived. Rather, the tendency in American nature pantheism is to construct the world somehow out of the self.… If the mystical quest is pursued far enough, it may take on new forms of self-discipline, committed practice, and community, as in the case serious practitioners of Zen Buddhism. But more usually the languages of Eastern spirituality and American naturalistic pantheism are employed by people not connected with any particular religious practice or community.

Internal and External Religion

Radically individualistic religion, particularly when it takes the form of a belief in cosmic selfhood, may seem to be in a different world from conservative or fundamentalist religion. Yet these are the two poles that organize much of American religious life. To the first, God is simply the self magnified; to the second, God confronts man from outside the universe. One seeks a self that is finally identical with the world; the other seeks an external God who will provide order in the world. Both value personal religious experience as the basis of their belief. Shifts from one pole to the other are not as rare as one might think.

Sheila Larson is, in part, trying to find a center in herself after liberating herself from an oppressively conformist early family life.… The two experiences that define her faith took a similar form. One occurred just before she was about to undergo major surgery. God spoke to her to reassure her that all would be well, but the voice was her own. The other experience occurred when, as a nurse, she was caring for a dying woman whose husband was not able to handle the situation. Taking over care in the final hours, Sheila had the experience that "if she looked in the mirror" she "would see Jesus Christ." Tim Eichelberger's mystical beliefs and the "nonrestrictive" nature of his yoga practices allowed him to "transcend" his family and ethnic culture and define a self free of external constraint.

Conversely, cosmic mysticism may seem too threatening and undefined, and in reaction a religion of external authority may be chosen. Larry Beckett was attracted to Hinduism and Buddhism in his counter-cultural stage, but found them just too amorphous. The clarity and authority that he found in the New Testament provided him with the structure that till then had been lacking in his life.

Howard Crossland, a scientist and a member of Larry Beckett's congregation …, finds a similar security in his religion. He tends to view his Christianity as a matter of facts rather than emotion: "Because I have the Bible to study, it's not really relying on your emotions. There are certain facts presented and you accept the facts." Not surprisingly, Crossland is concerned about his own self-control and respects self-control in others. He never went through a countercultural phase, but he does have memories of a father who drank too much—an example of what can happen when control gets lost. In his marriage, in relation to his children, and with the several people who work under him, Crossland tries to be considerate and put the good of others ahead of his own. As he sees it, he is able to do that because of the help of God and His church: "From the help of other members of the congregation and with the help of the Holy Spirit, well, first of all you accept God, and then He gives you help to do good to your fellowman, to refrain from immorality, to refrain from illegal things."

Ruth Levy, [an] Atlanta therapist … comments on what she calls "born-again Jews," who are in many ways similar to born-again Christians. They come from assimilated families who haven't kept kosher in three generations, yet "incredibly, they do stuff that my grandparents may not even have done." What these born-again Jews are doing is "instilling structure, discipline, and meaning." They have found that "to be free to do anything you want isn't enough. There isn't anything you want to do."

Since these two types of religion, or two ways of being religious, are deeply interrelated, if our analysis is correct, some of the obvious contrasts between them turn out to be not quite what they seem. It is true that the first style emphasizes inner freedom and the second outer control, but we cannot say that the first is therefore liberating and the second authoritarian, or that the first is individualistic and the second collectivist. It is true that the first involves a kind of radical individualism that tends to elevate the self to a cosmic principle, whereas the second emphasizes external authorities and injunctions. But the first sees the true self as benevolent and harmonious with nature and other humans and so as incompatible with narrow self-seeking. And the second finds in external authority and regulation something profoundly freeing: a protection against the chaos of internal and external demands, and the basis for a genuine personal autonomy. Thus, though they mean somewhat different things by freedom and individuality, both hold these as central values. And while the first is clearly more focussed on expressive freedom, the second in its own way also allows important opportunities for expressive freedom in intensely participatory religious services and through emphasis on love and caring. Finally, though conservative religion does indeed have a potential for authoritarianism, particularly where a magnetic preacher gathers inordinate power in his own hands, so does extreme religious individualism. Where a guru or other religious teacher is thought to have the secret of perfect personal liberation, he or she may gain excessive power over adherents.

...

Article 9

The Code of the Street

Elijah Anderson

The hard reality of the world of the street can be traced to the profound sense of alienation from mainstream society and its institutions felt by many poor inner-city black people, particularly the young. The code of the street is actually a cultural adaptation to a profound lack of faith in the police and the judicial system—and in others who would champion one's personal security.

O f all the problems besetting the poor inner-city black community, none is more pressing than that of interpersonal violence and aggression. This phenomenon wreaks havoc daily on the lives of community residents and increasingly spills over into downtown and residential middleclass areas. Muggings, burglaries, carjackings, and drug-related shootings, all of which may leave their victims or innocent bystanders dead, are now common enough to concern all urban and many suburban residents.

The inclination to violence springs from the circumstances of life among the ghetto poor—the lack of jobs that pay a living wage, limited basic public services (police response in emergencies, building maintenance, trash pickup, lighting, and other services that middle-class neighborhoods take for granted), the stigma of race, the fallout from rampant drug use and drug trafficking, and the resulting alienation and absence of hope for the future. Simply living in such an environment places young people at special risk of falling victim to aggressive behavior. Although there are often forces in the community that can counteract the negative influences—by far the most powerful is a strong, loving, "decent" (as inner-city residents put it) family that is committed to middle-class values—the despair is pervasive enough to have spawned an oppositional culture, that of "the street," whose norms are often consciously opposed to those of mainstream society. These two orientations—decent and street—organize the community socially, and the way they coexist and interact has important consequences for its residents, particularly for children growing up in the inner city. Above all, this environment means that even youngsters whose home lives reflect mainstream values—and most of the homes in the community do—must be able to handle themselves in a street-oriented environment.

This is because the street culture has evolved a "code of the street," which amounts to a set of informal rules governing interpersonal public behavior, particularly violence.[1] The rules prescribe both proper comportment and the proper way to respond if challenged. They regulate the use of violence and so supply a rationale allowing those who are inclined to aggression to precipitate violent encounters in an approved way. The rules have been established and are enforced mainly by the street-oriented; but on the streets the distinction between street and decent is often irrelevant. Everybody knows that if the rules are violated, there are penalties. Knowledge of the code is thus largely defensive, and it is literally necessary for operating in public. Therefore, though families with a decency orientation are usually opposed to the values of the code, they often reluctantly encourage their children's familiarity with it in order to enable them to negotiate the inner-city environment.

At the heart of the code is the issue of respect—loosely defined as being treated "right" or being granted one's "props" (or proper due) or the deference one deserves. However, in the troublesome public environment of the inner city, as people increasingly feel buffeted by forces beyond their control, what one deserves in the way of respect becomes ever more problematic and uncertain. This situation in turn further opens up the issue of respect to sometimes intense interpersonal negotiation, at times resulting in altercations. In the street culture, especially among young people, respect is viewed as almost an external entity, one that is hard-won but easily lost—and so must constantly be guarded. The rules of the code in fact provide a framework for negotiating respect. With the right amount of respect, individuals can avoid being bothered in public. This security is important, for if they are bothered, not only may they face physical danger, but they will have been disgraced or "dissed" (disrespected). Many of the forms dissing can take may seem petty to middle-class people (maintaining eye contact for too long, for example), but to those invested in the street code, these actions, a virtual slap in the face, become serious indications of the other person's intentions. Consequently, such people become very sensitive to advances and slights, which could well serve as a warning of imminent physical attack or confrontation.

The hard reality of the world of the street can be traced to the profound sense of alienation from mainstream society and its institutions felt by many poor inner-city black people, particularly the young. The code of the street is actually a cultural adaptation to a profound lack of faith in the police and the judicial system—and in others who would champion one's personal security. The police, for instance, are most often viewed as representing the dominant white society and as not caring to protect inner-city residents. When called, they may not respond, which is one reason many residents feel they must be prepared to take extraordinary measures to defend themselves and their loved ones against those who are inclined to aggression. Lack of police accountability has in fact been incorporated into the local status system: the person who is believed capable of "taking care of himself" is accorded a certain deference and regard, which translates into a sense of physical and psychological control. The code of the street thus emerges where the influence of the police ends and where personal responsibility for one's safety is felt to begin. Exacerbated by the proliferation of drugs and easy access to guns, this volatile situation results in the ability of the street-oriented minority (or those who effectively "go for bad") to dominate the public spaces.

Note

1. For a plausible description tracing the tradition and evolution of this code, with its implications for violence on the streets of urban America, see Fox Butterfield, *All God's Children* (New York: Knopf, 1995).

Article 10

Hate in the Suburbs
The Rise of the Skinhead Counterculture

Randy Blazak

In 1988, skinheads seemed to be everywhere—on *Geraldo* and *The Morton Downey, Jr. Show*, as the mindless thugs on episodes of *The Equalizer*, and as real-life thugs on the news after the murder of Mulugeta Serraw in Portland, Oregon.[1] Skinheads were the new bad guys. Monitoring organizations like the Southern Poverty Law Center and the Anti-Defamation Leagues of B'nai B'rith[2] released dire reports on the rise of hate crimes in America. Some were saying that the waning days of the Reagan era were strikingly similar to the waning days of Germany's Weimar Republic,[3] opening the doors to a substantial fascist movement.[4]

As a young activist and sociologist, I wanted to understand this trend. It seemed too easy to demonize skinheads as devils. Many hung out in the same punk rock clubs I did. They seemed fairly human and vulnerable to me. Some were racist and some were not. Some were criminal and others were not. I needed to find out what drew so many of my peers into such a dramatic counterculture, one characterized by an almost religious attachment to violence and intolerance.

Growing Up with the Klan

The first step to understanding the skinheads was to drop the good/evil dichotomy and see myself in their eyes. I grew up in Stone Mountain, Georgia, a suburb of Atlanta. In racist

---

[1] Mulugeta Serraw, an Ethiopian, was murdered by three skinheads. A civil court later ruled that a branch of the Aryan movement was ultimately responsible for the murder; the court award nearly bankrupted the Aryans.—Ed.

[2] The B'nai B'rith is an American Jewish organization established in 1843. In 1913, in response to an upsurge of prejudice and discrimination against Jews, the B'nai B'rith created the Anti-Defamation League to combat anti-Semitism.—Ed.

[3] The Weimar Republic was established in Germany in 1919 when the National Constituent Assembly met at Weimar to draw up a constitution. In 1933, two months after becoming chancellor of Germany, Adolf Hitler suspended the constitution.—Ed.

[4] Fascism is an undemocratic political philosophy that places the well-being of the nation over that of individuals.—Ed.

"Hate in the Suburbs; The Rise of the Skinhead Counterculture" by Randy Blazak as appeared in *The Practical Skeptic: Readings in Sociology* ed. Lisa J. McIntyre, 2002. Reprinted by permission of Randy Blazak, Portland State University.

circles, Stone Mountain is well known as the birthplace of the modern Ku Klux Klan in 1915. The annual Labor Day Klan rally was always a source of wonder to us as kids. When I was 12, my friend Kenny and I sat on our bikes and watched the Klansmen march through town in their robes to their annual cross lighting at the foot of the mountain. It was frightening and empowering at the same time. Even though I was taught that racism was not "polite." I knew that the Klan was there for me, to defend me. I had heard my father worry aloud about black families moving into our suburban Atlanta neighborhood and driving property values down. Maybe the Klan could help.

A few years later, I slipped a bit further into the defensive mode. I wrote an editorial in an eleventh-grade journalism class about the hypocrisy of celebrating Black History Month and not having a White History Month (nobody bothered to point out that every month is white history month). I saw black kids busing into my white high school and white kids moving out. I saw the ban on displaying the Confederate flag and singing "Dixie" at peprallies. Nobody was explaining what was happening to my community. There was no new crime. No gangs or riots. Just change. Well, the Klan had an explanation. They began handing out literature to my classmates and me after school, which revealed the dark plot to unseat whites from their "natural" position of dominance. I was fascinated.

Fortunately, I made it into the shrinking federal college loan program and escaped to a liberal arts college where I learned a few things. I learned how groups like the Klan twist facts to fit their philosophy. I learned how appealing conspiracy theories are to young people and how we can trick ourselves into believing our stereotypes. I was lucky. My friend Kenny, who never went to college, became an Exalted Cyclops in the Southern White Knights of the Ku Klux Klan.

Deciding to Study Skinheads

My first encounter with skinheads came in 1982. I was 18 and on a study-abroad program in London. One day I hopped onto a train at Victoria Station with three toughs with shaven heads and heavy dockworker boots. At the time, I claimed membership in a punkish subculture called "Mod," and my first thought upon seeing the three was, "Here we are, four alienated youths full of rebelling." But this was no opportunity for male bonding. It soon became clear that I was an enemy. They took out markers and began graffiti-ing swastikas and "Kill a Mod Today" inside the train car. Then they came after me. I jumped out at the next stop. So much for youth unity.

Back home in Atlanta, where I was in graduate school, skinheads began popping up around 1985. They still didn't like Mods (proved to me when a group of skinheads stole my Vespa scooter and set it on fire), but clearly they had other, more serious targets: blacks,

Asians, feminists, gays, communists, the homeless, and so on. Things became very political quickly. At any demonstration against Reagan's policies (the arms race, the secret wars in Central America, apartheid in South Africa, CIA recruiting) the skinheads would be there to break things up. They raised images of 1933 and the Nazi brownshirts. [5] As a 21-year-old graduate student, I had my research question: What impels suburban middle-class kids to become violent skinheads?

It was a question that would take me ten years to answer. I often wished I had picked an easier question. Qualitative fieldwork takes a lot of time and patience. My plan was to use my "white maleness" to get inside this counterculture and to try to see the world through their eyes. I spent years traveling around the country drinking beer with skinheads and attending Klan rallies and "white family picnics." I slam danced, fought attended secret meetings, and even sang in a skinhead band. As the 1980s became the 1990s, and the Berlin Wall came down, I headed off to Eastern Europe to talk to skinheads there as well as back in London. Needless to say, I drank a lot of beer.

My method was participant observation. Others, like Raphael S. Ezekial in his pioneering work *The Racist Mind* (1995), had gained access to hate groups by asking permission. Ezekial was an older Jew. But I was a young WASP and I wanted them to trust me, so I played the role of a potential recruit. Drawing upon my Stone Mountain upbringing, I could talk the talk of the white man who feared change. It was relatively easy to gain acceptance into the group. Then, at a certain point, I would ask to interview individual members for a local newspaper or school project. I told them they should have their story heard by others. I ended up doing more than seventy interviews with young skinheads.

There were a few frightening moments. In Orlando, Florida, a skinhead recruiter threatened to torture me unless I gave him my Social Security number. In Berlin, I found myself suddenly surrounded by Nazi skinheads who thought I was a Jew. In Atlanta, I got caught up in the middle of a brawl between racist and antiracist skinheads in which one of the combatants had his ear bit off. These frightening encounters notwithstanding, I generally found the skinheads to be warm and engaging with me. They wanted to be understood. They needed to explain the plight of white males in the rapidly changing culture of America in the 1980s and 1990s.

Finding a Theory in Bill Cosby

Ethnographers usually work inductively. That is, instead of entering the field with a hypothesis to test, they use what they observe to help them generate a theory. I had several ideas

---

[5] Nazi brownshirts were the *Sturmabteilung* or Storm Troops; members of this private army of Nazis wore brown uniforms—Ed.

about what was going on with the skinheads, but it took me a while to put together the pieces into some sort of theory. At the beginning of my study, I spent thirteen months with a group of skinheads in Orlando, Florida. Away from the tourist attractions, Orlando had a large underground youth scene that included dozens of skinheads. Much of our time together was spent in parking lots outside music clubs. And a recurring topic was *The Cosby Show*, which, in 1988, was the most popular TV show in America.

Cosby was almost an obsession with these boys. The show was about a very well-off black family—doctor father, lawyer mother, and private school kids. The consensus of the Orlando skinheads was that the show was a sign of the end of white hegemony. Otto, 18, asked me: "What kind of a country is it where the Cosbys have everything and I have nothing? It isn't right!" While they would not have known the sociological term for it, the notion of ascribed status was very powerful to these boys: *They* had a birth right to the good things in life. The Cosbys *did not*.

Such comments about *The Cosby Show* helped lead me to a theoretical understanding of skinheads. These youths clearly were experiencing "status frustration" with respect to their positions as white males. In other words, they felt that they were not getting the status rewards to which they felt entitled. The more time I spent with them, the more I saw this frustration as economically based. In the postindustrial eighties, these boys were seeing an evaporation of their hopes of attaining the American Dream. As their parents were being laid off, downsized, and forced into low-wage service jobs, they were beginning to experience anomie. Building on Robert Merton's anomie theory,[6] criminologist Albert Cohen wrote in his book. *Delinquent Boys* (1955) that economically frustrated boys will look to subcultures for "solutions" to their problems.

What Happened in the 1980s to Explain the Rise of Skinheads?

The Reagan-Bush years (1980–1992) were a time of great change in America. Along with the structural changes that attended "trickle down" economics,[7] there was a racial dynamic. In the wake of the changes fueled by civil rights legislation (including affirmative action), there was perceived to be a great movement of blacks into the middle class. In a kind of

---

[6] Blazak draws here on Robert Merton's conception of anomie (discussed in chapter 11 of *The Practical Skeptic Core Concepts in Sociology*). In brief, Merton suggested people share certain goals (especially success) in American society. When people find that the legitimate means to achieve these goals are blocked, they experience frustration, or what Merton called *anomie*.—Ed.

[7] The trickle-down theory is based on the simplistic assumption that whatever benefits the wealthiest members of society will ultimately benefit the entire society. For example, the trickle-down theory would justify reducing the amount of income taxes paid by wealthy people by saying that wealthy people will use the savings to create businesses that will, in turn, create jobs for poor people.—Ed.

backlash, the leftist organizations of the 1960s and 1970s lost ground to rabid right-wing, anti-communist groups that adopted the extremes of Ronald Reagan's philosophy.

As the civil rights movement faded, a new taboo emerged—race talk. Now that the race issue had been "solved," it was deemed impolite to raise the issue in public. This meant that the generation of parents who had come of age in the civil rights era neglected to teach their Gen X children about the dynamics of racism. This neglect was relevant, but not sufficient to drive kids into countercultural movements. More important were the following things: (1) the downward mobility of the increasingly downsized white middle class, (2) the frustration of straight males with the increasing gains of women and homosexuals in the public arena, and (3) the integration of the suburbs as millions of African Americans moved out of both urban and rural areas.

Downward Mobility in the American Middle Class

The 1992 presidential campaign promoted the theory that "this will be the first generation of Americans to be worse off than their parents." The notion of a contracting American middle class had first gained strength in the mid-1980s, and by the early 1990s, the reality of the economic threat came to be accepted by the wider social audience. The 6.8 percent unemployment rate of the 1992 election year included a great number of lower-middle-class/blue-collar workers who had lost jobs in the manufacturing, retail sales, and construction sections (Rose 1993).

The shrinking proportion of the middle class relative to other classes, and particularly the economic impact on the lower ranks of the middle class, has altered our conception of what the middle class actually is. Based on Department of Labor definitions, the middle-income group (families with incomes of $19,000 to $47,000 in 1986) has been shrinking: from 52.3 percent in 1978 to 44.3 percent in 1986. Using standardized family incomes, the middle class represented 46.7 percent of the population in 1979, but only 41.5 percent in 1989 (Rose 1993). The 1990 census revealed that the trend has continued: There was a significant decrease in the size of the middle class. Most importantly, most of those who had moved out of the middle class had moved downward. In 1979, the poverty rate was 11 percent. By the end of the 1980s, it hovered around 13 percent (U.S. Statistical Abstract 1991).

The recession of the early 1980s played a large role in changing people's perceptions.[8] Defining middle income as having a family income of between $20,000 and $49,000, Bradbury (1986) found that, after deflating incomes back to 1973 levels, the middle class had shrunk from 53 percent to 48 percent of all families in 1984. Again, the majority of those

---

[8] Technically, the health of the economy is generally defined in terms of general business activity (as measured by the total market value of the goods and services brought into use; that is, the Gross National Product). If a decline in the GNP persists for six to nine months, a *recession* exists. A serious recession is called a depression.—Ed.

who left the middle class experienced downward social mobility. A primary factor in this movement was the displacement of workers. In 1986, the U.S. Department of Labor reported that about 10.8 million workers (age 20 and above) had lost their jobs owing to plant closings or employment cutbacks between 1981 and 1986 (Horvath 1987). Of these, 5.1 million had been on the job for three years or more. Fewer than a third (3.4 million) of those displaced workers later found work; and only 2.7 million of them found full-time wage or salary jobs. Of the fully re-employed, 44 percent took jobs that paid less than their previous jobs. This represented a significant level of downward mobility within the lower middle class.

> *A frequently mentioned example of displaced workers is the steel or automobile worker, who had been employed at a relatively high paying production job and who, upon losing that job, finds little prospect of replacing the earnings to which he and his family had become accustomed. (Hovrath 1984, 4)*

In 1988, new studies mostly confirmed earlier Department of Labor findings. The level of re-employment was up from 66.7 percent to 71 percent, but still, 44 percent of those took lower-paying jobs and 30.4 percent were making at least 20 percent less than they had been earning in their previous jobs (Herz 1990). In addition, the types of jobs that were being created were much lower-paying service sector jobs that did not offer many benefits (health insurance. paid leave and vacations, and the like).

The replacement of good jobs with lower-paying ones was a new phenomenon. The growth of white-collar positions after World War II had brought people up from blue-collar and agricultural jobs into the swelling middle class (Macionis 1991). The bulk of jobs created in the 1960s and 1970s were in the high-income ($30,000 or more a year in 1988 dollars) or middle-income ($15,000 to $30,000) range. During the first half of the 1980s, the proportion of these jobs decreased dramatically, while the proportion of low-income jobs (under $15,000) increased to 40 percent of new jobs (Thurow 1987).

The shrinking middle class also adversely affected the working class. First, it reduced the opportunities for upward mobility as the number of those positions contracted. Second, it increased competition within the working class by adding the often overqualified down-wardly mobile to the labor market. And third, the forces that were behind the economic contraction, primarily deindustrialization and the rise of the service economy, hit the working class hardest. Before the downturn, a young unionized laborer with little education could find a secure position on the factory line. But when the factories moved abroad, the only jobs available were low-paying service sector jobs or jobs that generally require some educational training. So both the middle and working classes lost, even if it was only the potential for upward mobility.

Despite the brief economic upswing in the mid-1980s, the 1990s economy remained stagnant in terms of job opportunities for the lower middle class. The jobs that were created were largely in the service sector. Adding to real economic woes was the general perception of a slackening employment market. Nightly news stories featured factory closings, merger-fueled layoffs and downsizing, and thousands of applicants standing in line in the snow for a few hundred jobs. Even people who have not experienced real downward mobility may hold the perception that "it's happening and could happen to me." Rose wrote that

> *we all seem to want to "keep up with the Joneses" (what economists call consum-ing potential goods) and measure our self-worth by how successful we are in meeting this challenge. In a society bombarded with advertisements on televi-sion, billboards, newspapers—virtually everywhere, everyone has a chance to covet what is available to those with money. So as the incomes of the rich have moved farther away from those in the middle, this decline in relative standing has made people feel worse irrespective of the fact that their absolute standard of living may be a tad better. (1993, 16)*

The widespread perception that "the American Dream is going down the tubes" argu-ably affects some groups more than others. Among the most affected seem to be young white males. Despite the traditional emphasis on social equality, the United States has long had, and still has, an informal status system based on ascribed characteristics. But now "white" no longer seems to carry the same benefits it once did, and "male" no longer provides the same guarantee of economic security. Skin-heads and political conservatives alike often play up the image of the "straight white male" as a victim of a liberal society. In an uncertain economic environment, the loss of status once guaranteed to this group has created an envi-ronment of blame. Selective perception focuses on the haves of the previously disenfran-cised—*The Cosby Show* family, for example—and the have-nots of the white working class.

Patriarchal Reaction

The structure of gender power relations has changed as well. This is most evident in the work force. In 1950, 33 percent of adult women were in the paid work force. By 1990, that figure had risen to 58 percent and included an increase in the number of women in typi-cally male-dominated professions. Add to this the fact that corresponding to the women's rights movement in the 1970s was the gay rights movement that followed the Stonewall riots in 1969.[9] Via the popular media (Madonna, *Melrose Place*. Ellen DeGeneres) the number of homosexuals "coming out" in the 1980s and 1990s snowballed, and nearly one

---

[9] On June 28, 1969, the New York police raided a gay bar called the Stonewall Inn in Greenwich Village. Frequently violent, such raids were almost a tradition in New York City and other places where it was illegal to associate with known homosexuals in an establishment that served alcohol. Until the Stonewall raid, closeted lesbians and gays took their judicial and nonjudicial lumps quietly, fearing that any protest would bring them media exposure. The Stonewall rebellion marked a running point, leading to the gay rights movement—Ed.

million gays and lesbians attended a rally in Washington, DC, in 1993 (Houston 1993). "Gay bashing" hate crimes also increased during this period. In her book *The Chalice and the Blade* (1988), Riane Eisler presents an interesting theory about why patriarchal systems endure. Based on her extensive examination of history, Eisler suggests that ruling systems have followed a pattern: Societies that give an elevated status to women and approach some level of sex-role partnership ("gylanic" societies) are short-lived. They are ultimately defeated by an active patriarchal system in which males dominate ("androcratic" society). The pattern, then, is one in which, when male domination is lost, it is soon re-established. Thus, the patriarchal tone of the New Testament was a response to the elevated position of women in the original Christian cults. The Victorian era prohibitions were a response to the artistic, more gylanic activities of the Elizabethan era. Likewise, the macho arms race and the men's movements of the Reagan years can be seen as responses to the hippie and women's movements of the 1960s and 1970s. This is the "backlash" against feminism about which Susan Faludi warned:

> Unlike classic conservatives, these *"pseudoconservatives"*—as Theodore Adorno dubbed the constituents of such modern right-wing movements—perceive them-selves as social outcasts rather than guardians of the status quo. They are not so much defending the prevailing order as resurrecting an out-moded or imagined one. (1991, 231)

Following this argument, the skinhead movement can be seen as a reassertion of the androcratic system. American skinheads in the 1980s followed the Reagan model. Skinheads in the 1990s can be seen as reacting against the gylanic tendencies of the political correct-ness movement associated with much of youth culture and with the Clinton administration, which has made the rights of women and gays and lesbians something of a priority. This negative view of women and homosexuals is shared by racist and antiracist skinheads. For example, skinheads of every stripe tend to see women as totally subordinate—to the point at which, in many Nazi groups, women's role is simply to produce "healthy white babies for the master race." Homophobia is similarly institutionalized in these countercultures.[10] Gay bashing and harassment are accepted forms of skinhead behavior.

The Changing Face of the Suburbs
Add to economic and gender threats the changing face of suburban neighborhoods. Formerly all-white enclaves where members of the dominant group could escape from the problems of

---

[10] The term *homophobia* was coined by G. K. Lehne in 1976 to refer to the widespread irrational fear and intolerance of homosexuals. See Lehne, "Homophobia Among Men," in D. S. David and R. Brannon (eds.). *The Forty-Nine Percent Majority.*

TABLE 3.1 Suburban Racial Shifts Between 1980 and 1990 in Two Georgia Counties

Cobb County					
1980			1990		
White	281,625	(94.6%)	White	391,949	(87.5%)
Black	13,055	(4.4%)	Black	44,154	(9.9%)
Other	3,038	(1.0%)	Other	11,632	(2.6%)
Dekalb County					
1980			1990		
White	344,254	(71.3%)	White	292,310	(53.6%)
Black	130,980	(27.0%)	Black	230,425	(42.2%)
Other	7,790	(1.6%)	Other	23,102	(4.2%)

Source: 1990 U.S. Census Abstracts.

urban life—including interaction with members of minority groups—the suburbs now are seeing an influx of urban dwellers. In the 1980s, the proportion of black residents in the city of Atlanta dropped by 7 percent (Hiskey 1993), as those with the money to do so joined the growing number of blacks in middle-class suburbs. William J. Wilson (1991) argues that the eroding job base in urban centers led to an out-migration of African Americans to formerly all-white suburban areas. Two suburban Atlanta counties from my research (see table 3.1) reflect this shift. Between 1980 and 1990, 150,027 minorities moved into Cobb County, an increase of 7.1 percent. Dekalb County saw an even larger shift. Minority residents increased by 17.8 percent while the number of whites decreased by 17.7 percent. Woodridge Elementary School in Dekalb County, from which I graduated with a nearly all-white class in 1976, lost 57 percent of its white students between 1991 and 1993 (White 1993).

Along with this racial shift came a noticeable increase in the number of racist skinheads in these areas. A 1990 article in the *Atlanta Constitution* entitled "More Skinheads Cropping up in suburbs: Recruitment Reported in Middle, High Schools" discussed the rise in skinhead violence in metropolitan suburbs:

> *Racist skinheads—once rarely seen in Georgia outside Atlanta's inner city—are cropping up in predominantly middle-class and affluent North Georgia suburbs. And they are apparently taking their message to the schools. In a national report completed last June, the Anti-Defamation League of B'nai B'rith said Lassiter and Sprayberry high schools in Cobb County have a noticeable skinhead presence, and "about 28 neo-Nazi skinheads are reliably reported active at Sprayberry."* (Burson 1990, D1)

The new suburban skinheads may have been in more affluent areas, but these were still regions with a significant blue-collar and middle-class work force. Now the typical 16-year-old male was also competing with African, Asian, and Mexican Americans for the same service sector jobs.

Skinheads as Problem Solvers

To explain the relatively sudden appearance of skinheads on the American scene, it is important to look at macrolevel economic and social trends as well as microlevel subcultural trends. In the 1980s and 1990s, many people, particularly white males, have had to come to terms with their actual class position. Not only have there been threats to the status of white males on the economic front, but other social dynamics have shifted as well. The 1980s also saw the ascribed position of heterosexual males threatened by the gains made by gays and women. Some white males, then, saw their positions as being attacked on several fronts: economic, racial, gender, and sexual.

Many of the stories I heard were heart-breaking. A whole neighborhood plunged into poverty when the Ford Taurus plant laid off half its workers. White kids who were picked on as they became minorities in their own right. A bright 16-year-old with college plans forced to work construction after his father was downsized in a merger. There was real anger and real frustration. The influence of right-wing groups led many of those affected to regard these changes as the "fault" of minorities who had been given unfair advantages through Affirmative Action programs, or of Jews who controlled the suburban real estate market, or of gay rights advocates who were seeking to destroy traditional gender roles. In this way, the very real frustration about the loss of status felt by these boys was channeled into the problem-solving mode of the skinhead counterculture. The good news is that most of the boys left the counterculture after they realized that, ultimately, it didn't solve their problems. The bad news is that as the ascribed status of the straight white suburban male continues to lose value for its incumbents, it is likely that racist groups will continue to recruit alienated youths who seek simplistic solutions.

References

Adorno, T. 1950. *The Authoritarian Personality*. New York: Harper and Brothers.

Appelbaum, Richard, and William J. Chambliss. 1995. *Sociology*. New York: HarperCollins.

Blazak, Randy. 1991. "Status Frustration and Racism: A Case Study of Orlando Skinheads." Masters thesis, Emory University.

Burson, Pat. 1990. "More Skinheads Cropping Up in Suburbs." *Atlanta Journal Constitution*, May 20, p. D1.

Cloward, Richard A., and Lloyd E. Ohlin. 1960. *Delinquency and Opportunity*. Glencoe. IL: Free Press.

Cohen, Albert. 1955. *Delinquent Boys*. New York: Free Press.

Eisler, Riane. 1987. *The Chalice and the Blade*. San Francisco: HarperCollins.

Ezekial, Raphael S. 1995. *The Racist Mind: Portraits of American Neo-Nazis and Klansmer*. New York: Anchor.

Faludi, Susan. 1991. *Backlash*. New York: Anchor.

Heiz, Diane. 1990. "Worker Displacement in a Period of Rapid Job Expansion: 1983-1957." Monthly Labor Review. 13(5). 21–31.

Hiskey, Michelle. 1993. "The Atlanta Paradox," *Atlanta Journal Constitution*, September 19, p. G1.

Horrigan, M., and S. Hayen. 1988. "The Declining Middle-Class Thesis: A Sensitivity Analysis," *Monthly Labor Review* 10(6): 3–6.

Macionis, John J. 1991. *Sociology*. Englewood Cliffs, New Jersey: Prentice Hall.

Merton, Robert. 1938. "Social Structure and Anomie," *American Sociological Review* 3: 672–682.

Newman, Katherine. 1988. *Falling from Grace: The Experience of Downward Mobility in the American Middle Class*. New York: Free Press.

Phelps, Christopher. 1989. "Skinheads: The New Nazism." *Against the Current*, September/October, pp. 17–23.

Robertson, Ian. 1981. *Sociology*. New York: Worth.

Rose, Stephen J. 1993. *The Bunker Mentality of the Middle Class: The Real and Imagined Problems Facing America Today*. New York: New Press.

Statistical Abstract of the United States. 1991. Washington, D.C.: U.S. Dept. of Commerce.

Thurow, Lester C. 1987. "A Surge of Inequality." *Scientific American*, May, pp. 30–37.

White, Betsy. 1993. "Dekalb's Changing Schools," *Atlanta Journal Constitution*, March 29, p. A1.

Wilson, William Julius. 1991. "Studying Inner-City Dislocations: The Challenge of Public Agenda Research." *American Sociological Review* 56: 1–14.

Article 11

The McDonald's System

George Ritzer

The Dimensions of McDonaldization: From Drive-Throughs to Uncomfortable Seats

Even if some domains are able to resist McDonaldization, this book intends to demonstrate that many other aspects of society are being, or will be, McDonaldized. This raises the issue of why the McDonald's model has proven so irresistible. Four basic and alluring dimensions lie at the heart of the success of the McDonald's model and, more generally, of the process of McDonaldization.

First, McDonald's offers *efficiency*. That is, the McDonald's system offers us the optimum method for getting from one point to another. Most generally, this means that McDonald's proffers the best available means of getting us from a state of being hungry to a state of being full.... Other institutions, fashioned on the McDonald's model, offer us similar efficiency in losing weight, lubricating our cars, filling eyeglass prescriptions, or completing income tax forms. In a fast-paced society in which both parents are likely to work, or where there may be only a single parent, efficiently satisfying the hunger and many other needs of people is very attractive. In a highly mobile society in which people are rushing, usually by car, from one spot to another, the efficiency of a fast-food meal, perhaps without leaving one's car while passing by the drive-through window, often proves impossible to resist. The fast-food model offers us, or at least appears to offer us, an efficient method for satisfying many of our needs.

Second, McDonald's offers us food and service that can be easily *quantified* and *calculated*. In effect, McDonald's seems to offer us "more bang for the buck." (One of its recent innovations, in response to the growth of other fast-food franchises, is to proffer "value meals" at discounted prices.) We often feel that we are getting a *lot* of food for a modest amount of money. Quantity has become equivalent to quality; a lot of something means it must be good. As two observers of contemporary American culture put it, "As a culture, we tend to believe—deeply—that in general 'bigger is better.'" Thus, we order the *Quarter Pounder*, the *Big* Mac, the *large* fries. We can quantify all of these things and feel that we are getting a lot of food, and, in return, we appear to be shelling out only a nominal sum of money. This calculus, of course, ignores an important point: the mushrooming of fast-food outlets, and the spread of the model to many other businesses, indicates that our calculation is illusory and it is the owners who are getting the best of the deal.

There is another kind of calculation involved in the success of McDonald's—a calculation involving time. People often, at least implicitly, calculate how much time it will take them to drive to McDonald's, eat their food, and return home and then compare that interval to the amount of time required to prepare the food at home. They often conclude, rightly or wrongly, that it will take less time to go and eat at the fast-food restaurant than to eat at home. This time calculation is a key factor in the success of Domino's and other home-delivery franchises, because to patronize them people do not even need to leave their homes. To take another notable example, Lens Crafters promises us "Glasses fast, glasses in one hour." Some McDonaldized institutions have come to combine the emphases on time and money. Domino's promises pizza delivery in one-half hour, or the pizza is free. Pizza Hut will serve us a personal pan pizza in five minutes, or it, too, will be free.

Third, McDonald's offers us *predictability*. We know that the Egg McMuffin we eat in New York will be, for all intents and purposes, identical to those we have eaten in Chicago and Los Angeles. We also know that the one we order next week or next year will be identical to the one we eat today. There is great comfort in knowing that McDonald's offers no surprises, that the food we eat at one time or in one place will be identical to the food we eat at another time or in another place. We know that the next Egg McMuffin we eat will not be awful, but we also know that it will not be exceptionally delicious. The success of the McDonald's model indicates that many people have come to prefer a world in which there are no surprises.

Fourth and finally, *control*, especially through the *substitution of nonhuman for human technology*, is exerted over the human beings who enter the world of McDonald's. The humans who work in fast-food restaurants are trained to do a very limited number of things in precisely the way they are told to do them. Managers and inspectors make sure that workers toe the line. The human beings who eat in fast-food restaurants are also controlled, albeit (usually) more subtly and indirectly. Lines, limited menus, few options, and uncomfortable seats all lead diners to do what the management wishes them to do—eat quickly and leave. Further, the drive-through (and in some cases walk-through) window leads diners to first leave and then eat rapidly. This attribute has most recently been extended by the

Domino's model, according to which customers are expected to *never* come, yet still eat speedily.

McDonald's also controls people by using nonhuman technology to replace human workers. Human workers, no matter how well they are programmed and controlled, can foul up the operation of the system. A slow or indolent worker can make the preparation and delivery of a Big Mac inefficient. A worker who refuses to follow the rules can leave the pickles or special sauce off a hamburger, thereby making for unpredictability. And a distracted worker can put too few fries in the box, making an order of large fries seem awfully skimpy. For these and other reasons, McDonald's is compelled to steadily replace human beings with nonhuman technologies, such as the soft-drink dispenser that shuts itself off when the glass is full, the french-fry machine that rings when the fries are crisp, the preprogrammed cash register that eliminates the need for the cashier to calculate prices and amounts, and, perhaps at some future time, the robot capable of making hamburgers. (Experimental robots of this type already exist.) All of these technologies permit greater control over the human beings involved in the fast-food restaurant. The result is that McDonald's is able to reassure customers about the nature of the employee to be encountered and the nature of the service to be obtained.

In sum, McDonald's (and the McDonald's model) has succeeded because it offers the consumer efficiency and predictability, and because it seems to offer the diner a lot of food for little money and a slight expenditure of effort. It has also flourished because it has been able to exert greater control through nonhuman technologies over both employees and customers, leading them to behave the way the organization wishes them to. The substitution of nonhuman for human technologies has also allowed the fast-food restaurant to deliver its fare increasingly more efficiently and predictably. Thus, there are good, solid reasons why McDonald's has succeeded so phenomenally and why the process of McDonaldization continues unabated.

A Critique of McDonaldization: The Irrationality of Rationality

There is a downside to all of this. We can think of efficiency, predictability, calculability, and control through nonhuman technology as the basic components of a *rational* system. However, as we shall see in later chapters, rational systems often spawn irrationalities. The downside of McDonaldization will be dealt with most systematically under the heading of the *irrationality of rationality*. Another way of saying this is that rational systems serve to deny human reason; rational systems can be unreasonable.

For example, the fast-food restaurant is often a dehumanizing setting in which to eat or work. People lining up for a burger, or waiting in the drive-through line, often feel as if they are dining on an assembly line, and those who prepare the burgers often appear to be working on a burger assembly line. Assembly lines are hardly human settings in which to eat, and they have been shown to be inhuman settings in which to work. As we will see, dehumanization is only one of many ways in which the highly rationalized fast-food restaurant is extremely irrational.

Of course, the criticisms of the irrationality of the fast-food restaurant will be extended to all facets of our McDonaldizing world. This extension has recently been underscored and legitimated at the opening of Euro DisneyLand outside Paris. A French socialist politician acknowledged the link between Disney and McDonald's as well as their common negative effects when he said that Euro Disney will "bombard France with uprooted creations that are to culture what fast food is to gastronomy."

Such critiques lead to a question: Is the headlong rush toward McDonaldization around the world advantageous or not? There are great gains to be made from McDonaldization, some of which will be discussed below. But there are also great costs and enormous risks, which this book will focus on. Ultimately, we must ask whether the creation of these rationalized systems creates an even greater number of irrationalities. At the minimum, we need to be aware of the costs associated with McDonaldization. McDonald's and other purveyors of the fast-food model spend billions of dollars each year outlining the benefits to be derived from their system. However, the critics of the system have few outlets for their ideas. There are no commercials on Saturday morning between cartoons warning children of the dangers associated with fast-food restaurants. Although few children are likely to read this book, it is aimed, at least in part, at their parents (or parents-to-be) in the hope that it will serve as a caution that might be passed on to their children.

A legitimate question may be raised about this analysis: Is this critique of McDonaldization animated by a romanticization of the past and an impossible desire to return to a world that no longer exists? For some critics, this is certainly the case. They remember the time when life was slower, less efficient, had more surprises, when people were freer, and when one was more likely to deal with a human being than a robot or a computer. Although they have a point, these critics have undoubtedly exaggerated the positive aspects of a world before McDonald's, and they have certainly tended to forget the liabilities associated with such a world. More importantly, they do not seem to realize that we are *not* returning to such a world. The increase in the number of people, the acceleration in technological change, the increasing pace of life—all this and more make it impossible to go back to a nonrationalized world, if it ever existed, of home-cooked meals, traditional restaurant dinners, high-quality foods, meals loaded with surprises, and restaurants populated only by workers free to fully express their creativity.

While one basis for a critique of McDonaldization is the past, another is the future. The future in this sense is what people have the potential to be if they are unfettered by the constraints of rational systems. This critique holds that people have the potential to be far more thoughtful, skillful, creative, and well-rounded than they now are, yet they are unable to express this potential because of the constraints of a rationalized world. If the world were less rationalized, or even derationalized, people would be better able to live up to their human potential. This critique is based not on what people were like in the past, but on what they could be like in the future, if only the constraints of McDonaldized systems were eliminated, or at least eased substantially. The criticisms to be put forth in this book are animated by the latter, future-oriented perspective rather than by a romanticization of the past and a desire to return to it.

The Advantages of McDonaldization: From The Cajun Bayou to Suburbia

Much of this book will focus on the negative side of McDonald's and McDonaldization. At this point it is important, however, to balance this view by mentioning some of the benefits of these systems and processes. The economic columnist, Robert Samuelson, for example, is a strong supporter of McDonald's and confesses to "openly worship McDonald's." He thinks of it as "the greatest restaurant chain in history." (However, Samuelson does recognize that there are those who "can't stand the food and regard McDonald's as the embodiment of all that is vulgar in American mass culture.")

Let me enumerate some of the advantages of the fast-food restaurant as well as other elements of our McDonaldized society:

- The fast-food restaurant has expanded the alternatives available to consumers. For example, more people now have ready access to Italian, Mexican, Chinese, and Cajun foods. A McDonaldized society is, in this sense, more egalitarian.

- The salad bar, which many fast-food restaurants and supermarkets now offer, enables people to make salads the way they want them.

- Microwave ovens and microwavable foods enable us to have dinner in minutes or even seconds.

- For those with a wide range of shopping needs, supermarkets and shopping malls are very efficient sites. Home shopping networks allow us to shop even more efficiently without ever leaving home.

- Today's high-tech, for-profit hospitals are likely to provide higher quality medical care than their predecessors.

- We can receive almost instantaneous medical attention at our local, drive-in "McDoctors."

- Computerized phone systems (and "voice mail") allow people to do things that were impossible before, such as obtain a bank balance in the middle of the night or hear a report on what went on in their child's class during the day and what home-work assignments were made. Similarly, automated bank teller machines allow people to obtain money any time of the day or night.

- Package tours permit large numbers of people to visit countries that they would otherwise not visit.

- Diet centers like Nutri/System allow people to lose weight in a carefully regulated and controlled system.

- The 24-second clock in professional basketball has enabled outstanding athletes such as Michael Jordan to more fully demonstrate their extraordinary talents.

- Recreational vehicles let the modern camper avoid excessive heat, rain, insects, and the like.

- Suburban tract houses have permitted large numbers of people to afford single-family homes.

Conclusion

The previous list gives the reader a sense not only of the advantages of McDonaldization but also of the range of phenomena that will be discussed under that heading throughout this book. In fact, such a wide range of phenomena will be discussed under the heading of McDonaldization that one is led to wonder: What isn't McDonaldized? Is McDonaldization the equivalent of modernity? Is everything contemporary McDonaldized?

While much of the world has been McDonaldized, it is possible to identify at least three aspects of contemporary society that have largely escaped McDonaldization. First, there are phenomena traceable to an earlier, "premodern" age that continue to exist within the modern world. A good example is the Mom and Pop grocery store. Second, there are recent creations that have come into existence, at least in part, as a reaction against McDonaldization. A good example is the boom in bed and breakfasts (B&Bs), which offer rooms in private homes with personalized attention and a homemade breakfast from the proprietor. People who are fed up with McDonaldized motel rooms in Holiday Inn or Motel 6 can instead stay in so-called B&Bs. Finally, some analysts believe that we have moved into a new, "postmodern" society and that aspects of that society are less rational than their predecessors. Thus, for example, in a postmodern society we witness the destruction of "modern" highrise housing projects and their replacement with smaller, more livable communities. Thus, although it is ubiquitous, McDonaldization is *not* simply another term for contemporary society. There *is* more to the contemporary world than McDonaldization.

In discussing McDonaldization, we are *not* dealing with an all-or-nothing process. Things are not either McDonaldized or not McDonaldized. There are degrees of McDonaldization; it is a continuum. Some phenomena have been heavily McDonaldized, others moderately McDonaldized, and some only slightly McDonaldized. There are some phenomena that may have escaped McDonaldization completely. Fast-food restaurants, for example, have been heavily McDonaldized, universities moderately McDonaldized, and the Mom and Pop grocers mentioned earlier only slightly McDonaldized. It is difficult to think of social phenomena that have escaped McDonaldization totally, but I suppose there is local enterprise in Fiji that has been untouched by this process. In this context, McDonaldization thus represents a process—a process by which more and more social phenomena are being McDonaldized to an increasing degree.

Overall, the central thesis is that McDonald's represents a monumentally important development and the process that it has helped spawn, McDonaldization, is engulfing more and more sectors of society and areas of the world. It has yielded a number of benefits to society, but it also entails a considerable number of costs and risks.

Although the focus is on McDonald's and McDonaldization, it is important to realize that this system has important precursors in our recent history.... That is, McDonaldization is not something completely new, but rather its success has been based on its ability to bring together a series of earlier innovations. Among the most important precursors to McDonaldization are bureaucracy, scientific management, the assembly line, and the original McDonald brothers' hamburger stand.

…

Part 4

Social Class and the Economy

Article 12

The Communist Manifesto

Karl Marx and Frederich Engels

Bourgeois and Proletarians

The history of all hitherto existing society is the history of class struggles....

Modern industry has established the world market, for which the discovery of America paved the way. This market has given an immense development to commerce, to navigation, to communication by land. This development has, in its turn, reacted on the extension of industry; and in proportion as industry, commerce, navigation, railways extended, in the same proportion the bourgeoisie developed, increased its capital, and pushed into the background every class handed down from the Middle Ages.

We see, therefore, how the modern bourgeoisie is itself the product of a long course of development, of a series of revolutions in the modes of production and of exchange....

The bourgeoisie has at last, since the establishment of modern industry and of the world market, conquered for itself, in the modern representative state, exclusive political sway. The executive of the modern state is but a committee for managing the common affairs of the whole bourgeoisie.

The bourgeoisie, historically, has played a most revolutionary part.

The bourgeoisie, wherever it has got the upper hand, has put an end to all feudal, patriarchal, idyllic relations. It has pitilessly torn asunder the motley feudal ties that bound man to his "natural superiors," and has left remaining no other nexus between man and man than naked self-interest, than callous "cash payment." It has drowned the most heavenly ecstasies of religious fervour, of chivalrous enthusiasm, of philistine sentimentalism, in the icy water of egotistical calculation. It has resolved personal worth into exchange value, and in place of the numberless indefeasible chartered freedoms, has set up that single, unconscionable freedom—free trade. In one word, for exploitation, veiled by religious and political illusions, it has substituted naked, shameless, direct, brutal exploitation.

The bourgeoisie has stripped of its halo every occupation hitherto honoured and looked up to with reverent awe. It has converted the physician, the lawyer, the priest, the poet, the man of science, into its paid wage labourers.

The bourgeoisie has torn away from the family its sentimental veil, and has reduced the family relation to a mere money relation....

The need of a constantly expanding market for its products chases the bourgeoisie over the whole surface of the globe. It must nestle everywhere, settle everywhere, establish connections everywhere.

The bourgeoisie has through its exploitation of the world market given a cosmopolitan character to production and consumption in every country. To the great chagrin of reactionists, it has drawn from under the feet of industry the national ground on which it stood. All old-established national industries have been destroyed or are daily being destroyed. They are dislodged by new industries, whose introduction becomes a life and death question for all civilized nations, by industries that no longer work up indigenous raw material, but raw material drawn from the remotest zones; industries whose products are consumed, not only at home, but in every quarter of the globe. In place of the old wants, satisfied by the productions of the country, we find new wants, requiring for their satisfaction the products of distant lands and climes. In place of the old local and national seclusion and self-sufficiency, we have intercourse in every direction, universal interdependence of nations. And as in material, so also in intellectual production. The intellectual creations of individual nations become common property. National one-sidedness and narrow-mindedness become more and more impossible, and from the numerous national and local literatures, there arises a world literature.

The bourgeoisie, by the rapid improvement of all instruments of production, by the immensely facilitated means of communication, draws all, even the most barbarian, nations into civilization. The cheap prices of its commodities are the heavy artillery with which it batters down all Chinese walls, with which it forces the barbarians' intensely obstinate hatred of foreigners to capitulate. It compels all nations, on pain of extinction, to adopt the bourgeois mode of production; it compels them to introduce what it calls civilization into their midst, i.e., to become bourgeois themselves. In one word, it creates a world after its own image.

The bourgeoisie has subjected the country to the rule of the towns. It has created enormous cities, has greatly increased the urban population as compared with the rural, and has thus rescued a considerable part of the population from the idiocy of rural life. Just as it has made the country dependent on the towns, so it has made barbarian and semi-barbarian countries dependent on the civilized ones, nations of peasants on nations of bourgeois, the East on the West.

The bourgeoisie keeps more and more doing away with the scattered state of the population, of the means of production, and of property. It has agglomerated population, centralized means of production, and has concentrated property in a few hands. The necessary consequence of this was political centralization. Independent, or but loosely connected provinces, with separate interests, laws, governments and systems of taxation, became lumped together into one nation, with one government, one code of laws, one national class interest, one frontier and one customs tariff....

The weapons with which the bourgeoisie felled feudalism to the ground are now turned against the bourgeoisie itself.

But not only has the bourgeoisie forged the weapons that bring death to itself; it has also called into existence the men who are to wield those weapons—the modern working class—the proletarians.

In proportion as the bourgeoisie, i.e., capital, is developed, in the same proportion is the proletariat, the modern working class, developed—a class of labourers, who live only so long as they find work, and who find work only so long as their labour increases capital. These labourers, who must sell themselves piecemeal, are a commodity, like every other article of commerce, and are consequently exposed to all the vicissitudes of competition, to all the fluctuations of the market.

Owing to the extensive use of machinery and to division of labour, the work of the proletarians has lost all individual character, and, consequently, all charm for the workman. He becomes an appendage of the machine, and it is only the most simple, most monotonous, and most easily acquired knack, that is required of him. Hence, the cost of production of a workman is restricted, almost entirely, to the means of subsistence that he requires for his maintenance, and for the propagation of his race. But the price of a commodity, and therefore also of labour, is equal to its cost of production. In proportion, therefore, as the repulsiveness of the work increases, the wage decreases. Nay more, in proportion as the use of machinery and division of labour increases, in the same pro-portion the burden of toil also increases, whether by prolongation of the working hours, by increase of the work exacted in a given time or by increased speed of the machinery, etc.

Modern industry has converted the little workshop of the patriarchal master into the great factory of the industrial capitalist. Masses of labourers, crowded into the factory, are organized like soldiers. As privates of the industrial army they are placed under the com-mand of a perfect hierarchy of officers and sergeants. Not only are they slaves of the bour-geois class, and of the bourgeois state; they are daily and hourly enslaved by the machine, by the overseer, and, above all, by the individual bourgeois manufacturer himself. The more openly this despotism proclaims gain to be its end and aim, the more petty, the more hateful and the more embittering it is.

The less the skill and exertion of strength implied in manual labour, in other words, the more modern industry becomes developed, the more is the labour of men superseded by that of women. Differences of age and sex have no longer any distinctive social validity for the working class. All are instruments of labour, more or less expensive to use, according to their age and sex....

But with the development of industry the proletariat not only increases in number; it becomes concentrated in greater masses, its strength grows, and it feels that strength more. The various interests and conditions of life within the ranks of the proletariat are more and more equalized, in proportion as machinery obliterates all distinctions of labour, and nearly everywhere reduces wages to the same low level. The growing competition among the bourgeois, and the resulting commercial crises, make the wages of the workers ever more fluctuating. The unceasing improvement of machinery, ever more rapidly developing, makes their livelihood more and more precarious; the collisions between individual workmen and individual bourgeois take more and more the character of collisions between two classes. Thereupon the workers begin to form combinations (trade unions) against the bourgeois....

This organization of the proletarians into a class, and consequently into a political party, is continually being upset again by the competition between the workers themselves. But it ever rises up again, stronger, firmer, mightier. It compels legislative recognition of particular interests of the workers, by taking advantage of the divisions among the bourgeoisie itself....

Altogether, collisions between the classes of the old society further, in many ways, the course of development of the proletariat. The bourgeoisie finds itself involved in a constant battle: at first with the aristocracy; later on, with those portions of the bourgeoisie itself, whose interests have become antagonistic to the progress of industry; at all times, with the bourgeoisie of foreign countries. In all these battles it sees itself compelled to appeal to the proletariat, to ask for its help, and thus to drag it into the political arena. The bourgeoisie itself, therefore, supplies the proletariat with its own elements of political and general education, in other words, it furnishes the proletariat with weapons for fighting the bourgeoisie.

Further, as we have already seen, entire sections of the ruling classes are, by the advance of industry, precipitated into the proletariat, or are at least threatened in their conditions of existence. These also supply the proletariat with fresh elements of enlightenment and progress.

Finally, in times when the class struggle nears the decisive hour, the process of dissolution going on within the ruling class, in fact within the whole range of old society, assumes such a violent, glaring character, that a small section of the ruling class cuts itself adrift, and joins the revolutionary class, the class that holds the future in its hands. Just as, therefore, at an earlier period, a section of the nobility went over to the bourgeoisie, so now a portion of the bourgeoisie goes over to the proletariat, and in particular, a portion of the bourgeois ideologists, who have raised themselves to the level of comprehending theoretically the historical movement as a whole.

Of all the classes that stand face to face with the bourgeoisie today, the proletariat alone is a really revolutionary class. The other classes decay and finally disappear in the face of modern industry; the proletariat is its special and essential product....

Article 13

The Class Structure of the United States

Jerry Kloby

H ow is class determined and what does the class structure of the United States look like? The subject of social class is a controversial one both within sociology and outside of it. Most generally, *social classes are large groups of people who occupy similar positions in the social order, particularly the economic system.* Social structure is an important concept to understand if one is to grasp the full impact of social class. *Social structure refers to the enduring patterns of relationships that exist in society.* These include the individual positions (such as those in the family, the government, or some other institution), whole collections of positions (a formal or informal group) and the relationship among those individuals, groups, and other segments of the broader social structure. Individuals entering into a society enter into a pre-existing social structure that operates guided by formal and informal rules independent of the individuals. Some people have greater ability to shape the social structure and the course of history, but the vast majority have little influence on it.

Social structure acts like an invisible force and its power has been demonstrated in social-psychological experiments, including classics such as Stanley Milgram's experiment on obedience to authority and Philip Zimbardo's mock prison experiment. But it is also seen in the larger grand sweeps of history that can lead to war or peace, conquest or cooperation, economic depression or social progress. Social structure, like physical structure, is something that can constrain or enable. It is the pattern of relationships that carries people along, some to desirable outcomes, some to disastrous ones. Social class is a powerful component of social structure.

How is Class Determined?

The key indicators commonly used to define social class are wealth, income, occupational status, and education. Where wealth is what one owns, income is the money received over the course of a year (income can come from many sources, not just one's job). Occupational status refers to the esteem that other hold of a particular occupation; it has a great deal to do with the skill level, the authority, and the autonomy (level of control) of the occupation.

Education, although frequently associated with class, is not so much a determinant of class as it is a benefit of class. We typically see that people with more education generally get the better jobs and hence greater incomes, but if we take a step back in the equation we will see that, by and large, families of higher economic standing typically provide a better learning environment for their children outside of school, make sure their children attend quality elementary and secondary schools, and are able to afford to send them to college to get a bachelor's degree or higher.

Many books dealing with stratification tend to focus on the fact that people with more education generally have better paying jobs, and that families with two income earners are usually much better off than those with one. The impression is given that inequality in the United States is a lot like a ladder—with a little more education you can move up a rung. If you are married and your spouse works, that's another step up. More time on the job will bring raises and maybe promotions and you'll gradually move up a step or two. The strata (layers) in such a system are depicted as not that far apart and not that difficult to climb. Success is simply the result of a little more education and a good dose of perseverance. There are several ideological factors that come into play when thinking about inequality in the United States. One is the belief that success is a result of individual factors (education, hard work, a little luck). In other words, there is an implicit belief in meritocracy—that people get ahead based on merit, on their own abilities. The second is that there is a good deal of social mobility, that lots of people move up and down the ladder and there are no major structural factors inhibiting them.

However, the research on inequality and social mobility contradicts these ideological lynch pins. But the things that might be most important about popular beliefs is not what they get wrong but what they leave out all together. What we will look at in the pages ahead will help the reader gain a much fuller picture of class and social mobility in the United States. What does the class structure of the United States look like? Is the existing inequality simply the result of differences in individual characteristics such as skill levels and motivation? Are there structural elements that empower or enable people in some classes some while constraining those in other classes?

In the United States there is a dominant upper class. It owns a vastly disproportionate amount of the nation's wealth, income is generally much higher than the other classes and, perhaps as important, the source of its income is the ownership of income-producing assets such as corporate stocks, government bonds, investment real estate, and similar assets. The upper class has great power and influence. The German sociologist Max Weber defined *power* as *the ability to get one's way even over the resistance of others*. Influence is something we can define a little differently—the ability to affect the actions of others that comes from people being willing to listen to what one has to say. The words or

TABLE 4.1. Classes in Contemporary United States

Class		Economic Position/ Occupation	Degree of Power and influence; autonomy	Typical Income	Average Net Worth	Size
Upper Class/Corporate Class		Capitalists, major stockholders, CEOs, directors	High	Over $500,000 but some make tens of millions	$15 million	1%
Professional Managerial Class	Semi-autonomous professionals	Doctors, Lawyers, Engineers, Architects, Upper managers and supervisory personnel in medium to large corporations.	Medium to High	$100,000 to $400,000	$1–3 million	12–15%
	Upper level managers					
	Owners of medium size businesses					
Working Classes	Upper Middle Class	Some professionals, college professors, middle-level Managers, skilled craftsmen (electricians, plumbers, etc.)	Low to medium	$60,000 to 100,000	$200,000 to $500,000	25–30%
	Middle	Firemen, Police, Teachers, Nurses, etc. Better paid manual workers	Low to medium	$30,000 to 70,000	$70,000 to 90,000	25–30%
	Lower Middle Class	Low-skill manual and white collar workers (many retail and clerical workers)	low	$20,000 to 35,000	zero to $10,000	15%
	Working Poor	Lowest paid manual, retail and service workers	low	$20,000	zero or less	10%
	Unemployed or marginal workers	Unemployed or part-time, part-year workers.	low	$10,000	zero or less	5–10%

Note: In constructing this model I have based the theoretical framework (the class categories, economic position/occupations, and degree of power and influence) on the work of many including especially G. William Domhoff, Gilbert and Kahl, Harold Kerbo, Scott Sernau, and Erik Olin Wright. For the occupational and income information I drew upon data published by the Bureau of Labor Statistics and the Census Bureau. Wealth and income figures are, in part, from the Census Bureau's P-60 series, but mainly from the work of Edward N. Wolff, especially Wolff 2007.

desires of a person of influence are more likely to be taken into account than an ordinary citizen. The influence that a person has, more often than not, comes from their economic standing but also from their educational credentials and other lesser factors.

The factors that ultimately distinguish one class from another:

1. *Ownership.* Class is largely determined by whether or not one owns some significant portion of the means of production.

2. *Wealth and income.* As stated, for the upper class the amount of wealth and income is far greater than the society's norm.

3. *Power.* Power includes an ability to determine or influence government policy but it also includes the investment decisions that the upper class makes and it includes control over what other people do. Decisions made by investors can put thousands of people out of work, leave whole cities starved for investment capital, and can determine whether socially valuable goods and services are produced or frivolous ones are.

4. *Autonomy.* Autonomy means control of over one's own labor (mental and physical labor). Generally a person with power also has autonomy. There are some workers who have very little power over other people but do have a good deal of control over their own work and their working conditions. One example might be a lawyer. A lawyer may be able to pick and choose which cases he or she takes on. He or she may decide to take a two week vacation or a five week vacation. He or she will make decisions about which part of town to set up his/her office, who is going to work for him/her, and so on. Such autonomy does not exist for all lawyers so it is not possible to make precise claims regarding autonomy about the profession as a whole. Some lawyers, such as public defenders or lawyers who are part of a large firm, have cases assigned to them that they can't turn down. Their schedules are determined by their employers and must suit courtroom schedules and other external constraints.

In defining social class many theorists also include *education* as a key variable, as well as the prestige of one's occupation. But I take the position that education is more of a dependent variable than an independent one. That is to say, one's educational success largely depends on one's class background. Similarly, occupational prestige is a product of the power, authority, autonomy, and income of one's economic status and not an independent factor.

The major class categories outlined in Table 4.1 are the upper class, the professional-managerial class, and the working classes. There are divisions within these categories but they are not as clear nor as rigid as the divisions that separate the major classes. The upper class, for example, can be viewed as having three subdivisions. One group concerns itself primarily with the operation of its businesses. Another portion of the upper class is more concerned with, and gets involved in, the affairs of government. They are often referred to as the power elite and may be very influential in local, state, or federal government. A third segment, very rich and very autonomous, appears to be much more concerned with enjoying the luxuries that their class position enables them to buy. These are what the economist and social theorist Thorstein Veblen (1857–1929) called the "leisure class." Their stocks, bonds, and trust funds, provide them with plenty of money to live a life of luxury but they leave the running of their businesses to professionals who are far more capable than themselves. All three segments of the upper class share one overriding characteristic: They own sufficient income-producing wealth to provide themselves with a very comfortable life even if they were to chose not to work.

The professional-managerial class may be the class category with the greatest internal variation. This class includes highly educated professionals who may have a great deal of autonomy in their work. It includes the people who manage much of the corporate empires that dominate the economic scene today. It includes highly skilled professionals who do research and development for those corporations. It also includes owners of small- to medium-size businesses who share some of the characteristics of big business (they employ some people, they make investment decisions that affect others, they tend to support a pro-business political agenda, etc.) but the owners of these smaller businesses do not have much political influence. Their single most defining characteristic may be that their businesses do not provide them with enough income that they can live comfortably without working. Smaller business owners often work a great deal in order to keep their business viable and their income flowing.

Within the working classes I've grouped together a number of categories that, superficially, have some very noticeable differences. Incomes, for instance, in the upper middle class occupations are much higher than the working poor. Educational attainment can be extreme. Status and lifestyle may also be drastically different. Why then are they grouped together? Because they serve a common purpose in the economic order. The upper class owns the economy, the professional–managerial class plans and manages it, and the working classes do the productive labor that creates the wealth. And they do it by selling their labor power, either to private businesses or government and non-profits that help maintain the social and economic order.

A number of social theorists have proposed the idea that an "underclass" exists in contemporary society (Wilson 1987, 1996). The term refers to the existence of a large number of people (several million) in the United States who live and function outside of the formal economy. They are largely located in older central cities, are chronically unemployed, and they survive by dealing drugs or stealing. Within the underclass are pervasive problems of poverty, drug and alcohol abuse, violence, and hopelessness. But the existence of this class is directly the result of the actions of the upper class, including its business leaders and the power elite. The massive withdrawal of investment capital from older industrial cities, especially in the northern portion of the country, coupled with governmental policies that concentrated the poor in urban neighborhoods, brought on the development of concentrated urban poverty and isolation. The disinvestment and abandonment that is, or was, rampant in such cities as Detroit and Flint, Michigan, and Cleveland and Youngstown, Ohio, can only be understood by looking at the broader economic forces than produced it. The underclass, to the extent it truly exists, is a product of contemporary economic trends and not an independent phenomenon. Thus the people who are part of it ultimately are connected to the economic order, just as the hundreds of millions of people occupying the urban slums of the third world are.

In addition, those poorest and most economically marginalized members of society who comprise the underclass do function as a reserve army of labor when redevelopment projects are undertaken and cheap unskilled labor is needed. They may even serve as forced labor working as prisoners picking up trash on the roadside or stitching T-shirts for nationally known brands while serving a prison term.

Article 14

Four Modes of Inequality

William M. Dugger

The Inequality Tableau

A mode of inequality is a social process whereby a powerful group of humans (top dogs) reaps benefits for itself at the expense of a less powerful group (underdogs). The process involves an institutionalized struggle over power, status, and wealth. Four modes of inequality will be discussed: (1) gender, (2) race, (3) class, and (4) nation. These do not include all of the ways in which humans take advantage of each other, but they do cover much of the ground. Moreover, the four modes overlap and reinforce each other.

Corresponding to each mode is a set of practices whereby the top dogs take advantage of the underdogs. These practices ensure that the top dogs win. Corresponding to each mode of inequality is also a set of enabling myths that culturally enforce the practices and "make the game seem fair" to both the top dogs and the underdogs. A focal point also exists for each mode of inequality. The focal point is a particular institution where the inequality resides—where the myths justifying it are learned and the practices realizing it actually take place. These focal points frequently change as the particular mode of inequality evolves. Moreover, corresponding to each mode is an antidote—a set of values, meanings, and beliefs—that can debunk the enabling myths. Inequality, then, is a whole complex of modes, practices, enabling myths, focal points, and antidotes. This complex does not reach a balance of forces. It is not an equilibrium system, but an interacting process of cumulative causation in which inequality either gets worse or better. Seldom, if ever, does it stay the same.

Values are central to inequality. They either rationalize it by making it seem fair and true, or they debunk it by pointing out its injustice and falsehood. We can pretend to be value neutral about inequality, but we never are.

TABLE 4.2. The Inequality Tableau

Modes	Practices	Myths	Antidotes
Gender	Domination	Sexism	Feminism
Race	Discrimination	Racism	Civil Rights
Class	Exploitation	Classism	Economic Democracy
Nation	Predation	Jingoism	Internationalism

Four Modes of Inequality Defined

Gender inequality is the domination of one gender by another. In our time and place (the twentieth century in the Western Hemisphere), men dominate women through a whole series of gendered practices. These practices are supported and justified by myths about female inferiority and male superiority. These myths are the substance of sexism. Sexist myths enable men to dominate women without feeling guilty and also enable women to be dominated without mass rebellion or suicide. The antidote to gender inequality is feminism.

Race inequality is practiced by one race discriminating against another. In our time and place, the most significant form is the discrimination of white Europeans against black Africans or other people of color. It is justified by myths about African, Asian, and Latin American inferiority and about European superiority. These myths are the substance of today's racism. Racist myths enable white Europeans to discriminate against non-European people of color without feeling guilty and also enable those people of color to adjust to their unfair treatment without fully realizing that it is unfair. The antidote to discrimination is civil rights.

Class inequality in capitalism is practiced through the exploitation of the workers by the capitalists. In Soviet communism, the workers were exploited by the nomenklatura. Class exploitation is supported by its own myths. In the West, the myths are about market efficiency, while in the East, the myths were formerly about the dictatorship of the proletariat. Class myths enable a powerful class to exploit a powerless class and are comparable to racist and sexist myths in terms of effect, if not in terms of content. The antidote to exploitation is economic democracy (see Dugger 1984).

Nation inequality is practiced through the predation of powerful nations on weak nations and is supported by jingoistic myths about national honor and foreign treachery. Jingoistic myths allow the members of powerful nations to take pride in the killing of the members of weak nations rather than feel shame. The antidote to national predation is internationalism. Table 4.2 summarizes all the modes, practices, myths, and antidotes.

Four Modes of Inequality Explained Institutionally

Mode of inequality refers to the way in which people are grouped for giving offense and for receiving it. The groups are separate and unequal. Individuals do not choose to join one group or the other, but rather are assigned to a particular group by the operation of law, tradition, and myth. Culture and coercion, not individual preference and choice, are the operative factors.

Grouping (1): The Class Mode of Inequality

When individuals are grouped into classes, the boundaries are based mainly on how they appropriate their incomes, but also on how large the incomes are. The upper class is composed of capitalists and people who have managed to appropriate large incomes for themselves. An exact number cannot be placed on just how large that income has to be, but the inexact nature of its boundary does not mean an upper class does not exist. It exists because its members have acquired and used differential economic advantages and have kept the lower strata from doing the same. The appropriation of large incomes can be done through the control of wealth or important services. Those who own or control industrial and financial capital—wealthy families, corporate executives, investment bankers, and the like—can use their capitalist position to enlarge their income. Such capitalists are the most powerful members of the upper class; they set its ideological tone and make it essentially a capitalist class. Those who control the delivery of financially important services—corporate lawyers, lobbyists, politicians, and the like—can also appropriate large incomes. The middle class is composed of the "wannabe" groups—those who want to appropriate large incomes but lack the differential advantage needed to do so. They are contenders but were born to the wrong parents; they were sent to the wrong schools, had access to the wrong social connections, or were steered into the wrong professions. Members of the lower class are not in contention, whether they themselves realize it or not. Enough class overlap and circulation between classes exists to allow a limited role for individual choice, merit, and luck. Nonetheless, membership in a particular class is determined primarily by what class a person is born into rather than that individual person's rise or fall (see Osberg 1984).

Although class is an economic category, it is also strongly influenced by cultural factors. The kind of school attended and the kind of learning that takes place there vary by class, as do family structures, religions, beliefs, values, and meanings. (For a conservative view of cultural factors and class, see Berger and Berger 1983. For a liberal view, see Jencks et al. 1972, 1979. For a radical view, see Green 1981; Harrington 1983.) All the basic institutions teach the youth of each class the values, beliefs, and meanings appropriate to their economic station in life. When the class role has been learned and accepted, the person will be well adjusted, perhaps even happy. When the class role is rejected, unhappiness and maladjustment result, and either a change in class will be attempted or a rebel will be made. (For further discussion see Moore 1978.)

Grouping (2): The Race Mode of Inequality

When individuals are grouped into races, the boundary between discriminating and discriminated groups is based on race, but race itself is as much a cultural heritage as it is a biological endowment. The particular form that the race mode of inequality takes in the United States will illustrate the point. (The classic work is Myrdal 1962.) "African American" is as much a cultural as a biological grouping. It does not necessarily include all people whose skin is black. Many people from India, Melanesia, and Sri Lanka are black, as are Native Australians. Many have their own problems and face their own injustices, but they are not in the racially discriminated group of African Americans. Even though the group of African Americans excludes many people whose skin is black, it also includes some people whose skin is white. People with white skins are African Americans if their ancestors were seized for slaves in Africa and forcibly transported to the Americas, where miscegenation and a whole myriad of laws, traditions, and myths forced generation after generation of, not only the dark-skinned, but also the fair-skinned, members of the group into an inferior position relative to "white" Europeans. Cultural learning, not genetics, was the principal factor operating throughout the period.

Grouping (3): The Gender Mode of Inequality

Females (those with ovaries) are assigned to the group called women and males (those with testicles) are assigned to the group called men. However, gender, like race, is as much cultural as it is biological. Female humans are taught to be women by their culture; male humans are taught to be men by their culture as well. What the assignees learn to become is determined by what the culture teaches them, not by their gonads. Humans with ovaries are expected to learn to be women. Humans with testicles are expected to learn to be men. That is, they learn how they are expected to behave in their assigned roles. Their genitals do not teach them; their culture does. (The classic is Mead 1949.) The males of today are expected to be superior to the females, and the females are expected to be inferior to the males.

Grouping (4): The Nation Mode of Inequality

When people are grouped into nations, arbitrary geopolitical boundaries separate the groups into the chosen people and the foreigners. Such groupings are also based on ethnic differences within individual nations, and can produce a considerable degree of inequality.

However, when ethnic differences are combined with the power of the nation-state, an even more effective mode of inequality is formed. (Religion plays a role as well but will not be discussed in this chapter.) A nation is an area controlled by one state, where allegiance is to that state rather than another. Cultural and language differences may further differentiate the people in one state from those in another. Moreover, the controlling states may accentuate the differences through state education, state religion, and other forms of propaganda. The individuals who happen to find themselves identified as French, German, Italian, or Russian are not so by nature. They must be taught these identities. Since the nation mode of grouping people is particularly arbitrary, it relies very heavily on the teaching of alleged group differences. People must be taught that foreigners are untrustworthy, ignorant, brutal, and inferior. Only then can national leaders use their jingoism for supporting attacks against other nations or for mounting a defense against (imagined) attacks. Those members of the underlying population who do not accept their assigned roles in these jingoistic activities are exiled, ridiculed, imprisoned, or executed. A complex system of passports and identification papers keeps track of people and makes sure they are assigned to the "correct" national group—whether they want to be or not. Formidable security agencies are created by each nation to implement the groupings. Security agencies such as the former Soviet State Security Committee (KGB) and the U.S. Central Intelligence Agency (CIA) and Federal Bureau of Investigation (FBI) become focal points of nationalism.

Four Practices of Inequality

The practices of inequality are interrelated forms of parasitic collective action. They cannot be reduced down to just one abstract practice without doing great damage to the multifaceted reality of inequality. The domination of women by men is really not the same as the exploitation of workers by capitalists, nor is the discrimination against African Americans by European Americans the same as the German invasion of Poland. Consequently, each practice will be discussed separately.

Practice (1): Domination

The domination of women by men has an institutionalized focal point in patriarchal societies—the family. An institution—and the family is no exception—is made up of people performing activities according to a set of rules that are justified by a set of values, beliefs, and meanings. As people perform their activities according to the rules, they internalize the values, beliefs, and meanings that justify the rules. Domination within the patriarchal family involves the male parent telling the female parent and her offspring (if any) how to conduct family activities. The patriarch exercises power over the other family members, assigning them most of the burdens and appropriating for himself most of the benefits of the family's activities. The patriarch enjoys liberties, and the other family members suffer exposure to the liberties. The patriarch appropriates most of the family status, wealth, and power. In full-blown patriarchy, the family becomes the extension of the patriarch's will. The other family members cannot own property or appropriate income in their own names; they cannot display status on their own behalves, nor exercise power to serve their own authentic wills.

Following the path of least resistance, as most of us do, the members of the family accept the rules that support the male parent's practices because they accept the values, beliefs, and meanings that support them. Male parents come to believe that they are the best judges of what is best for the other members of the family and that resistance to their will is not just inconvenient to them, but harmful for the family and immoral as well. Female parents come to believe that *family* means the patriarchal family only, and that no other types of families or meanings are possible. The female parent also learns to value her subservient role in patriarchy and to feel a real loss if deprived of it.

The values, beliefs, and meanings that support male domination within the family also spread to other social institutions. The acceptance of the subservient wife/mother role generalizes to the acceptance of a subservient worker role—including the acceptance of low-paid occupations or of lower pay for the same kind of work that males do. In the twentieth century, domination originating in the family has been picked up by a new and rising social control mechanism—bureaucracy. As women have moved into paid work outside the home, they have partially escaped the practices of domination within the home only to become enmeshed in the practices of domination within the modern bureaucracy, which now controls the workplace in both capitalist enterprises and government agencies. Access to the highest-paying jobs is controlled by a web of rules and traditions favoring males over females; so, too, is access to status and power within the workplace. Furthermore, if women turn from the family to the welfare agency instead of the workplace, the story is largely the same. State and federal welfare agencies control access to the welfare system through a web of rules and regulations formulated by males and based on the traditional roles of the patriarchal family.

Practice (2): Discrimination

I will focus on discrimination against African Americans. While the focal point for patriarchy begins with the family and the process of procreation, the focal point for discrimination began with slavery and the process of production. Although slavery varied from state to state and even from region to region within the same state, it always was supported by a racist culture in which Europeans were considered to be the superiors and Africans, the inferiors. The racist culture dehumanized Africans, turning them into property that could be bought and sold at will. Although the brutality of slavery varied, it always was coercive. Although the frequency of selling slaves varied, the owner's right to sell a human being as a commodity always was retained.

Agitation by whites for reform and resistance from slaves generally hardened the attitudes of slave owners and increased their coercive hold over their slaves. Neither the slaves' resistance nor the abolitionists' moral outrage led to reform. Slavery was an either/or institution. It could not be reformed; it could only be abolished. It was not amenable to institutional adjustment. In this lies a lesson: incremental institutional adjustment, though desirable on its own merits, can lead to a hardening of inequality. Incremental institutional adjustment can act more like a vaccine against progress toward equality than a means of actually attaining equality. The Civil War finally ended slavery. (For further discussion, see Fogel and Engerman 1974; Genovese 1965, 1969; Hirshson 1962; Mellon 1988; Oates 1975; Stampp 1956; Low and Clift 1981, 756–96.)

Racism did not end with slavery; it has continued for 130 years. After reconstruction in the South, Jim Crow laws and sharecropping replaced slave codes and slavery itself. Now, however, instead of supporting slavery or sharecropping, racism supports a whole series of discriminatory practices diffused throughout the economy, society, and polity. In developments similar to those that are moving male domination over females out of the old focal point in the family and into the larger arena of the modern bureaucracy, the focal point for discrimination has moved, first out of slavery into sharecropping, and now out of sharecropping into bureaucracy. Now, educational bureaucracies control access to good education and training, while corporate and government bureaucracies control access to good jobs. Zoning laws, public housing bureaucracies, lending agent bureaucracies, and municipalities all control access to good housing. The bureaucratic rules and regulations are stacked against the African American in favor of the European American. The practice of discrimination has become institutionalized in the bureaucratic life of modern society. It has moved out of the production processes of the old agrarian South into the whole of society, where it is joined by male domination over females, upper class exploitation of the lower class, and the predation of the chosen people on foreigners.

Practice (3): Exploitation

The practice of class inequality is exploitation. Its focal point in capitalism is the hierarchical workplace, where owners hire workers and use them for producing commodities for a profit. The owners try to enlarge the flow of income that goes to them after all contractual costs are paid and after all costs that can be avoided are avoided (externalities). As in gender and race inequality, the practice of class inequality has become bureaucratized, and far more so than in the other modes of inequality. The production and sale of commodities for a profit is now organized by corporate bureaucracies. The income appropriated by the wage workers, middle managers, engineers, equity owners, and debt owners (rentier capital) is now the subject of bureaucratic rules, state regulations, court decisions, and continual struggle between different organizations and different hierarchical levels within organizations. The struggle is to obtain a differential economic advantage that will allow the appropriation of more income at the expense of those who have no such advantages. Such advantages are usually obtained through property ownership, but physicians, hospital administrators, lawyers, lobbyists, politicians, and even celebrities are also involved in the acquisition and use of differential economic advantages. The practices of exploitation are quite varied. Owners enlarge their incomes by pushing down wages and pushing up the prices of their products and by paying out higher dividends, interest, and rent to themselves. Chief executive officers of corporations enlarge their incomes by downsizing their companies and upsizing their own compensation packages. Physicians and hospital administrators charge exorbitant fees, perform unneeded services, and reap their rewards. Celebrities in the sports and entertainment fields push up their fees and salaries, endorsements, and such. We pay the higher ticket prices and wish that we could raise our "rates" as well. Lobbyists and politicians work out agreements between conflicting factions and pass new legislation that affects us all. Then they collect their fees for service rendered or leave public service for more lucrative private service, hoping the rest of us will not come to see whom they really serve.

Practice (4): Predation

The nation state is the focal point for predation, which is practiced through war and diplomacy. Favorable treatment is sought for the nation's elite groups of capitalist corporations and state bureaucracies (military or civilian). Successful predator nations build empires by forming shifting alliances with other predators, occupying opposing nations, subjecting opposing nations to unfavorable trade relations, or setting up puppet regimes within opposing nations.

Predation also allows the predatory apparatus of each state to extract status, power, and wealth from the underlying population of that state. The underlying population is induced to grant the state's predatory apparatus exceptional power in the name of defending the homeland. The liberties of citizens are reduced in the name of national security, and their exposure to arbitrary action by security, and their exposure to arbitrary action by security officials is increased. Dissent becomes treason. Power is concentrated in the internal security apparatus and the external predatory apparatus. The status of the nation's predatory apparatus is increased by instilling in the underlying population the great importance of defending the homeland and of honoring those who do. Numerous medals and awards are granted to the national heroes as they fill up the cemeteries, hospitals, and prisons. The wealth of the nation's predatory apparatus is increased by inducing the underlying population to grant it exemplary taxing authority. (For further discussion see Melman 1983; Dumas 1986.)

Opposing predatory nations are busy doing the same thing. The activities of the one predatory apparatus gives the other predators stronger motivation to step up their own war preparations to a more feverish pitch. Each nation's predatory apparatus comes to serve as the reason for each other nation's predatory apparatus to expand itself. They are as much allies in their predation of their underlying populations as they are adversaries in their struggle against each other.

Enabling Myths: The Cultural Support of Inequality

Enabling myths are composed primarily of the stereotypes men believe about women, European Americans believe about African Americans, the upper class believes about the lower class, and the chosen people believe about foreigners. However, enabling myths are more than the stereotypes believed by the beneficiaries of inequality. Inequality must be justified, in the minds of both its victims and its beneficiaries. To avoid unrest among the victims, they must be taught that their treatment is not really unfair. To avoid guilty consciences among the beneficiaries—which is not nearly as important nor as difficult as avoiding unrest among the victims—the beneficiaries must be taught that their advantages are due them. Such learning is not resisted. It is easy to be convinced that one deserves all the good things that come one's way. Teaching acceptance to the victims is much harder and more important than teaching it to the beneficiaries, so it is the primary function of enabling myths. It is not easy to be convinced that one deserves all the bad things that come one's way.

Enabling myths also create "otherness" and this involves more than just instilling superiority in the top dogs and inferiority in the underdogs but also centrality and marginality For one to be superior, an "other" must be inferior. For one to be the center of things, an "other" must be on the margin. The enabling myths of sexism, for example, put males at the center of humanity and females on the margin. Simone de Beauvoir explained;

> *Thus humanity is male and man defines woman not in herself but as relative to him; she is not regarded as an autonomous being.... She is defined and differentiated with respect to man and not be with reference to her; she is the incidental, the inessential as opposed to the essential. He is the Subject, he is the Absolute— she is the Other.*
>
> *(Beauvoir [1952] 1989, xxii–xxiii)*

(1) Sexism: The Myths Supporting Gender Inequality

Sexist myths begin with the category of "otherness." Males are the ones; they are the center. Females are the others; they are the margin. Thus, when categorizing the human species we say "mankind" or "man." However, when we say "womankind" or "woman," we do not mean the human species. We mean women, the margin. Men are the categorically human; women are other. The justification for males dominating females begins here. Then it ranges far and wide. Public activities—those that yield wealth, status, and power—are the realm of men. Private activities—those that do not yield wealth, status and power—are the realm of women. Men can speak better than women in public. Men are more intelligent and articulate. Men make better bosses. They are less emotional than women, more straightforward and honest in the pursuit of goals. Women are too emotional and intuitive, less straightforward. Their place is in the home. Man's place is in the world. Women who internalize these myths find it easier to accept their narrowed role in life. Men who internalize these myths find it easier to keep women in their narrowed role to exclude them with no regrets. Well-adjusted men and women may even succeed in putting the confined role of women on a pedestal, and idealizing it as the embodiment of feminine truth and beauty.

This feminine mystique is a myth about the proper role of woman (Friedan [1963] 1983). It contains positive inducements to reward women for accepting it—they are put on a pedestal, and raised to the height of feminine truth and beauty. The myth also contains negative sanctions (taboos) to punish women for violating it—they are put in the pit, and accused of being untrue to their femininity and ugly to boot. (Just three centuries ago, we burned such women as witches.)

(2) Racism: The Myths Supporting Race Discrimination

Like sexist myths, racist myths also begin with "otherness." In the United States, literature refers to the writings of white Europeans; art means the works of white Europeans; culture, in short, means Greco-Roman culture. African writings are other; African art is other. Some exceptions exist: blues and jazz in music, and Pablo Picasso's adaptations of African art in painting and sculpture are notable. Nonetheless, in the United States, the African American is still *the other*, and the European is still *the one*.

From the foundation of otherness, the myths of racism spring forth. Racist beliefs, like the other enabling myths, are opportunistic. They serve a purpose, even though their propagation and acceptance need not be consciously opportunistic. Racial myths are resistant to evidence contradicting them. They exist in the realm of magic and superstition, not that of fact and experience (Myrdal 1962, 100). They are related directly to the otherness of the African American in the mind of the European American. Racial myths are rational in the sense that they serve the purpose of enabling "whites" to take advantage of "blacks."

However, racial myths are also profoundly irrational in the sense that they are psychologically grounded in magic and in superstitious dread of the unknown, of the other.

(3) Classism: The Myths Supporting Class Explotation

Classist myths are the most sophisticated of all, as they are layered. The first layer of class myths supports the denial of class exploitation, while the second layer of myths supports the belief that the capitalist/Western world is a free market system. The third layer supports the belief that a free market system is neutral with respect to class, and that it involves no class exploitation, but only individual competition, which results in benefits for all.

We are constantly aware of class and of our own class standing relative to others. However, while we constantly think in terms of class, we do not think in terms of class exploitation. One of the most profound discoveries of Thorstein Veblen was that Americans in the lower strata seldom think of the upper strata in the bitter terms of exploitation. Rather than feel resentment, those in the lower strata feel envy. They do not want to overthrow their exploiters. They want to move up into the higher strata themselves (Veblen [1899] 1975). Americans do not think straight when it comes to class because they do not think of it in terms of exploitation (For further discussion, see DeMott 1991.)

The denial of class exploitation is supported by the belief that ours is a free market system. Beneficial market competition, not differential economic advantage, is believed to be the way in which our economy distributes income. Milton Friedman's two works for the general reader, *Capitalism and Freedom* (1962) and *Free to Choose* (with Rose Friedman; 1980), are the most popular representations of the myth of the market system. In the mythical world of these two popular books, free markets are those that are unfettered by government interference. In such markets, monopolies cannot exist for long, and so the freedom of the market becomes the foundation for the freedom of the polity and the society. Furthermore, in these free markets, individuals are "free to choose," not only what they will buy and what they will sell, but also how prosperous they will become. If they are thrifty, innovative, willing to take risks, and hard working, they can rise very far. No barriers hold them back, unless government interferes with their efforts or unions either keep them out of lucrative employment or take away their profits with exorbitant wages.

The Friedmans do qualify their market utopia. They add in a central bank that provides a framework of monetary stability by following a growth rate rule for the money stock, if we could just agree how to measure the money stock. They also add in a negative income tax to help the poor and maybe also an educational voucher, allegedly to help poor children. They even recognize the need for a limited court system—one that enforces the rules and makes sure that contracts are performed. Nonetheless, the market utopia they describe will benefit us all, provided we keep government interference at a minimum.

There is no class exploitation in the Friedmans' world; no gender domination, racial discrimination, or national predation—unless it is instigated by government interference. The Friedmans' utopia sounds very much like the utopia of Adam Smith, with his system of natural liberty. However, a major difference destroys the similarity. Smith's utopia was used to attack the tyranny of the monarchy's mercantilism. It was used by the underdogs of the time to push their way through the barriers erected by the top dogs of the time. It was used by the upstart merchants and mechanics to rise up against the resistance of the landed aristocracy and against the power of the great, royally-chartered, monopoly-granted, trading companies (Smith 1937; Dugger 1990). While Smith's utopia was used to defend the efforts of the upstarts, the Friedmans' utopia is used to attack the efforts of the upstarts. The upstarts of Smith's time were the merchants and mechanics, but they have grown rich and become established. They are no longer the underdogs but rather the top dogs. The upstarts of the Friedmans' time now must push against the former merchants and mechanics, who have become great retailing corporations, giant industrial conglomerates, and entrenched managerial and professional groups.

The upstarts of the Friedmans' time are women dominated by men, African Americans discriminated against by European Americans, workers and communities exploited by corporate capital, and foreign devils preyed upon by the predatory apparatus of powerful nations. Moreover, the way they push up against the top dogs is to call upon the state, particularly the welfare state, to aid them in their struggle. However, the Friedmans insist that the underdogs should not call for help, or try to improve their position through state aid. Instead, they should simply aid themselves by working harder, being smarter, and saving more. If they do not thrive, it is their own fault. They were not talented enough or did not work hard enough. If the victims of domination, discrimination, exploitation, and predation actually believe that, the top dogs are safe.

What a powerful enabling myth this is. It not only enables class inequality, it enables all the other forms of inequality as well. The wretched of the earth have only themselves to blame for their wretchedness. Here is another important intersection of the different modes of inequality. They are all enabled by the market utopian myth. In fact, the market utopian myth is so powerful that its pull became irresistible to even the former Soviet nomenklatura, who abandoned the myth of the dictatorship of the proletariat for the myth of the utopian market. No longer able to keep the former Soviet masses in their subservient places with the old myth, the nomenklatura adopted a new myth. The new propaganda is for free markets, while the reality involves reconstructed centers of differential economic advantage hidden by a new cover of darkness.

(4) Jingoism: The Myths Supporting National Predation

Jingoism supports national predation. In the United States, jingoism means that "Americans" are "the one" and foreigners, "the other." We are the ones with the manifest destiny. This belief has been with us for a very long time and needs little further discussion here (see Baritz 1985; Slotkin 1985). Jingoism also involves denial and projection, which form an effective mechanism to justify attack and this requires further elaboration.

When the predatory apparatus of the United States attacks another nation, the attack is accompanied by a denial of our own hostile intentions and by projection of hostile intentions onto the nation being attacked. The best recent example of the denial-projection mechanism involved stories circulated in the United States about Libyan hit squads infiltrating the country with instructions to assassinate important U.S. leaders. We subsequently learned that the stories and other alleged hostilities were not true, but they did provide us with the opportunity to justify an air raid against Libya by projecting our own hostile intentions onto the Libyans (see Woodward 1987).

The denial and projection mechanism also allowed us to take a number of hostile actions against the Sandinista government in Nicaragua. It is the foundation of our great fear of international terrorism. We see Saddam Hussein of Iraq as being at the center of a vast network of terrorists who are poised for a myriad of attacks against the United States, both at home and abroad. (For further discussion of the "terrorism terror" see Perdue 1989; Herman and O'Sullivan 1990.)

Jingoism differs from the other enabling myths in a very important and tragic way. In gender, class, and race inequality the enabling myths of sexism, classism, and racism can be inculcated in their negative forms in the underdog groups. However, this is far less possible in nation inequality. Leaders of one nation are hardpressed to convince the people of the opposing nation that they are inferior foreign devils, which makes the nation mode of inequality a particularly unstable and violent form. With the underdog groups harder to fool, inequality between nations requires more violence to enforce. Husbands have killed their wayward wives in patriarchal societies. European Americans have killed disrespectful African Americans, and capitalists have killed revolting workers. However, such killing does not occur on the same vast scale as it does in nation inequality. Indeed, "chosen peoples" (nations) have killed tens of millions of foreigners in the last century alone. It seems easier to kill foreigners than to pacify them with myths.

Enabling myths do four related things simultaneously: (1) they provide an opportunistic rationalization of privilege, (2) they create a superstitious dread of the unknown in the minds of the top dogs, (3) they create the otherness of the victim, and (4) they make it possible to deny that injustice occurs by encouraging the underdogs to blame themselves.

The Antidotes for Inequality

Means of debunking myths are readily available. However, debunking specific myths is not enough because as long as the practices of inequality persist, innovative minds will create new myths to support them. The practices of inequality must be changed, and doing so will take more than just a change of heart. It takes collective action to change social practices. The adage that "you cannot legislate morality" is exactly wrong. In fact, you cannot change morality unless you legislate change in practices. Change the practices and the morals will follow. What people come to believe derives, in large part, from what they do (see Veblen 1919, 1–31, 32–55). Then, however, they use some of their beliefs to justify what they do. In the first instance, their beliefs come from their habits of life; beliefs are largely habitual constructs. Thus, to change the beliefs, the myths that support inequality, the practices of inequality must also be changed.

Inequality, then, must be attacked from two directions simultaneously. First, the irrational myths that support inequality must be debunked. This is the responsibility of the churches, the schools, the sciences, the arts, and the social movements. Second, the actual practices of inequality must be transformed through collective action. This is the responsibility of the unions, the professional associations, the corporate boards, the courts, the legislatures, and, again, the social movements. The following remarks deal with debunking the myths rather than changing the practices.

Debunking the Myths

Unfortunately, rumors of evil foreign intentions spring up eternally, so they must continually be investigated and the truth or falsehood of them exposed on a case-by-case basis. The only way to deal with them as they arise is to have faith and insist upon an open society, an aggressive press, and an informed citizenry. Racist, sexist, and classist myths already have been debunked at length by numerous researchers. For my purposes here, only a brief discussion of the highlights of these debunking efforts is necessary.

With social Darwinism, enabling myths became "scientific." Biological differences between the races and sexes were measured and listed by researchers of high standing in scientific circles. One of the most infamous "scientific" myths supporting racism and sexism had to do with the allegedly biologically determined mental superiority of men over women and of the "white" race over the "black" race. The biological determinists were avid bone collectors and skull measurers—rigorously mathematical and objective. They created the "science" of craniometry. The craniometricians "proved" that the white race was mentally superior to the black race and that men were mentally superior to women because the craniums of men were larger than those of women and the craniums of whites were larger than those of blacks. Of course, many of their measurements were inaccurate and their samples biased. Nevertheless, their findings were accepted in wide university and scientific circles. However, when cranium size was finally related to body size, the results took a dramatic turn. Women were found to have larger craniums relative to their body size than men! Thus, the craniometricians lost heart, and face. How could they admit that women were actually more mentally advanced than men? Of course, the craniometricians were men, and white ones at that. Moreover (needless to say), no evidence of any kind exists that can link mental ability to the size of the cranium of a healthy human of any color or sex (see Gould 1981; Montagu 1974; Ayres [1927] 1973). These first biological determinists, who were supporters of racism and sexism, were eventually debunked by other, better scientists. However, a new crop of biological determinists has stepped into the cultural vacuum to conjure up deceptive bell curves in place of cranium sizes.

Although the keepers of the sacred truths of classism behave much like the biological determinists before them, the myths of classism have a very different origin. The market myth goes back to Adam Smith, in whose hands it was not an enabling myth. It did not justify the inequality of the status quo; instead, it attacked that inequality. The market myth now defends inequality, but it did not start out that way. The market myth's origin is noble, not base, so debunking it is much harder.

The Dynamics of Inequality: Circular Process

Inequality is not an equilibrium state but a circular process. Inequality either gets worse or better, but it does not reach an equilibrium. The continued practice of inequality strengthens the myths that support it, and the stronger myths then lend even greater support to the practice. The resulting circular process is not characterized by offsetting forces that reach a balance but by cumulative causation that continues to move an inegalitarian society toward more inequality or continues to move an egalitarian society toward more equality. The inequality process is a vicious circle, but the equality process is a virtuous circle. Both processes are cumulative, not offsetting.

The Vicious Circle

Collective action of the top dogs against the underdogs establishes the practices of inequality. White Europeans established the great Atlantic slave trade. Males established patriarchy; state leaders established the system of nation-states; and property holders established capitalism. They all did so through collective action. Then, the myths of each form of inequality strengthened the practices of inequality. White Europeans came to believe themselves racially superior to black Africans. Black Africans, who were trapped in slavery, were taught that they must adjust to it or perish. The practice of patriarchy strengthened sexist myths, and the sexist myths then strengthened the sexist practices. State leaders established nation-states. We learned that we were English or French or German and that the foreigners were plotting against us. This strengthened the hands of the state leaders as they extracted more income, status, and power from the underlying populations. They used their gains in foreign plots, teaching us the truth in jingoism. Feudal property holders pushed us off the commons and taught us to value their private property. We believed them and worked ever harder for them, hoping that we could save enough to get some property for ourselves. In each mode of inequality, parasitic practices are established through collective action, and then enabling myths make the practices seem legitimate. The practices then become more entrenched because of the myths, and the myths begin to seem like truths because of the practices. The process is circular.

The Virtuous Circle

If the vicious circle were all there is to the story, we humans would probably have destroyed ourselves long ago. However, there is more. Just as there is a vicious circle of inequality, there is a virtuous circle of equality. Collective action of the underdogs against the top dogs can put an end to the practices of inequality, albeit perhaps only to establish another set of parasitic practices whereby the old underdogs attack the old top dogs. The first become last and the last become first; the meek inherit the earth. Perhaps however, the practices of inequality can be replaced with the practices of equality. The possibility of a virtuous circle replacing the vicious circle is not that remote. The religious leaders of the American civil rights movement did not seek to replace white racism with black racism. Malcolm X became an enlightened antiracist, an egalitarian. Setting the example for the rest of us to fol-low, African-American collective action took the high road. African Americans took collective action against inequality and made considerable progress in eliminating racist practices and myths. Of course, much more needs to be done. Nevertheless as racist practices were resisted by collective action and as racist myths were debunked, it became harder for white people to believe the myths and continue the practices. Thus, a virtuous circle was begun. Then, however, racial progress was interrupted, and then reversed by the Ronald Reagan administration and retrenchment. The vicious circle has replaced the virtuous, once again.

Concluding Remarks

This chapter supplied a simple vocabulary for describing inequality and suggested a dynamic framework of circular and cumulative causation for showing how the forces of inequality move in a reinforcing, rather than offsetting, fashion. The vocabulary includes the modes, practices, myths, focal points, and antidotes for inequality. A few examples and a bit of institutional context were provided to illustrate the concepts. The overall purpose was to help elucidate inequality and the different forms it takes, and to put the forms in an appropriate context. The treatment was introductory and exploratory, not exhaustive or definitive.

References

Ayres, Clarence E. [1927] 1973. *Science: The False Messiah*. Clifton, NJ: Augustus M. Kelley.

Baritz, Loren. 1985. *Backfire*. New York: William Morrow.

Beauvoir, Simone de. [1952] 1989. *The Second Sex*. Translated and edited by H. M. Parshley. New York: Random House.

Becker, Gary S. 1971. *The Economics of Discrimination*. 2d ed. Chicago: University of Chicago Press.

—.1981. *A Treatise on the Family*. Cambridge: Harvard University Press.

Berger, Brigitte, and Peter L. Berger. 1983. *The War over the Family*. Garden City, NY: Anchor Press/Doubleday.

Braverman, Harry. 1974. *Labor and Monopoly Capital*. New York: Monthly Review Press.

Coleman, Richard P., and Lee Rainwater, with Kent A. McClelland. 1978. *Social Standing in America*. New York: Basic Books.

DeMott, Benjamin. 1991. *The Imperial Middle*. New York: William Morrow.

Dugger, William M. 1984. "The Nature of Capital Accumulation and Technological Progress in the Modern Economy." *Journal of Economic Issues*, 18 (Sept.): 799–823.

—.1989a. *Corporate Hegemony*. Westport, CT: Greenwood Press.

—.1989b. "Instituted Process and Enabling Myth: The Two Faces of the Market." *Journal of Economic Issues*, 23 (June): 606–15.

—.ed. 1989c. *Radical Institutionalism*. Westport, CT: Greenwood Press.

—.1990. "From Utopian Capitalism to the Dismal Science: The Effect of the French Revolution on Classical Economics." In Warren J. Samuels, ed., *Research in the History of Economic Thought and Methodology*. Vol. 8. Greenwich, CT.: JAI Press, pp. 153–73.

Dumas, Lloyd Jeffry. 1986. *The Overburdened Economy*. Berkeley: University of California Press.

Fogel, Robert William, and Stanley L. Engerman. 1974. *Time on the Cross*. Boston: Little, Brown and Company.

Friedan, Betty. [1963] 1983. *The Feminine Mystique*. New York: Dell Publishing.

Friedman, Milton. 1962. *Capitalism and Freedom*. Chicago: University of Chicago Press.

Friedman, Milton, and Rose Friedman, 1980. *Free to Choose*. New York: Avon Books.

Genovese, Eugene D. 1965. *The Political Economy of Slavery*. New York: Pantheon.

—.1969. *The World the Slaveholders Made*. New York: Vintage Books.

Gould, Stephen Jay. 1981. *The Mismeasure of Man*. New York: W. W. Norton.

Green, Philip, 1981. *The Pursuit of Inequality*. New York: Pantheon.

Hacker, Andrew. 1995. *Two Nations*. New York: Ballantine Books.

Harrington, Michael. 1983. *The Politics at God's Funeral*. New York: Holt, Rinehart and Winston.

Herman, Edward S., and Gerry O'Sullivan. 1990. *The "Terrorism" Network*. New York: Pantheon.

Hirshson, Stanley P. 1962. *Farewell to the Bloody Shirt*. Chicago: Quadrangle Books.

Jencks, Christopher, and Marshall Smith, Henry Acland, Mary Jo Bane, David Cohen, Herbert Gintis, Barbara Heyns, Stephan Michelson. 1972. *Inequality*. New York: Basic Books.

Jencks, Christopher, and Susan Bartlett, Mary Corcoran, James Crouse, David Eaglesfield, Gregory Jackson, Kent McClelland, Peter Mueser, Michael Olneck, Joseph Schwartz, Sherry Ward, Jill Williams. 1979. *Who Gets Ahead?* New York: Basic Books.

Low, W. Augustus, and Virgil A. Clift. 1981. *Encyclopedia of Black America*. New York: Da Capo Press.

Mead, Margaret. 1949. *Male and Female*. New York: Dell Publishing.

Mellon, James, ed. 1988. *Bullwhip Days*. New York: Avon Books.

Melman, Seymour. 1983. *Profits without Production*. New York: Alfred A. Knopf.

Montagu, Ashley. 1974. *The Natural Superiority of Women*. Rev. ed. New York: Macmillan Publishing Company.

Moore, Barrington, Jr. 1978. *Injustice: The Social Bases of Obedience and Revolt*. White Plains, NY: M. E. Sharpe.

Myrdal, Gunnar. 1962. *An American Dilemma*. New York: Harper and Row.

Oates, Stephen B. 1975. *The Fires of Jubilee*. New York: Harper and Row.

Osberg, Lars. 1984. *Economic Inequality in the United States*. Armonk, NY: M. E. Sharpe.

Perdue, William D. 1989. *Terrorism and the State*. New York: Praeger.

Slotkin, Richard. 1985. *The Fatal Environment*. New York: Atheneum.

Smith, Adam. 1937. *The Wealth of Nations*. Edited by Edwin Canaan. New York: Modern Library.

Stampp, Kenneth M. 1956. *The Peculiar Institution*. New York: Vintage Books.

Stanfield, J. Ron. 1982. "Toward a New Value Standard in Economics." *Economic Forum*, 13 (Fall): 67–85.

Veblen, Thorstein. [1899] 1975. *The Theory of the Leisure Class*. New York: Augustus M. Kelley.

—.1919. The Place of Science in Modern Civilization and Other Essays. New York: B. W. Huebsch.

Woodward, Bob. 1987. *Veil*. New York: Simon and Schuster.

Article 15

Address the Pain, Reap the Gain

Why Our Nation's Future Demands That Political Leaders Take Seriously the Economic Plight of America's Young

Tamara Draut

T oday's young adults are very likely to be the first generation to not surpass the living standards of their parents. Evidence of their declining economic opportunity and security abound, from widespread debt to lower earnings in today's labor market for all but those with advanced degrees.

While this new generation is intensely engaged in the 2008 primary process, their pocketbook concerns remain on the margins of our political debate. A candidate visiting a college campus throws in something about the need for good jobs and lower tuition. But the stump speeches and debates are aimed primarily at middle-aged voters, using broad phrases like "strengthening the middle class" and ignoring the extreme economic insecurity of the young.

There are two compelling reasons why our politics needs a platform centered on the promise of expanding economic opportunity and security for a new generation. First, any effective agenda to shore up America's middle class will have to address young people. After all, it's between the ages of 18 and 34 that the major decisions affecting the trajectory of one's life are made: how much education to complete, what to do for a living, and when to start a family. Second, it could be a winning electoral strategy—attracting not just the youth vote but that of parents and grandparents, voters who worry about the ability of their children and grandchildren to build a better life for themselves. Indeed, polls now show that the majority of Americans do not believe the next generation will be better off than they are.

It's not surprising when you consider what has changed in just one generation. Back in the 1950s, 1960s, and early 1970s, three factors helped facilitate the transition to adulthood. First, there were jobs that provided good wages even for high school graduates. A college degree wasn't necessary to earn a decent living. And if you wanted to go, college was far more affordable. The second was an economy that lifted all boats, with productivity gains shared by workers and executives alike. The result was a massive growth of the middle class, which provided security and stability for families. Third, a range of public policies helped facilitate this economic mobility and opportunity: a strong minimum wage, grants for low-income students to go to college, generously subsidized state college tuition, a reliable unemployment insurance system, enforcement of the right to join a union, major incentives for homeownership, and a solid safety net for those falling on hard times.

This world no longer exists. Relationships between employers and employees have become more tenuous, as corporations face global competitors and quarterly bottom-line pressures from Wall Street. Fringe benefits like health care and pension plans have been evaporating. As most families see their incomes stagnate or decline, they increasingly need two full-time incomes just to stay afloat, creating new demands and pressures on working parents. Getting into the middle class now requires a four-year college degree, and even that is no guarantee of the American dream.

But this increased insecurity for the young is not mainly the result of changes in the economy, for the economy is always changing. Rather, the insecurity reflects the failure of public policy to keep pace with the changes by providing the kind of buffers and counterweights that were widespread just a generation ago.

Today's young adults are trying to establish themselves in a society that has grown widely unequal and less responsive to the needs of ordinary citizens—with no real help from their government. At each step in the obstacle course to adulthood—getting an education, finding a job, starting a family, and buying a home—our nation's public policies have failed to keep up. Far too often, social critics blame a supposed poor work ethic or out-of-control spending habits. But the statistics paint an economic portrait much more troubling than a penchant for $4 lattes.

College: A Luxury-Priced Necessity

Today, rapidly rising tuition and anemic federal financial aid has created a "debt-for-diploma system." With two out of three undergraduates leaving school with student-loan debts averaging $19,200 ($17,250 for those attending four-year public universities), the debt-for-diploma system is a financial undertow on young adults long after graduation.

Back in the 1970s, before college became essential for a middle-class lifestyle, our nation was more committed to helping students afford college. Students from modest economic backgrounds received almost free tuition through Pell grants, and middle-class households could afford to send their kids to college because states kept tuition at public universities and colleges within reach. A generation later, state spending on higher education is at a 25-year low and federal financial aid is increasingly debt-based, with only 38 percent in the form of grants (chart below). We no longer help students afford college; we simply help them go into debt for college.

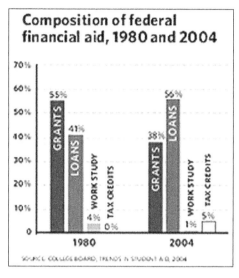

Composition of federal financial aid, 1980 and 2004

SOURCE: COLLEGE BOARD, TRENDS IN STUDENT AID, 2004

After sitting idly by for more than a decade, Congress last September passed The College Cost Reduction and Access Act, which will provide an additional $20 billion in student aid over the next five years. The act was heralded as a major improvement, but its impact on college access will be negligible. Behind the lofty rhetoric are modest improvements at best: the law increases the maximum Pell grant by about $500 each year over the next five years, to $5,400 in 2012. The act also creates an income-based repayment system that caps the amount student borrowers would pay on their loans to 15 percent of their discretionary income (discretionary is defined as any income above 150 percent of poverty, or about $15,000 for a single individual). Finally, the law reduces the interest rate charged on certain new student loans, cutting it in half by 2012. These improvements are paid for by reducing the subsidies the government currently provides to student-loan companies.

These measures provide some progress in fixing our financial aid system, but it's important to remember that in 1972 when the Pell grant was established, it was designed to cover three-quarters of the cost of attending a public university. In 2007, the maximum Pell grant only covered about one-third of the costs at a public four-year college. By the time it reaches the new maximum under the act in 2012, it will still likely only cover about one-third of the cost of college because tuitions are likely to have risen faster.

The Disappearing "Real Job"

The term "real job" used to mean the first job you got after completing school. A real job allowed you to pay rent, buy groceries, make car payments, and have enough left over for spending money. A real job also came with fringe benefits such as health care and some type of retirement savings plan. Today's 20- and 30-somethings are discovering that real jobs are hard to come by in reality.

Incomes for full-time workers aged 25 to 34 are lower today than they were a generation ago, except among workers with college degrees. Among young workers without college degrees, young women's earnings have remained relatively flat, while young men's earnings have declined considerably. Young males with high school diplomas are earning 29 percent less than they did in 1974, with young black men experiencing the steepest drop in incomes. Unemployment among young men of color is particularly high for this generation, with half of black men in their 20s jobless in 2004, up from 46 percent in 2000.

The paycheck decline experienced by this new generation of young workers can partly be explained by the disappearance of manufacturing jobs that offered good wages for workers without college degrees, and the proliferation of low-wage service-sector jobs in their place, with no public policy for professionalizing those jobs or helping unions to organize them. In addition to lackluster wages, these jobs offer little room for advancement and few, if any, fringe benefits. Today, about 29 percent of young adults—a full 18.2 million 19- to 34-year-olds—don't have health insurance, making this the age group with the largest percentage uninsured.

In addition to often working in a benefit-free zone, moving up the wage or career ladder in the new economy is more difficult than it was a generation ago. The well-paying middle-management jobs that characterized the workforce up to the late 1970s have been eviscerated. Corporate downsizing in the 1980s and 1990s slashed positions in the middle of the wage distribution, and now outsourcing threatens to take millions more. And unions, which also helped facilitate upward mobility particularly for those outside the professional ranks, have been pummeled by illegal management tactics and government failure to enforce the right to organize. The same government has allowed corporations to misclassify permanent jobs as contract work, denying employees other hard-won legal protections.

Generation Debt

Between college debt and the spillover effects of lower earnings amid a higher cost of living, credit card debt has become a new rite of passage into adulthood. It's not exactly the kind of generation-defining characteristic one wishes for, but debt is perhaps the one shared experience of this diverse generation. Young adults between the ages of 18 and 24 have 22 percent higher credit card debt than those who were that age in 1989. Young adults between the ages of 25 and 34 are also deeper in debt. In 2004, 25- to 34-year-olds averaged $4,358 in credit card debt—47 percent higher than it was for baby boomers who were in that age group in 1989. Additional survey research conducted by Dēmos of low- to middle-income households found that in 2005 the average indebted adult under age 34 had slightly more than $8,000 in credit card debt. According to these households, the most common reasons for their credit card debt were car repairs, loss of a job, and home repairs. Forty-five percent of those under age 34 reported using credit cards in the last year to pay for basic living expenses, such as rent, mortgage payments, groceries, and utilities.

The rise in credit card debt, coupled with the surge in student-loan debt, is the main reason why today's young adults are spending much more on debt payments than the previous generation. On average, 25- to 34-year-olds spend nearly 25 cents out of every dollar of income on debt payments, according to the Federal Reserve's data. That's more than double what baby boomers of the same age spent on debt payments in 1989. The fact that young adults are already spending a quarter of their income on debt is particularly worrisome because most in the 25 to 34 age group aren't homeowners. So that 25 cents is going to non-mortgage debt: primarily student loans, car loans, and credit cards—making it harder to ever become homeowners.

High-Cost Housing

The average person now leaves his or her parents' home at the age of 24. But four out of 10 young people will end up circling back to their parents' home at least once after leaving. Most grown-ups do not look forward to continuing to live with their parents. A prime reason for these "boomerang kids" is that housing costs have risen faster than inflation and faster than entry-level wages. For college graduates, big cities are still the best place to go for launching a career. But chasing a good job comes with a steep price. Between 1995 and 2002, median rents in nearly all the largest metropolitan areas rose by more than 50 percent. Median rents in San Francisco ballooned by 76 percent; Boston, 61 percent; and Denver, 62 percent. And the last five years haven't been any kinder to renters.

First-time homebuyers have also become particularly vulnerable in the wake of rapidly rising home prices and a deregulated mortgage market. In 2006, the National Association of Realtors reported that 43 percent of first-time homebuyers purchased their home with zero money down. Many are financing 100 percent of their homes and taking out massive mortgages that eat up as much as half of their income. An unregulated mortgage industry has unleashed a tidal wave of "innovative products" designed to bilk new homeowners with extra fees, points, and complex pricing schemes that can spell disaster for the unwary—as the sub-prime meltdown continues to demonstrate. As a result of surging home prices and lower down payments, the typical monthly mortgage payment of a young homeowner is one-third larger than it was in 1980.

The Perils of Parenthood

For middle-income families, the cost of raising a child born in 1960 to age 18 was $155,141 (in 2003 dollars). Four decades later, the cost of raising a child born in 2003 to age 18 rose to $178,590—a 15 percent increase.

Why does it cost more today to raise a child than it did back then? You might look around at all the techno toys and frivolous clothing in parents' magazines, but the real culprit is child care and health care. Today the average two-parent family with two children under age 5 spends 11 percent of its budget on child care—up from only 1 percent in 1960. Paying for a child's health care eats up significantly more of the budget too, absorbing 7 percent compared to 4 percent a generation ago.

Limited subsidies are available to help lower-income parents, mostly single women transitioning off welfare, pay for child care. But income limits are too low for moderate or middle-income families to qualify. As a result, child care remains one of the biggest expenses in a young family's household budget, often second only to the mortgage or rental payment. Having access to nurturing and developmentally sound day care for infants and toddlers is something young families can take for granted in virtually every other developed nation in the world. But in our society it's something only the most well-off can procure.

If progressives want to win the youth vote and begin building a sustainable new progressive majority, then it's time to take the economic insecurity and downward mobility of today's young people seriously. The economic concerns facing young people should be the backbone of the promise to strengthen the middle class and create more opportunity. The reality is that it has become much more difficult for this generation to either work or educate their way into the middle class. It's a reality their parents and grandparents are witnessing firsthand. It's a reality few politicians talk about but most Americans understand.

Creating a broader, stronger, and more inclusive middle class demands new public policies aimed at young people just starting out. Right now they have the most to lose. With the right mix of politics and real policy change, they could have the most to gain. This Prospect special report, co-sponsored with Demos and underwritten through the generosity of the W.K. Kellogg Foundation, provides a blueprint for both the policies and the politics.

Article 16

Reclaiming Middle-Class America

If Progressives Want a Winning Theme That the Right Can't Match, this is it

Jacob S. Hacker

"Middle class" is more than an income category. It's an image of a certain kind of society—a nation in which the gains of prosperity are broadly shared and those who work hard have a good shot at upward mobility and the security of a basic safety net.

Today, that image is badly tarnished. In a September 2010 ABC News/Yahoo! poll, only half of Americans agreed that "the American Dream—that if you work hard you'll get ahead—still holds true"; more than four in 10 said it no longer did. This dark mood undoubtedly reflects hard economic times, but middle-class discontent runs much deeper than the current downturn, and its roots are at least as much political as economic. To reclaim America as a middle-class nation, we need to understand what's gone wrong—and what can be done to fix it.

The Eroding Foundations of Middle-Class America

Like all ideals, the American dream is an aspiration, not a guarantee. Yet, for 30-odd years after World War II, the aspiration came remarkably close to reality. Thanks to the GI bill, millions gained college degrees or vocational training, bought a home, or started a business. Pressed by labor unions, employers provided decent wages and developed extensive health and pension benefits that provided security to workers and their families. Social Security and then Medicare transformed secure retirement into a mass experience.

Most important, earnings rose rapidly for workers at the bottom, the middle, and the top. This was no accident. It was grounded in an implicit social contract that emphasized joint economic gains and financial security. This contract, in turn, was grounded in broadly distributed power. Strong labor unions, cross-class civic organizations, and political institutions less

Jacob Hacker, "Reclaiming Middle Class," *The American Prospect Online*: Feb. 16, 2011. http://www.prospect.org. The American Prospect, 1710 Rhode Island Avenue, NW, 12th Floor, Washington, DC 20036. All rights reserved. Reprinted with permission.

inundated by and responsive to money—these were the foundations of what my co-author Paul Pierson and I call "middle-class democracy."

Under the midcentury social contract, workers received job security, guaranteed benefits, and good pay, and employers got loyal, productive workers who invested in skills specific to their jobs. Prosperity, mobility, and security were not just ideals espoused by politicians. They were lived realities for an increasing share of workers and their families.

That bargain has unraveled. In the middle of the earnings ladder, wages have risen only modestly over the last generation; below the middle, they have stagnated or fallen. Even a college-educated entry-level male worker earns barely more than his counterpart did a generation ago. The story of the last 40 years is of a huge divorce between aggregate productivity, which has continued to rise handsomely, and wages for most workers, which have stagnated or declined.

The 1990s economic boom temporarily reduced the pay-productivity gap. In the 2000s, however, the underlying gap returned with a vengeance. Indeed, the 2002–2007 expansion was the first on record in which median family incomes ended lower than they had at the close of the last expansion.

The other, closely linked story of the post-1970s economic reversal is the growing income divide between the rich and the rest. While wages in the middle stagnated, those at the top flourished. The richest 0.1 percent of Americans have seen their share of pre-tax national income rise from less than 3 percent in 1970 to more than 12 percent in 2007—the highest rate since the creation of the income tax in 1913. An ethic of shared prosperity has given way to one of winner-take-all.

As job security has eroded and gains have shifted toward the top, other pillars of the American dream have also weakened.

Education and Social Mobility

Class lines have hardened. American inequality is sky high; American social mobility is below the advanced industrial norm. The United States has gone from the world leader in college completion to a middling performer. More and more of skyrocketing college costs are financed through loans, burdening many students and their parents. Children of the rich, however, gain a huge head start.

Pensions and Social Insurance

America's job-based framework of economic security has gone from basic to broken. Defined, secure pensions—once the hallmark of a good job—are vanishing. Tax-deferred savings accounts such as 401(k)s aren't filling the gap. As medical costs continue to outstrip inflation, employment-based health-insurance benefits are becoming rarer and less protective.

Housing and Economic Assets

Besides their homes, most middle-class families have strikingly little in the way of private assets to cushion economic shocks or build their futures. And, of course, those homes look far less secure than they once did. The traditional strategy of gradually accumulating wealth through housing has taken a perhaps fatal hit, with implications for the economic security not just of the middle-aged but also of the young, aspiring middle class.

What Went Wrong

Who killed the old social contract? To some, the culprit is the unstoppable forces of technology and globalization. Computers and automation have reduced the rewards to routine skills and encouraged outsourcing and offshoring. The entry of hundreds of millions of literate, low-wage workers into the global workforce has undermined the earning power of less-educated Americans and elevated the well-educated. Compared with these vast tides, conventional wisdom suggests, American politics and policy have played only a bit role—and can only do a limited amount to reclaim the American dream.

Technological change and globalization matter immensely. But all rich countries have experienced their impact—most more so than the U.S.—yet few have seen anything like America's sharp upward shift of economic rewards, implosion of unions, or breakdown of social benefits. Moreover, in many nations where wage inequality has risen, policymakers have pushed back through active labor-market policies, taxes, and public spending designed to reduce the remaining income gaps. Not so in the United States. Despite the Earned Income Tax Credit and expansion of Medicaid, low-wage workers have continued to fall behind. According to the Congressional Budget Office, even after all public and private benefits and federal taxes are included, almost 40 percent of all household income gains between 1979 and 2007 accrued to the richest 1 percent of Americans—more than received by the bottom 90 percent combined.

The recent tax-cut deal, extending huge tax cuts for the richest, highlighted the long-term role of our tax system in abetting inequality. Far more important and less recognized have been ways in which Washington has remade markets to advantage the top. Failure to enforce the Wagner Act has undermined labor unions as a force for good pay and benefits. Corporate-governance rules all but asked top executives to drive up their own earnings. Financial deregulation brought great riches for some while crashing the rest of the economy.

Perhaps the least visible policy changes were passive—aggressive—deliberate failures to address changing economic and social conditions, such as the need to balance work and family. Entire categories of support that have become essential to middle-class life, such as good child care, are not a public responsibility. Meanwhile, responsibilities once shouldered by corporations are shifting back to families. Uniquely among industrial nations, the U.S. came to rely on employers as mini welfare states, providing health insurance, pensions, and other benefits that elsewhere enjoyed state sponsorship. But as employers have pulled back, government has not filled the gap, leaving families more vulnerable.

Perhaps it's not surprising, then, that so many middle-class Americans feel abandoned. Asked in mid-2010 whom government had helped "a great deal" during the downturn, 53 percent of Americans said banks and financial institutions. Forty-four percent fingered large corporations. Just 2 percent thought economic policies had helped the middle class a great deal.

Americans are skeptical because government hasn't delivered. The great social-policy breakthrough of 2010, health reform, falls far short of a long-term vision for rebuilding the middle class. Emergency actions such as the stimulus package and bank bailout sought to stabilize the economy without challenging its imbalances. The recently enacted tax-cut deal means two more years of huge tax cuts for the richest. In return, the middle class received grudging extensions of unemployment insurance and a partial payroll tax holiday that will create few good jobs. While Americans say that their highest priority is to restart the economy and their most cherished programs are Social Security and Medicare, political leaders from the center and the right are embracing a deficit-reduction agenda that will threaten those two programs and preclude serious investment in the middle class to restore broadly shared prosperity.

Unequal Income, Unequal Power

What explains this disconnect? The imbalance in organizational power and resources between the middle and the top is certainly a big part of the answer. In the late 1970s, corporate America organized on an unprecedented scale to influence government policy—not just through campaign giving but also through vast lobbying efforts. At the same time, with campaign costs skyrocketing, money has become a far more important resource for politicians—and, as we have seen, a far more unequally distributed resource in American society.

Another part of the answer, however, is the bitter fruit of this imbalance: an increasingly radicalized Republican Party, a divided Democratic Party, and powerful, growing currents of public hostility toward American government itself. For the contemporary

GOP, the increased organizational might of business and influence of money—along with the party's success in locking down the conservative evangelical vote—have encouraged the party to shift ever rightward on economic issues. Democrats, by contrast, have been cross-pressured, torn between their historical commitment to the "little guy" and the pull of money from the big guys, including, for much of the 1990s and early 2000s, the ascendant titans of Wall Street. The result has been an increasingly polarized economic debate in which a significant faction of one party, the Democrats, has been willing to cut deals that undermine the middle class' standing.

For progressives, reclaiming the high political ground by addressing the bread-and-butter concerns of the middle class is the key to not just broadly shared prosperity but also long-term political success. As the last two years suggest, however, picking the ball back up won't be easy. Progressives will have to grapple with the decline of the organizations, like labor unions and broad-based civic associations, that informed Americans about what was at stake in political debates and helped them shape what government did. They will have to break the Democrats' unholy alliance with Wall Street. Above all, they will need to put forth a clear alternative to the anti-government mantra of tax cuts, deregulation, and programmatic cutbacks—one that is far more compelling than the grab bag of deficit reduction and modest new initiatives that defined the Democratic economic message for so much of the 1990s and 2000s.

Progressives will also have to confront an inconvenient truth: They are losing on economic issues not because Americans' judgments are clouded by social issues or racial animosity but because, battered by the economic trends just described and bombarded with mixed messages, many middle-class Americans are wondering whether progressives can really deliver a better economic life. And, perhaps most challenging, progressives are losing because the well of public trust in government has been so badly poisoned by the failures of government to deliver that life in the recent past.

It is a myth that Americans do not care about inequality or put unbridled faith in corporate America or believe they all will be rich one day. In fact, Americans are strikingly egalitarian in many respects (ask ordinary people how they feel about Wall Street) and relatively realistic about their own economic prospects. But one common presumption is true: Many Americans have lost their faith in government. A generation ago, the majority of Americans said they trusted public officials to do what was right. No more: In 2008, 69 percent of Americans agreed that "government is pretty much run by a few big interests looking out for themselves" rather than for "the benefit of all the people"; only 29 percent disagreed. In 1964—the first year this question was asked by the American National Election Studies—the numbers were reversed: 64 percent disagreed; 29 percent agreed. This loss of faith is the most destructive legacy of a cynical right that has torn down government to gain power and a feeble center that has too often gone along.

Today's anti-government tide is deeply corrosive. It feeds excess suspicion, fuels the disconnect between citizens and leaders, and pushes voters—who still overwhelmingly embrace current middle-class programs—toward tax cuts, spending cutbacks, and other policies that feed on anti-government sentiments. It is impossible to imagine a political movement centered on middle-class concerns that somehow avoids using activist government. Rebuilding the middle class requires rebuilding a sense that government can make a positive difference.

If progressives do not seize the moment, they will not only lose the votes of the middle class; they will also lose their chance to craft a governing philosophy that can shape the economic future of our nation.

Article 17

Champions of the Middle Class

Can Organized Labor Lead a Movement to Restore Broad Economic Security? It's Hard to Imagine Who Else Will

Robert Kuttner

The labor movement has long been a potent force for promoting a broad economic middle. Though no longer centered in auto and steel factories, unions continue to offer lower-income Americans a path into the middle class—just ask a newly organized janitor, hotel worker, security guard, hospital paraprofessional, home-care worker, or warehouse, call-center, or food-service employee. In 2003, the Economic Policy Institute found that the wage premium for unionized jobs relative to comparable jobs is about 20 percent, and union workers are far more likely to have decent health and pension benefits as well as a voice at work. Unions are also the single most powerful lobby for good social legislation such as Social Security, Medicare, and college aid, helping anchor the middle class generally.

Unions are also central to electing Democrats. For two decades, Steve Rosenthal, former political director of the AFL-CIO, has been providing the numbers with a regularly updated slide show to political candidates, operatives, donors, and activists. In 2010, even with turnout down, unemployment up, and the working middle class anxious and skeptical, union households voted Democratic by a margin of 60-to-38, only slightly below the 64-to-34 margin in 2008.

Comparable unorganized workers voted heavily Republican. In 2010, working-class (non-college-educated) whites from nonunion households backed Republicans by a devastating margin of 68 percent to 31 percent—more than 2-to-1. But working-class white voters from union families cast their ballot for Democrats by 55 percent to 45 percent.

This stunning 24-point gap does not reflect some fundamental differences in the character of, say, truckers at nonunion FedEx versus unionized UPS drivers, or workers at

Robert Kuttner, "Champions of the Middle Class," *The American Prospect Online*: March 1, 2011, http://www.prospect.org. The American Prospect, 1710 Rhode Island Avenue, NW, 12th Floor, Washington, DC 20036. All rights reserved. Reprinted with permission.

unionized hotels in Las Vegas and nonunion ones in Phoenix. The different consciousness of union workers is the result of a shared experience of bargaining collectively to improve working life, coupled with union efforts on economic education and political campaigns. "Union workers have more solidarity, more leadership, and more understanding of economic issues," says Sen. Sherrod Brown of Ohio.

The union share of votes cast, though smaller than it once was, still matters immensely in swing states. In 2010, it was 26 percent in Ohio, Illinois, and Wisconsin, and 24 percent in Pennsylvania. Nevada's majority-unionized hotel and casino industries delivered an otherwise impossible re-election victory for Sen. Harry Reid.

Another of Rosenthal's slides extrapolates these voting propensities to show how a larger labor movement would transform American politics. Five million more union members, assuming that they voted roughly like existing members, would flip at least five Senate seats from Republican to Democrat and would flip a far larger number in the House. Ten million new unionists would produce something close to a Democratic lock on Congress.

Until the blowout of November 2010, the unions' ability to deliver votes for Democrats was growing stronger with every recent election. The rank-and-file Democratic vote increased from 54 percent in 1992 to 59 percent in 1996 to 64 percent in 2006 and 2008, before falling back slightly to 60 percent in 2010. Unionization, even with a depleted labor movement, still provides Democrats with about 5 million votes they would not otherwise have. Several Democrats from swing states who narrowly won in 2006 will be up in 2012. Many would not have been elected in the first place, but for labor's strong support, including Missouri's Claire McCaskill, Montana's Jon Tester, Minnesota's Amy Klobuchar, and Virginia's Jim Webb. The labor movement put about a third of a billion dollars into the 2008 campaign, and a quarter billion in 2006, according to the Center for Responsive Politics and *The Wall Street Journal*. With spending at an all-time high in 2010, labor's numbers are most likely higher for the last election, and that's in addition to knocking on millions of doors.

But the labor movement has been steadily losing members in recent decades and is now down to just 7 percent of the private-sector workforce. "At this rate," says a leader of Change to Win, a coalition of four major unions, "there will be no private-sector labor movement in another 10 years." To counteract the decline, AFL-CIO and Change to Win are planning major campaigns, not just to unionize workers but to mobilize Americans on behalf of a broad middle-class agenda. Though details are still being debated, that agenda has to include jobs and major social investment—the traditional tonic of the liberal-labor coalition updated for the 21st century.

Republicans and corporate elites are all too aware of what a stronger labor movement would mean. On the eve of President Barack Obama's election, Sen. John Ensign of Nevada, chair of the National Republican Senatorial Committee, warned that enactment of the Employee Free Choice Act, which would streamline union representation elections, "would make Republicans the minority party for the next 40 to 50 years." When it looked as if the Obama administration might make EFCA a priority, Randel Johnson, a vice president at the U.S. Chamber of Commerce, described the coming battle as "Armageddon." Business groups warned the White House to forget cooperation on other issues if they made a serious push for EFCA.

But while business lobbyists and Republican strategists are fully aware of what a stronger labor movement would mean for the Democratic Party as well as wages and benefits, their appreciation is not entirely reciprocated by Democrats. Early in 2009, the Obama administration made some fateful decisions. The president wanted common ground, not polarization. Health reform came first and required the collaboration, or at least not the active opposition, of major industries. EFCA had to wait.

Labor leaders report being told by the White House in early 2009 that if they could produce the votes, President Obama would gladly sign the bill, but he would not actively work Congress on its behalf. That stance effectively doomed the reform law, since at least six senators from states with weak unions and powerful business interests were disinclined to vote to break a Republican filibuster on EFCA. Obama is not unique. His is the third consecutive Democratic administration that benefited greatly from labor's voter-mobilization efforts only to respond with disinterest that effectively killed labor-law reform.

In January 2009, partly as a sop to the labor movement and partly to signal symbolic concern for the middle class, the president did create a task force on middle-class working families, chaired by Vice President Joe Biden. But the task force has only two part-time professional employees, stages purely symbolic events, and is not taken seriously by other Cabinet departments. Such is the administration's unease about discussing class that a major debate ensued about whether to call it a task force on working families or a task force on the middle class. The ungainly final name was a hybrid of both.

If a stronger labor movement is so good for middle-class incomes and for the Democratic Party, what explains the Democrats' ambivalence? The problem is far more structural than personal, says Larry Cohen, president of the Communication Workers of America. Two factors are labor's declining membership and geographic concentration. Organized labor is not just a diminished share of the workforce—its strongholds are geographically concentrated in New York, California, and a few Midwestern states. Democrats can't win without those states, but most senators and representatives neither appreciate unions nor have to answer to them politically.

"Democrats get that we're politically useful," Cohen says. "But I'm not sure that enough Democrats grasp the economic argument that collective bargaining allows the economy to build the middle class."

Says a senior union political strategist: "Democrats think that all the union has to do is endorse them, and that's all it takes. They don't understand that it takes a lot of effort and political education to convince voters what is in their economic self-interest. We have to work to get out people to support the Democrat—often in spite of these Democratic candidates."

The shift from economic to social issues since the 1960s has also diminished labor's role. "After Vietnam, the civil-rights movement, and the emergence of issues like gay rights and abortion, the Democratic Party was reconstituted," says a senior labor leader. "There was a cultural revolt against the kind of society into which the older labor movement fit well."

"An increasing number of Democratic elected officials and their consultants come from the business and professional class," says an influential pollster. "They are successful individuals. They tend to identify more with the boss than the worker. Their view of labor is instrumental, antiseptic, and transactional. Labor is seen as a source of funds and votes—'I'll do this for you, if you do this for me.' But there's no real appreciation of what unions do for their members."

This pollster adds that a related problem is the functional separation of union staffers who do politics from staffers who do organizing: "The political types interact with other political types, so party operatives never see the labor movement at its most inspiring."

According to another Democratic operative, senators, governors, and their spouses and advisers just don't spend much time with union leaders, much less with union members. "If they oppose gay rights or abortion rights, they are going to get a lot of static from people they value, including their wives. But if they support NAFTA [the North American Free Trade Agreement] or don't push labor-law reform, does anyone come up to them at a cocktail party the next day and say, why did you do that?"

Of course, big money has also displaced ordinary people. Beginning in the early 1980s, Congressman Tony Coelho of California, then chair of the Democratic Congressional Campaign Committee, realized that the Democrats, as the majority party in Congress, could raise bushels of money from organized business. Getting too cozy with labor undercut that strategy.

Money tends to crowd out respect for labor's strongest suit—mobilizing voters. "We've spent the past 15 years building on-the-ground infrastructure—door knocking, organizing. But the whole system is marinated in money," says United Steelworkers President Leo Gerard. "I remember a political consultant telling us, 'Don't give me any shit about yard signs, just give me money for TV.'"

Labor does give Democrats a lot of money, but it is only one source among many. The other big money sources include Hollywood, Wall Street, trial lawyers, and business renegades like oil wildcatters and socially liberal entrepreneurs. None of the elite Democratic

Party donors wants a politics that emphasizes class differences. They tend to be center-left on cultural and foreign-policy issues but have little in common with organized labor.

Stan Greenberg, the pollster who crafted Bill Clinton's strategy of winning with a middle-class, pocketbook populism, sees a paradox: "There's more of an opportunity today for a populist middle-class message, because the middle class feels more squeezed. But there is increased structural pressure in a capitalist economy for political leaders not to be populist."

The labor movement, seemingly, is the natural counterweight to elite pressures to deregulate, privatize, reduce social outlay, and otherwise leave the middle class at risk. First, however, labor needs to be seen as more than a narrow interest group. Says Leo Gerard, "The labor movement has to do a better job explaining to the general public that we aren't what we're perceived to be on Fox News. We're the voice not just for the represented middle class but for the middle class generally."

Certainly, the present trajectory is unsustainable—for progressives generally, for unions, and for a middle-class America. The organized middle class that the labor movement built is now the target of both newly elected Republican majorities and frightened voters looking for scapegoats. America's loss of competitiveness, for example, is often blamed on union pay scales (though Germany's highly competitive cars and well-managed auto companies have even better-compensated workers). Newly elected Republican governors are aggressively seeking to weaken public-sector unions, while even some Democrats such as New York's Andrew Cuomo and President Obama are imposing public-worker pay freezes, reinforcing the image of unions as a privileged minority rather than the voice of a working middle-class society generally.

"Rather than being honest about not enough revenues coming in because of the recession, they try to mask that by blaming the people who provide public services," says Randi Weingarten, president of the American Federation of Teachers. Wall Street billionaires were momentarily scorned for causing the crash that led to a generalized economic collapse, but that anger is now being focused on public-sector workers who earn around the median wage and autoworkers who have already taken steep pay cuts.

Instead of other citizens clamoring for what unionized workers have, organized labor is being asked to give up its hard-won pension and health benefits—of the sort that citizens of other advanced capitalist countries enjoy as a right.

America, in sum, is paying dearly for its one-sided class politics. It's hard to imagine a middle-class society without a labor movement—but it's hard to imagine organized labor thriving unless labor becomes the credible leader of a movement to reclaim a middle-class America. "Politicians put their fingers to the wind," says Mary Kay Henry, the new president of the Service Employees International Union. "We need to be the wind."

Article 18

The Collapse of Secure Retirement

The Dream of a Modestly Middle-Class Retirement is Fading

Teresa Ghilarducci

W hile many in Washington and on Wall Street are talking about cutting Social Security, the real problem is that America's patchwork retirement system is already eroding. Once, the majority of America's seniors could look forward to at least a modestly middle-class retirement. That dream is fading.

America's retirement system is said to be a three-legged stool made up of private savings, pension plans, and Social Security. But each leg of the stool is wobbly, while a fourth unacknowledged leg—asset accumulation from home equity—has also taken a huge hit. Absent drastic changes in retirement policy, more elderly Americans will be poor, and many more will be working, often in low-wage jobs, because they can't afford to retire.

Even without further cuts, the normal Social Security retirement age is set to increase to 67 in 2022. Compare to where it was before the last major changes enacted in 1983, Social Security has already been cut close to 20 percent, in terms of how much wage income it typically replaces.

The private pension part of our system is in even worse shape. Over half of workers have no pension plan. Of those who do, only 20 percent have traditional plans that provide a guaranteed benefit, while the other 80 percent have 401(k)-type plans that shift all the risks to the retiree. In 2009, the account balance for the average-income household with a 401(k) plan was only about $67,000. Even the oldest workers in the highest-earning households, of $100,000 annual income and over, have on average only about $173,000, which yields a lifetime monthly income of just $500.

According to the Center for Retirement Research at Boston College, less than half of American workers will have enough income to adequately maintain living standards into

Teresa Ghilarducci, "The Collapse of Secure Retirement," *The American Prospect Online*: Feb. 28, 2011. http://www.prospect.org. The American Prospect, 1710 Rhode Island Avenue, NW, 12th Floor, Washington, DC 20036. All rights reserved. Reprinted with permission.

retirement. The risk of insufficient income in old age is higher for workers today than it was for their parents and grandparents.

The 30-year experiment with 401(k)-type retirement plans has failed for six reasons: Only half of the workforce has access to a retirement account or pension plan; the plans are voluntary, making retirement savings rates too low and too inconsistent; 401(k) and individual retirement account (IRA) management fees are too high; financial markets are too volatile; many people cash out their accounts to meet immediate needs; and lopsided tax breaks go mainly to the richest taxpayers. So individuals bear too much risk of under-accumulation, unreliable returns, and the absence of a steady stream of lifelong retirement income.

In 2009, Vice President Joe Biden's Middle Class Task Force acknowledged the eroding retirement-income system. It urged more choices in retirement accounts and universal coverage. In the same year, the Government Accountability Office recognized the failure of 401(k)-type plans and reviewed four serious pension-reform ideas. The best of these was the Guaranteed Retirement Account plan.

GRAs, which I helped to develop working with the Economic Policy Institute and Rockefeller Foundation, would ensure everyone has a retirement plan that effectively supplements Social Security. Participation in a pension plan would be automatic for everyone; contributions would be required by both employers and employees and thus, would be consistent and adequate. Professional managers would invest the GRA money at low fees, and the accounts would have a guaranteed inflation-adjusted rate of return, provide automatic annuities, and prevent withdrawals before retirement. A $600 tax credit would be given to everyone, not just those taxpayers with large deductions, ensuring every worker gets help from the government.

GRAs are similar to plans available to university professors, nonprofit employees, members of Congress, and other public-sector employees. GRAs would also break the lock that Wall Street currently has on most retail and brokerage retirement products. The management of 401(k) and IRA plans is among the financial industry's most lucrative business. Fees are hidden and so large that they can easily erode the value of the fund by 20 percent.

Alternatives such as extending IRAs to Americans without pensions are no solution. With universal or automatic IRAs, people will still not save enough, pay too many fees for risky investments, and have no assured income stream for life.

So the current Social Security debate has it backward. The real issue is not how much to cut the system's already meager benefits but how to assure decent living standards for Americans in old age. Part of the answer is to restore decent wage growth for working Americans, so that their contributions to retirement will be more nearly adequate. But the retirement system itself is in need of major overhaul.

Part 5

Crime

Article 19

In Prison Reform, Money Trumps Civil Rights

Michelle Alexander

The legal scholar Derrick A. Bell foresaw that mass incarceration, like earlier systems of racial control, would continue to exist as long as it served the perceived interests of white elites.

Thirty years of civil rights litigation and advocacy have failed to slow the pace of a racially biased drug war or to prevent the emergence of a penal system of astonishing size. Yet a few short years of tight state budgets have inspired former "get tough" true believers to suddenly denounce the costs of imprisonment. "We're wasting tax dollars on prisons," they say. "It's time to shift course."

Newt Gingrich, the former House speaker, shocked many earlier this year when he co-wrote an essay for The Washington Post calling on "conservative legislators to lead the way in addressing an issue often considered off-limits to reform: prisons."

Republican governors had already been sounding the same note. As California was careering toward bankruptcy last year, Gov. Arnold Schwarzenegger lamented that more money was being spent on prisons than on education. Priorities "have become out of whack over the years," he said. "What does it say about any state that focuses more on prison uniforms than on caps and gowns?" Another Republican governor, John R. Kasich of Ohio, recently announced support for reducing penalties for nonviolent drug offenders as part of an effort to slash the size of the state's prison population.

A majority of those swept into our nation's prison system are poor people of color, but the sudden shift away from the "get tough" rhetoric that has dominated the national discourse on crime has not been inspired by a surge in concern about the devastating human toll of mass incarceration. Instead, as Professor Bell predicted, the changing tide is best explained by perceived white interests. In this economic climate, it is impossible to maintain the vast prison state without raising taxes on the (white) middle class.

Given this political reality, it is hardly a surprise to read a headline that says, "N.A.A.C.P. Joins With Gingrich in Urging Prison Reform," rather than the other way around. If there were ever an illustration of Professor Bell's theory that whites will support racial justice only to the extent that it is in their interests, this would seem to be it.

Of course, in the late 1970s, when Professor Bell, who now teaches at New York University School of Law, first advanced his theories, our prison population was much smaller. The Reagan revolution had not yet taken hold. No one knew that the war on drugs and the "get tough" movement would unleash a wave of punitiveness that would trap generations in ghettoes, and brand them criminals and felons. No one foresaw the caste-like system that would emerge, the millions who would be stripped of basic civil and human rights supposedly won in the civil rights movement—the right to vote, to serve on juries, and to be free of discrimination in employment, housing, education and public benefits.

Today, 2.3 million Americans are behind bars; the United States has the world's highest rate of incarceration. Convictions for non-violent crimes and relatively minor drug offenses—mostly possession, not sale—have accounted for the bulk of the increase in the prison population since the mid-1980s.

African-Americans are far more likely to get prison sentences for drug offenses than white offenders, even though studies have consistently shown that they are no more likely to use or sell illegal drugs than whites.

What to do now? Understandably, civil rights advocates and criminal justice reformers are celebrating this moment of what Professor Bell calls "interest convergence." They say we must catch the wave and ride it. Many have given up all hope of persuading the white electorate that they should care about the severe racial disparities in the criminal justice system or the racial politics that birthed the drug war. It's possible now, they say, to win big without talking about race or "making it an issue." Public relations consultants like the FrameWorks Institute—which dedicates itself to "changing the public conversation about social problems"—advise advocates to speak in a "practical tone" and avoid discussions of "fairness between groups and the historical legacy of racism."

Surely the Rev. Dr. Martin Luther King Jr. would have rejected that advice.

In 1963, in his "Letter From a Birmingham Jail," he chastised white ministers for their indifference to black suffering: "I have almost reached the regrettable conclusion that the Negro's great stumbling block in his stride toward freedom is not the White Citizens Counciler or the Ku Klux Klanner, but the white moderate who is more devoted to 'order' than to justice; who prefers a negative peace which is the absence of tension to a positive peace which is the presence of justice; who constantly says, 'I agree with you in the goal you seek, but I can't agree with your methods of direct action'; who paternalistically believes he can set the timetable for another man's freedom; who lives by a mythical concept of time and who constantly advises the Negro to wait for a 'more convenient season.'"

He continued: "We will have to repent in this generation not merely for the hateful words and actions of the bad people but for the appalling silence of the good people." Such language would not have tested well in a focus group. Yet it helped to change the course of history.

Those who believe that righteous indignation and protest politics were appropriate in the struggle to end Jim Crow, but that something less will do as we seek to dismantle mass incarceration, fail to appreciate the magnitude of the challenge. If our nation were to return to the rates of incarceration we had in the 1970s, we would have to release 4 out of 5 people behind bars. A million people employed by the criminal justice system could lose their jobs. Private prison companies would see their profits vanish. This system is now so deeply rooted in our social, political and economic structures that it is not going to fade away without a major shift in public consciousness.

Yes, some prison downsizing is likely to occur in the months and years to come. But we ought not fool ourselves: we will not end mass incarceration without a recommitment to the movement-building work that was begun in the 1950s and 1960s and left unfinished. A human rights nightmare is occurring on our watch. If we fail to rise to the challenge, and push past the politics of momentary interest convergence, future generations will judge us harshly.

Michelle Alexander, an associate professor of law at Ohio State University, is the author of "The New Jim Crow: Mass Incarceration in the Age of Colorblindness."

Article 20

Twenty Things You Should Know About Corporate Crime

Russell Mokhiber

Twenty years ago, *Corporate Crime Reporter*, a weekly print newsletter, was launched.

From the beginning, the most popular feature of *Corporate Crime Reporter* has been a question/answer format <u>interview</u>.

Over the years, we've interviewed hundreds of prosecutors, defense attorneys, law school professors, reporters, and activists.

Our first interview, which appeared in Volume One, Number One on April 13, 1987 was with the premier corporate crime prosecutor of his day.

That was Rudolph Giuliani, then U.S. Attorney in the Southern District of New York.

At the time, he was prosecuting the likes of Michael Milken, Ivan Boesky and Marc Rich.

President Clinton later pardoned Marc Rich.

Apparently Marc Rich's wife was dumping big cash into the Clinton library.

Rudy is now solidly in the hands of the corporate crime lobby. He prosecuted corporate crime as a way to achieve higher office. Then he learned one of the key lessons of corporate crime prosecution.

You can achieve higher office by prosecuting corporate crime. But as you move up the ladder, you have to make nice with the corporate powers that be. And so you turn your attention and rhetoric to various forms of street crime.

Now, Rudy is ready to be President.

So, corporate crime lesson number one—prosecute corporate crime to achieve higher office, then prosecute street crime to protect your political position.

Or to simplify it, corporate crime is all about power politics.

And the corporate crime game is a bi-partisan affair—it is played the same by Democrats and Republicans alike.

Eliot Spitzer, the former Attorney General of New York, prosecuted corporate crime to achieve higher office.

And now as Governor of New York, Spitzer is making nice with Wall Street.

To celebrate the 20th anniversary of *Corporate Crime Reporter*, I present to you the *Top 20 Things You Should Know About Corporate Crime.*

With a tip of the hat to David Letterman, let us proceed.

Number 20

Corporate crime inflicts far more damage on society than all street crime combined.

Whether in bodies or injuries or dollars lost, corporate crime and violence wins by a landslide.

The FBI estimates, for example, that burglary and robbery—street crimes—costs the nation $3.8 billion a year.

The losses from a handful of major corporate frauds—Tyco, Adelphia, Worldcom, Enron—swamp the losses from all street robberies and burglaries combined.

Health care fraud alone costs Americans $100 billion to $400 billion a year.

The savings and loan fraud—which former Attorney General Dick Thornburgh called "the biggest white collar swindle in history"—cost us anywhere from $300 billion to $500 billion.

And then you have your lesser frauds: auto repair fraud, $40 billion a year, securities fraud, $15 billion a year—and on down the list.

Number 19

Corporate crime is often violent crime.

Recite this list of corporate frauds and people will immediately say to you: but you can't compare street crime and corporate crime—corporate crime is not violent crime.

Not true.

Corporate crime is often violent crime.

The FBI estimates that, 16,000 Americans are murdered every year.

Compare this to the 56,000 Americans who die every year on the job or from occupational diseases such as black lung and asbestosis and the tens of thousands of other Americans who fall victim to the silent violence of pollution, contaminated foods, hazardous consumer products, and hospital malpractice.

These deaths are often the result of criminal recklessness. Yet, they are rarely prosecuted as homicides or as criminal violations of federal laws.

Number 18

Corporate criminals are the only criminal class in the United States that have the power to define the laws under which they live.

The mafia, no.

The gangstas, no.

The street thugs, no.

But the corporate criminal lobby, yes. They have marinated Washington—from the White House to the Congress to K Street—with their largesse. And out the other end come the laws they can live with. They still violate their own rules with impunity. But they make sure the laws are kept within reasonable bounds.

Exhibit A—the automobile industry.

Over the past 30 years, the industry has worked its will on Congress to block legislation that would impose criminal sanctions on knowing and willful violations of the federal auto safety laws. Today, with very narrow exceptions, if an auto company is caught violating the law, only a civil fine is imposed.

Number 17

Corporate crime is underprosecuted by a factor of say—100. And the flip side of that— corporate crime prosecutors are underfunded by a factor of say—100.

Big companies that are criminally prosecuted represent only the tip of a very large iceberg of corporate wrongdoing.

For every company convicted of health care fraud, there are hundreds of others who get away with ripping off Medicare and Medicaid, or face only mild slap-on-the-wrist fines and civil penalties when caught.

For every company convicted of polluting the nation's waterways, there are many others who are not prosecuted because their corporate defense lawyers are able to offer up a low-level employee to go to jail in exchange for a promise from prosecutors not to touch the company or high-level executives.

For every corporation convicted of bribery or of giving money directly to a public official in violation of federal law, there are thousands who give money legally through political action committees to candidates and political parties. They profit from a system that effectively has legalized bribery.

For every corporation convicted of selling illegal pesticides, there are hundreds more who are not prosecuted because their lobbyists have worked their way in Washington to ensure that dangerous pesticides remain legal.

For every corporation convicted of reckless homicide in the death of a worker, there are hundreds of others that don't even get investigated for reckless homicide when a worker is killed on the job. Only a few district attorneys across the country have historically investigated workplace deaths as homicides.

Corporate crime prosecutors are underfunded by a factor of say—100.

White collar crime defense attorneys regularly admit that if more prosecutors had more resources, the number of corporate crime prosecutions would increase dramatically. A large number of serious corporate and white collar crime cases are now left on the table for lack of resources.

Number 16

Beware of consumer groups or other public interest groups who make nice with corporations.

There are now probably more fake public interest groups than actual ones in America today. And many formerly legitimate public interest groups have been taken over or compromised by big corporations. Our favorite example is the National Consumer League. It's the oldest consumer group in the country. It was created to eradicate child labor.

But in the last ten years or so, it has been taken over by large corporations. It now gets the majority of its budget from big corporations such as Pfizer, Bank of America, Pharmacia & Upjohn, Kaiser Permanente, Wyeth-Ayerst, and Verizon.

Number 15

It used to be when a corporation committed a crime, they pled guilty to a crime.

So, for example, so many large corporations were pleading guilty to crimes in the 1990s, that in 2000, we put out a report titled <u>The Top 100 Corporate Criminals of the 1990s</u>. We went back through all of the Corporate Crime Reporters for that decade, pulled out all of the big corporations that had been convicted, ranked the corporate criminals by the amount of their criminal fines, and cut it off at 100.

So, you have your Fortune 500, your Forbes 400, and your Corporate Crime Reporter 100.

Number 14

Now, corporate criminals don't have to worry about pleading guilty to crimes.

Three new loopholes have developed over the past five years—the deferred prosecution agreement, the non prosecution agreement, and pleading guilty a closet entity or a defunct entity that has nothing to lose.

Number 13

Corporations love deferred prosecution agreements.

In the 1990s, if prosecutors had evidence of a crime, they would bring a criminal charge against the corporation and sometimes against the individual executives. And the company would end up pleading guilty.

Then, about three years ago, the Justice Department said—hey, there is this thing called a deferred prosecution agreement.

We can bring a criminal charge against the company. And we will tell the company—if you are a good company and do not violate the law for the next two years, we will drop the charges. No harm, no foul. This is called a deferred prosecution agreement.

And most major corporate crime prosecutions are brought this way now. The company pays a fine. The company is charged with a crime. But there is no conviction. And after two or three years, depending on the term of the agreement, the charges are dropped.

Number 12

Corporations love non prosecution agreements even more.

One Friday evening last July, I was sitting my office in the National Press Building. And into my e-mail box came a press release from the Justice Department.

The press release announced that Boeing will pay a $50 million criminal penalty and $615 million in civil penalties to resolve federal claims relating to the company's hiring of the former Air Force acquisitions chief Darleen A. Druyun, by its then CFO, Michael Sears—and stealing sensitive procurement information.

So, the company pays a criminal penalty. And I figure, okay if they paid a criminal penalty, they must have pled guilty.

No, they did not plead guilty.

Okay, they must have been charged with a crime and had the prosecution deferred.

No, they were not charged with a crime and did not have the prosecution deferred.

About a week later, after pounding the Justice Department for an answer as to what happened to Boeing, they sent over something called a non prosecution agreement.

That is where the Justice Department says—we're going to fine you criminally, but hey, we don't want to cost you any government business, so sign this agreement. It says we won't prosecute you if you pay the fine and change your ways.

Corporate criminals love non prosecution agreements. No criminal charge. No criminal record. No guilty plea. Just pay the fine and leave.

Number 11

In health fraud cases, find an empty closet or defunct entity to plead guilty.

The government has a mandatory exclusion rule for health care corporations that are convicted of ripping off Medicare.

Such an exclusion is the equivalent of the death penalty. If a major drug company can't do business with Medicare, it loses a big chunk of its business. There have been many criminal prosecutions of major health care corporations for ripping off Medicare. And many of these companies have pled guilty. But not one major health care company has been excluded from Medicare.

Why not?

Because when you read in the newspaper that a major health care company pled guilty, it's not the parent company that pleads guilty. The prosecutor will allow a unit of the corporation that has no assets—or even a defunct entity—to plead guilty. And therefore that unit will be excluded from Medicare—which doesn't bother the parent corporation, because the unit had no business with Medicare to begin with.

Earlier, Dr. Sidney Wolfe was here and talked about the criminal prosecution of Purdue Pharma, the Stamford, Connecticut-based maker of OxyContin.

Dr. Wolfe said that the company pled guilty to pushing OxyContin by making claims that it is less addictive and less subject to abuse than other pain medications and that it continued to do so despite warnings to the contrary from doctors, the media, and members of its own sales force.

Well, Purdue Pharma—the company that makes and markets the drug—didn't plead guilty. A different company—Purdue Frederick pled guilty. Purdue Pharma actually got a non-prosecution agreement. Purdue Frederick had nothing to lose, so it pled guilty.

Number 10

Corporate criminals don't like to be put on probation.

Very rarely, a corporation convicted of a crime will be placed on probation. Many years ago, Consolidated Edison in New York was convicted of an environmental crime. A probation official was assigned. Employees would call him with wrongdoing. He would write reports for the judge. The company changed its ways. There was actual change within the corporation.

Corporations hate this. They hate being under the supervision of some public official, like a judge.

We need more corporate probation.

Number 9

Corporate criminals don't like to be charged with homicide.

Street murders occur every day in America. And they are prosecuted every day in America. Corporate homicides occur every day in America. But they are rarely prosecuted.

The last homicide prosecution brought against a major American corporation was in 1980, when a Republican Indiana prosecutor charged Ford Motor Co. with homicide for the deaths of three teenaged girls who died when their Ford Pinto caught on fire after being rear-ended in northern Indiana.

The prosecutor alleged that Ford knew that it was marketing a defective product, with a gas tank that crushed when rear ended, spilling fuel.

In the Indiana case, the girls were incinerated to death.

But Ford brought in a hot shot criminal defense lawyer who in turn hired the best friend of the judge as local counsel, and who, as a result, secured a not guilty verdict after persuading the judge to keep key evidence out of the jury room.

It's time to crank up the corporate homicide prosecutions.

Number 8

There are very few career prosecutors of corporate crime.

Patrick Fitzgerald is one that comes to mind. He's the U.S. Attorney in Chicago. He put away Scooter Libby. And he's now prosecuting the Canadian media baron Conrad Black.

Number 7

Most corporate crime prosecutors see their jobs as a stepping stone to greater things.

Spitzer and Giuliani prosecuted corporate crime as a way to move up the political ladder. But most young prosecutors prosecute corporate crime to move into the lucrative corporate crime defense bar.

Number 6

Most corporate criminals turn themselves into the authorities.

The vast majority of corporate criminal prosecutions are now driven by the corporations themselves. If they find something wrong, they know they can trust the prosecutor to do the right thing. They will be forced to pay a fine, maybe agree to make some internal changes.

But in this day and age, in all likelihood, they will not be forced to plead guilty.

So, better to be up front with the prosecutor and put the matter behind them. To save the hide of the corporation, they will cooperate with federal prosecutors against individual executives within the company. Individuals will be charged, the corporation will not.

Number 5

The market doesn't take most modern corporate criminal prosecutions seriously.

Almost universally, when a corporate crime case is settled, the stock of the company involved goes up.

Why? Because a cloud has been cleared and there is no serious consequence to the company. No structural changes in how the company does business. No monitor. No probation. Preserving corporate reputation is the name of the game.

Number 4

The Justice Department needs to start publishing an annual Corporate Crime in the United States report.

Every year, the Justice Department puts out an annual report titled "Crime in the United States."

But by "Crime in the United States," the Justice Department means "street crime in the United States."

In the "Crime in the United States" annual report, you can read about burglary, robbery and theft.

There is little or nothing about price-fixing, corporate fraud, pollution, or public corruption.

A yearly Justice Department report on Corporate Crime in the United States is long overdue.

Number 3

We must start asking—which side are you on—with the corporate criminals or against?

Most professionals in Washington work for, are paid by, or are under the control of the corporate crime lobby. Young lawyers come to town, fresh out of law school, 25 years old, and their starting salary is $160,000 a year. And they're working for the corporate criminals.

Young lawyers graduating from the top law schools have all kinds of excuses for working for the corporate criminals—huge debt, just going to stay a couple of years for the experience.

But the reality is, they are working for the corporate criminals.

What kind of respect should we give them? Especially since they have many options other than working for the corporate criminals.

Time to dust off that age-old question—which side are you on? (For young lawyers out there considering other options, check out Alan Morrison's new book—Beyond the Big Firm: Profiles of Lawyers Who Want Something More.)

Number 2

We need a 911 number for the American people to dial to report corporate crime and violence.

If you want to report street crime and violence, call 911.

But what number do you call if you want to report corporate crime and violence?

We propose 611.

Call 611 to report corporate crime and violence.

We need a national number where people can pick up the phone and report the corporate criminals in our midst.

What triggered this thought?

We attended the press conference at the Justice Department the other day announcing the indictment of Congressman William Jefferson (D-Louisiana).

Jefferson was the first U.S. official charged with violating the Foreign Corrupt Practices Act.

Federal officials alleged that Jefferson was both on the giving and receiving ends of bribe payments.

On the receiving end, he took $100,000 in cash—$90,000 of it was stuffed into his freezer in Washington, D.C.

The $90,000 was separated in $10,000 increments, wrapped in aluminum foil, and concealed inside various frozen food containers.

At the press conference announcing the indictment, after various federal officials made their case before the cameras, up to the mike came Joe Persichini, assistant director of the Washington field office of the FBI.

"To the American people, I ask you, take time," Persichini said. "Read this charging document line by line, scheme by scheme, count by count. This case is about greed, power and arrogance."

"Everyone is entitled to honest and ethical public service," Persichini continued. "We as leaders standing here today cannot do it alone. We need the public's help. The amount of corruption is dependent on what the public with allow.

Again, the amount of corruption is dependent on what the public will allow."

"If you have knowledge of, if you've been confronted with or you are participating, I ask that you contact your local FBI office or you call the Washington Field Office of the FBI at 202.278.2000. Thank you very much."

Shorten the number—make it 611.

Number 1

And the number one thing you should know about corporate crime?

Everyone is deserving of justice. So, question, debate, strategize, yes.

But if God-forbid you too are victimized by a corporate criminal, you too will demand justice.

We need a more beefed up, more effective justice system to deal with the corporate criminals in our midst.

Thank you.

(This is the text of a speech delivered by Russell Mokhiber, editor of Corporate Crime Reporter to the Taming the Giant Corporation <u>conference</u> in Washington, D.C., June 9, 2007.)

Part 6

Politics

Article 21

Fewer Are Angry at Government, But Discontent Remains High

Republicans, Tea Party Supporters More Mellow

The Pew Research Center

Overview

The public remains deeply frustrated with the federal government, but fewer Americans say they are angry at government than did so last fall. Overall, the percentage saying they are angry with the federal government has fallen from 23% last September to 14% today, with much of the decline coming among Republicans and Tea Party supporters.

While anger at government has subsided, the public expresses no greater taste for political compromise today than it did last fall. As political leaders head into a tough political debate over the budget, 54% say they like elected officials who stick to their positions, while 40% prefer officials who make compromises with people they disagree with. This is virtually identical to the balance of opinion among registered voters last September.

By roughly two-to-one (63% vs. 32%), more Republicans say they like elected officials who stick to their positions rather than those who make compromises. About half of independents (53%) prefer politicians who stick to their positions compared with 41% who like elected officials who make compromises with people they disagree with. Democrats are evenly divided—48% like elected officials who stick to their positions, 46% like those who compromise.

The latest national survey by the Pew Research Center for the People & the Press, conducted Feb. 22-Mar. 1 among 1,504 adults, finds a modest recovery in public trust in government from historic lows last year. Yet even with this uptick, the general mood remains overwhelmingly negative.

Just 29% say they can trust the government in Washington to do what is right just about always or most of the time, up from 22% last March. About seven-in-ten (69%) say they trust the government only some of the time or never, compared with 76% a year ago.

"Fewer Are Angry at Government, But Discontent Remains High: Republicans, Tea Party Supporters More Mellow", by the Pew Research Center, For the People and the Press, a project of the Pew Researh Center. Reprinted by permission.

The proportion of Republicans saying they can trust the government always or most of the time has increased from 13% to 24% over the past year; opinions among Democrats are unchanged over this period, at 34%.

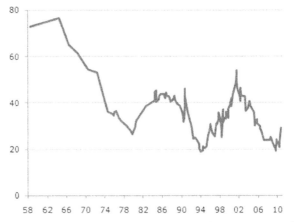

Public Trust in Government, 1958-2011

Trust the government in Washington to do what is right "just about always" or "most of the time"

PEW RESEARCH CENTER Feb. 22-Mar. 1, 2011. QA25. Trend sources: Pew Research Center. National Election Studies, Gallup, ABC/Washington Post, CBS/New York Times, and CNN Polls. From 1976-2010 the trend line represents a three-survey moving average.

The public continues to express negative views of Congress, as well as Republican and Democratic congressional leaders. Just 34% say they have a favorable opinion of Congress, up slightly from 26% a year ago; a majority (57%) has an unfavorable view. Comparable percentages say they approve of the job performance of Republican (36%) and Democratic (33%) congressional leaders.

By contrast, Barack Obama's job ratings remain positive. Currently, 51% approve of Barack Obama's job performance while 39% disapprove. That is little changed from early February, but Obama's ratings have shown significant improvement since last fall, when about as many approved as disapproved.

The survey finds a continuing rise in support for same-sex marriage since 2009. Currently, 45% say they favor allowing gays and lesbians to marry legally while 46% are opposed. In Pew Research surveys conducted in 2010, 42% favored and 48% opposed gay marriage and in 2009, just 37% backed same-sex marriage while 54% were opposed.

Over the same period, there has been movement toward a liberal position on abortion. In 2009, for the first time in many years, the public was evenly divided over whether abortion should be legal or illegal in all or most cases. But support for legal abortion has recovered and now stands at about the same level as in 2008 (55% then, 54% today).

Independents have become more supportive of both gay marriage and legal abortion since 2009. Roughly half of independents (51%) now favor same-sex marriage, up from 37% in 2009. And 58% of independents say that abortion should be legal in all or most cases, compared with 47% in Pew Research Center surveys two years ago.

Liberal Movement on Gay Marriage, Abortion

Allow gays and lesbians to marry legally...	2008	2009	2010	2011	09-11 change
	%	%	%	%	
Favor	39	37	42	45	+8
Oppose	51	54	48	46	-8
Don't know	<u>10</u>	<u>9</u>	<u>10</u>	<u>9</u>	
	100	100	100	100	
Abortion should be...					
Legal in all/most cases	55	47	50	54	+7
Illegal in all/most cases	39	44	44	42	-2
Don't know	<u>6</u>	<u>9</u>	<u>7</u>	<u>4</u>	
	100	100	100	100	

PEW RESEARCH CENTER Feb. 22-Mar. 1, 2011. Q461, A62. Figures may not add to 100% because of rounding. Gay marriage opinions based on yearly averages for 2008-2010; abortion opinions based on yearly averages for 2008-2009.

Labor Union Favorability Holds Steady through Wisconsin Dispute

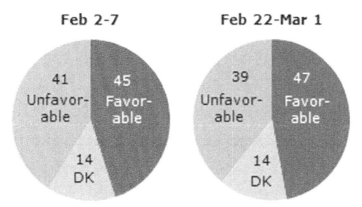

PEW RESEARCH CENTER Feb. 21-Mar. 1, 2011. QA4e.

The public's overall views of labor unions have changed little through the lengthy stalemate between Wisconsin's governor and the state's public employee unions over collective bargaining rights. About half (47%) say they have a favorable opinion of labor unions compared with 39% who have an unfavorable opinion. In early February, 45% expressed a favorable opinion of unions and 41% said they had an unfavorable view. However, liberal Democrats and people in union households are more likely to say they have a *very* favorable opinion of labor unions than they were just weeks ago.

Article 22

Six Things Everybody Knows About Deficits ... That Are Completely Untrue

Richard (RJ) Eskow

Thanks to the generous support of billionaires and self-interested corporations, think tanks have seeded our political discourse with a lot of mistaken ideas about government spending and deficits. For too many journalists, consultants, and policy makers, these ideas are "givens," things that everybody *knows* ... which also happen to be totally wrong.

Here are a few of them.

1. Deficits are caused by government spending.

That's like saying empty gas tanks are caused by driving. They're actually caused by *driving and not filling up the gas tank*. Sure, one way to prevent empty gas tanks is to just stop driving. But if you need to get somewhere—as either a person driving a car or a nation rebuilding its economy—you can also *stop at a gas station*. A rational person would drive when it's necessary, drive less when they can, and fill 'er up when the tank's running low.

The primary drivers of our current budget deficit are:
- **a)** The wars in Iraq and Afghanistan.
- **b)** Wall Street greed and corruption, and the resulting economic collapse.
- **c)** The Bush tax cuts.

So in a year when the president and the Republicans are trying to one-up each other on who can cut deficits the fastest, which three topics are almost never addressed as budget-busters in the media?
- **a)** The wars in Iraq and Afghanistan.
- **b)** Wall Street greed and corruption, and the resulting economic collapse.
- **c)** The Bush tax cuts.

"Six Things Everybody Knows About Deficits...That Are Completely Untrue" by Richard (RJ) Eskow, February 15, 2011 as appeared in *Huffington Post*. Reprinted by permission of the author.

169

Deficits aren't caused by spending. They're caused by *spending more than you collect*. Yet in a year when the mediasphere is breathlessly sounding the alarm over "entitlement" programs like Medicare and Medicaid, which will cost around $800 billion this year, it remains rather silent about ten years' worth of tax "entitlements"—sorry, tax "breaks"—to the wealthiest 2% of Americans, which cost more than $1 trillion.

Despite what you've heard, "deficit reduction" and "spending cuts" aren't synonyms.

To his credit, the president is proposing to raise taxes on the wealthiest 2% or Americans—or rather, not to renew the extension of these cuts agreed upon in last December's deal. But he's focused his rhetorical firepower on spending cuts, not raising revenue. And spending cuts account for two-thirds of his deficit reduction plan, while increased revenue only accounts for only one-third. (And that's before the backroom negotiations even begin.)

Maybe it's us, but so far the president's defense of his revenue-raising proposals seems … well, unenthusiastic. We'll find out soon whether he's proposing them in a got-to-have-them-or-there's-no-deal way, or whether he's proposing them in a I'm-planning-to-trade-them-away-like-I-did-the-public-option-and-the-same-tax-increase-last-year way. Either way, it's come to this: The president's proposed revenue hikes are modest, but our conservative-think-tank-generated, media-fueled reality distortion field is so pervasive that he must make needless, symbolic cuts to programs for the poor (including fuel oil to help them make it through the winter) in order to earn credibility on the topic of deficits.

In this reality warp, credibility can never be earned by tamping down the accumulation of wealth for top earners with a modest tax hike—one that comes after a forty-year period during which their taxes were cut by more than half. And it can only be earned with spending cuts for "programs the president cares about," not "programs Republicans care about."

2. Neither the Republican budget nor the president's budget propose cuts to Social Security benefits.

I've heard this one several times in the past few days, and it's wrong. The president's budget doesn't cut Social Security—at least not so far—but Rep. Eric Cantor says that the Republicans will propose cuts to both Social Security and Medicare. And while the Republican Continuing Resolution for Fiscal Year 2011 doesn't explicitly cut Social Security *benefits*, it provides $625 million less to *administer* those benefits than was provided last year—and nearly a billion dollars less than was originally budgeted.

That means that people will receive less in benefits, whether they're officially "cut" or not. There are already agonizing delays in the appeals process for people who have been denied disability benefits. Further cuts will deny even more people of benefits that in many cases they've paid for and deserve—and could lead to many more problems for people receiving retirement benefits, too.

The president deserves credit for trying to increase the administrative budget by a modest amount. But the Republicans, while claiming not to "cut" benefits, are cutting a tiny percentage from the overall budget when they propose to cut funding for the Social Security Administration. That won't make a dent in the deficit. They're doing that so that fewer people will collect the benefits that still exist—but which for them will only exist on paper.

3. "We have to live within our means so we can invest in the future."

This trope comes from Jacob Lew, Director of the White House Office of Management and the Budget, in a blog post defending some of the Draconian reductions in the White House's new budget. It encapsulates the "cut for growth" argument in a nutshell.

But in decades of private-sector work, I never heard an executive say that a company can or should "invest" and "cut" at the same time. If a corporation did something like that, chances are it would be sacrificing its core business while at the same time moving into uncharted waters.

What do businesses usually do when they want to invest? They *borrow*. They're especially happy to borrow at times like these, when money is so cheap. Economically and managerially, the "cut-to-invest" concept is financial mumbo-jumbo. Sure, sometimes you need to cut. And sometimes you need to invest. But they're separate issues and separate decisions, each of which requires its own justifications.

This is a perfect time for government to engage in short-term stimulus spending to get the economy moving, and to create jobs for people who will then start paying taxes ... which reduces the deficits. In other words, the next two years or so should be a time for any government with a smart, private-sector management mindset to invest in both its core "businesses" *and* in R&D for the future.

4. More concessions to Corporate America will lead to more jobs.

The logic goes like this: If we give more tax breaks to corporations they'll have more money, and they'll use it to hire people.

Wrong. Corporate America may not have as much cash on hand as the two trillion dollars you've read in the papers or heard the president say, but it has a lot. And the mega-corporations that dominate the economy also have access to very cheap credit.

What does that tell us? That the problem isn't cash. It's *demand*. They're holding on to the money because people aren't buying their products. Demand has picked up a little, but not nearly enough. That means the answer isn't to give corporations more cash, it's to give *consumers* more cash. Then they'll buy products, which will give businesses a reason to start hiring and investing again.

Corporations aren't sitting on that cash because they like to see big numbers in their bank account. If a CEO had willing customers lined up but wouldn't spend money to meet their demand profitably, she or he would be fired. Tomorrow. How do you create more demand? By creating more jobs, and by putting more money in the pockets of people who'll spend it rather than save it. That means stimulus spending for jobs and growth. And when it comes to Social Security, it would make more sense to *increase* benefits than it would to cut them. Most of that increase would be spent for goods and services—in other words, more demand.

Remember, we want to get businesses to spend their cash. Maybe they don't have two trillion on hand. But if we could get them to spend, say, $1.5 trillion, financed by a combination of cash and borrowing, it would be **more than our entire projected deficit for the year.** So why not put our money where it will more than pay for itself by stimulating private investment— and help people who are hurting? The alternative, after all, is years of ongoing joblessness—a plight that not only causes untold suffering, but also robs the government of tax revenue.

Targeted government spending can trigger more private-sector investment, leading to a cycle of growth and job creation. That way leaders in government and business can be both good managers and good people. It doesn't always work out that way, so when an opportunity like that comes along, why not grab it?

5. Government debt soared because of the last financial crisis … but we can fix the debt problem without ending the Wall Street behavior that will cause the *next* crisis.

The 2008 financial crisis caused the national debt to soar, both because of the increased expenditures that were needed and because the government lost revenue from millions of workers who lost their jobs and stopped paying taxes. Then there were the fiscal crises triggered in state and local governments, which caused even more damage.

"Deficit reduction" programs that don't rein in Wall Street's gambling and fraud are like bailing out a boat that's still got a hole in the bottom.

Could the financial crisis happen again? JPMorgan Chase CEO Jamie Dimon says it *will* happen again—every five to seven years. He should know: He's a fierce defender of "too big to fail" banks and a deregulated financial sector, two major causes of the last crisis. Dimon is now fretting that the deficit is a major threat, and saying that "governments have to show the will" to get them "under control."

But you can't get deficits under control when the Wall Street casino is designed to collapse every five to seven years, and when it will cause massive increases in debt every time it does.

6. Medicare, Medicaid, and Social Security are a huge deficit problem.

Jackie Calmes of the New York *Times* does some excellent work. But her coverage of the budget debate today is not one of her better moments. She writes that "… the most pressing long-term budget problem (is) the huge costs in the Medicare, Medicaid and Social Security programs as the population ages and medical costs rise." In fact, this statement—issued in the "paper of record" as undisputable fact—is objectively, factually incorrect.

The truth: Social Security "spending" for 2011 is projected to be $695 billion this year.

How much does that add to the Federal deficit or the overall budget and its deficits? Social Security is separately funded by a dedicated tax, not general revenues, and this year's projected shortfall between revenues from that tax and Social Security expenses $41 billion, not $695 billion. $41 billion is less than the cost of extending the estate tax break for one year—a $68 billion break (shouldn't that be "entitlement"?) that will benefit Paris Hilton or other rich heirs and heiresses.

So does that mean that Social Security is only adding $41 billion to the deficit this year, instead of the $695 billion I saw in the papers? No. It's adding *zero* to the deficit. This self-funded program is forbidden by law from *ever* adding to the deficit. It has a $2.6 trillion (that's "trillion" with a "t") surplus and will return to profitability in a couple of years, before finally using up its surplus so that it can pay "only" 75% of benefits—nearly three decades from now. There are easy fixes for that, especially lifting the cap on the payroll tax. But apparently anything that discommodes the glitterati doesn't fit the prevailing narrative. Whatever the reason, everybody's pretending that option doesn't exist.

I guess you could say that these "entitlement programs"—connected only in this case by the inflammatory-sounding word "entitlement" (as in "he acts, you know, *entitled*")—represent around 21% of the budget, since that's roughly what Medicare and Medicaid cost. But you might as well say that "Medicare, Medicaid, and Justin Bieber's haircuts contribute 21% to the Federal budget," or "Medicare, Medicaid, and those Egg McMuffins you keep ordering for breakfast are the most pressing budget problem the Federal government faces." It's nonsensical. When journalists who are supposed to be objective write in straight news pieces that the costs of "entitlements"—Medicare, Medicaid, *and Social Security*—"could overwhelm the government and crimp the economy if not addressed," as Calmes did, that's demonstrably untrue and calls for a formal correction.

Why don't reporters just say that "Medicare and Medicaid are the main cause of future deficits and must be addressed"? We don't know. We do know that a lot of funding has gone into promoting the "entitlements" slant to the story, rather than the more accurate "runaway health care costs" angle. And we know that our runaway health care costs raise some topics that are considered off-limits these days: The fact that countries with publicly-provided health care pay much less than we do. The role of for-profit insurers and hospitals in driving up costs. Income levels for some specialist physicians that are much higher than they are anywhere else in the world. Poorly designed incentives for doctors, hospitals, and other medical facilities.

Besides, they've wanted to dismantle the New Deal for 75 years, and Social Security's the heart of the New Deal. Like the man said: Never let a crisis go to waste.

Article 23

The Hollow Cry of 'Broke'

The New York Times, et al.

We're broke! We're broke! Speaker John Boehner said on Sunday. "We're broke in this state," Gov. Scott Walker of Wisconsin said a few days ago. "New Jersey's broke," Gov. Chris Christie has said repeatedly. The United States faces a "looming bankruptcy," Charles Koch, the billionaire industrialist, wrote in The Wall Street Journal on Tuesday.

It's all obfuscating nonsense, of course, a scare tactic employed for political ends. A country with a deficit is not necessarily any more "broke" than a family with a mortgage or a college loan. And states have to balance their budgets. Though it may disappoint many conservatives, there will be no federal or state bankruptcies.

The federal deficit is too large for comfort, and most states are struggling to balance their books. Some of that is because of excessive spending, and much is because the recession has driven down tax revenues. But a substantial part was caused by deliberate decisions by state and federal lawmakers to drain government of resources by handing out huge tax cuts, mostly to the rich. As governments begin to stagger from the self-induced hemorrhaging, Republican politicians like Mr. Boehner and Mr. Walker cry poverty and use it as an excuse to break unions and kill programs they never liked in flush years.

On Wednesday, to cite just the latest example, House Republicans successfully pressured the Senate to approve a bill cutting $4 billion in spending just to keep the federal government from shutting down for the next two weeks. In a matter of days, the Senate will be forced to take up the House bill to make more than $61 billion in ruinous cuts over the next seven months, all under the pretext of "fiscal responsibility." (At least the White House says it will be involved in the next round.) Many Republican governors are employing the same tactic.

But now voters are starting to notice the effects of these cuts and to get angry at the ideological overreach. A New York Times/CBS News poll published on Tuesday showed that Americans oppose ending bargaining rights for public unions by a majority of nearly two to one. And the poll sharply refutes the post-Reagan Republican mantra that the public invariably abhors all tax increases. Nearly twice as many people said they would prefer a tax increase to cutting benefits of public employees or to cutting spending on roads.

A Gallup poll last week showed that 61 percent of respondents nationwide reject Mr. Walker's attempt to revoke collective-bargaining rights for public unions, including 41 percent of the Republicans polled. Like the Times/CBS poll, Gallup found a mixed result about the overall popularity of unions, suggesting that labor is on firm ground in defending its basic rights but still needs to negotiate with the public good in mind.

Before the union uprising, Wisconsin voters might not have noticed when Mr. Walker approved business tax cuts earlier this year that made his budget gap worse. But now, with his cries of being "broke," they should listen more closely. On Tuesday, he unveiled a budget that would cut aid to school districts and local governments by nearly $1 billion over two years, while preventing those jurisdictions from raising property taxes at all to make up for the loss.

Perhaps because of the economic downturn, voting among union households was sharply down last November, which may help explain some of the Republican gains. Mr. Walker and his fellow Republicans, may wind up turning that around next year.

Article 24

The Shameful Attack on Public Employees

Robert Reich

In 1968, 1,300 sanitation workers in Memphis went on strike. The Rev. Martin Luther King, Jr. came to support them. That was where he lost his life. Eventually Memphis heard the grievances of its sanitation workers. And in subsequent years millions of public employees across the nation have benefited from the job protections they've earned.

But now the right is going after public employees.

Public servants are convenient scapegoats. Republicans would rather deflect attention from corporate executive pay that continues to rise as corporate profits soar, even as corporations refuse to hire more workers. They don't want stories about Wall Street bonuses, now higher than before taxpayers bailed out the Street. And they'd like to avoid a spotlight on the billions raked in by hedge-fund and private-equity managers whose income is treated as capital gains and subject to only a 15 percent tax, due to a loophole in the tax laws designed specifically for them.

It's far more convenient to go after people who are doing the public's work—sanitation workers, police officers, fire fighters, teachers, social workers, federal employees—to call them "faceless bureaucrats" and portray them as hooligans who are making off with your money and crippling federal and state budgets. The story fits better with the Republican's Big Lie that our problems are due to a government that's too big.

Above all, Republicans don't want to have to justify continued tax cuts for the rich. As quietly as possible, they want to make them permanent.

But the right's argument is shot-through with bad data, twisted evidence, and unsupported assertions.

They say public employees earn far more than private-sector workers. That's untrue when you take account of level of education. Matched by education, public sector workers actually earn less than their private-sector counterparts.

The Republican trick is to compare apples with oranges—the average wage of public employees with the average wage of all private-sector employees. But only 23 percent of private-sector employees have college degrees; 48 percent of government workers do. Teachers, social workers, public lawyers who bring companies to justice, government accountants who try to make sure money is spent as it should be—all need at least four years of college.

Compare apples to apples and and you'd see that over the last fifteen years the pay of public sector workers has dropped relative to private-sector employees with the same level of education. Public sector workers now earn 11 percent less than comparable workers in the private sector, and local workers 12 percent less. (Even if you include health and retirement benefits, government employees still earn less than their private-sector counterparts with similar educations.)

Here's another whopper. Republicans say public-sector pensions are crippling the nation. They say politicians have given in to the demands of public unions who want only to fatten their members' retirement benefits without the public noticing. They charge that public-employee pensions obligations are out of control.

Some reforms do need to be made. Loopholes that allow public sector workers to "spike" their final salaries in order to get higher annuities must be closed. And no retired public employee should be allowed to "double dip," collecting more than one public pension.

But these are the exceptions. Most public employees don't have generous pensions. After a career with annual pay averaging less than $45,000, the typical newly-retired public employee receives a pension of $19,000 a year. Few would call that overly generous.

And most of that $19,000 isn't even on taxpayers' shoulders. While they're working, most public employees contribute a portion of their salaries into their pension plans. Taxpayers are directly responsible for only about 14 percent of public retirement benefits. Remember also that many public workers aren't covered by Social Security, so the government isn't contributing 6.25 of their pay into the Social Security fund as private employers would.

Yes, there's cause for concern about unfunded pension liabilities in future years. They're way too big. But it's much the same in the private sector. The main reason for underfunded pensions in both public and private sectors is investment losses that occurred during the Great Recession. Before then, public pension funds had an average of 86 percent of all the assets they needed to pay future benefits—better than many private pension plans.

The solution is no less to slash public pensions than it is to slash private ones. It's for all employers to fully fund their pension plans.

The final Republican canard is that bargaining rights for public employees have caused state deficits to explode. In fact there's no relationship between states whose employees have bargaining rights and states with big deficits. Some states that deny their employees bargaining rights—Nevada, North Carolina, and Arizona, for example, are running giant deficits of over 30 percent of spending. Many that give employees bargaining rights—Massachusetts, New Mexico, and Montana—have small deficits of less than 10 percent.

Public employees should have the right to bargain for better wages and working conditions, just like all employees do. They shouldn't have the right to strike if striking would imperil the public, but they should at least have a voice. They often know more about whether public programs are working, or how to make them work better, than political appointees who hold their offices for only a few years.

Don't get me wrong. When times are tough, public employees should have to make the same sacrifices as everyone else. And they are right now. Pay has been frozen for federal workers, and for many state workers across the country as well.

But isn't it curious that when it comes to sacrifice, Republicans don't include the richest people in America? To the contrary, they insist the rich should sacrifice even less, enjoying even larger tax cuts that expand public-sector deficits. That means fewer public services, and even more pressure on the wages and benefits of public employees.

It's only average workers – both in the public and the private sectors—who are being called upon to sacrifice.

This is what the current Republican attack on public-sector workers is really all about. Their version of class warfare is to pit private-sector workers against public servants. They'd rather set average working people against one another—comparing one group's modest incomes and benefits with another group's modest incomes and benefits—than have Americans see that the top 1 percent is now raking in a bigger share of national income than at any time since 1928, and paying at a lower tax rate. And Republicans would rather you didn't know they want to cut taxes on the rich even more.

Part 7

Race

Article 25

American Apartheid

Douglas S. Massey and Nancy A. Denton

> *It is quite simple. As soon as there is a group area then all your uncertainties are removed and that is, after all, the primary purpose of this Bill [requiring racial segregation in housing].*
>
> Minister of the Interior,
> Union of South Africa legislative debate on the Group Areas
> Act of 1950

During the 1970s and 1980s a word disappeared from the American vocabulary. It was not in the speeches of politicians decrying the multiple ills besetting American cities. It was not spoken by government officials responsible for administering the nation's social programs. It was not mentioned by journalists reporting on the rising tide of homelessness, drugs, and violence in urban America. It was not discussed by foundation executives and think-tank experts proposing new programs for unemployed parents and unwed mothers. It was not articulated by civil rights leaders speaking out against the persistence of racial inequality; and it was nowhere to be found in the thousands of pages written by social scientists on the urban underclass. The word was segregation.

Most Americans vaguely realize that urban America is still a residentially segregated society, but few appreciate the depth of black segregation or the degree to which it is maintained by ongoing institutional arrangements and contemporary individual actions. They view segregation as an unfortunate holdover from a racist past, one that is fading progressively over time. If racial residential segregation persists, they reason, it is only because civil rights laws passed during the 1960s have not had enough time to work or because many blacks still prefer to live in black neighborhoods. The residential segregation of blacks is viewed charitably as a "natural" outcome of impersonal social and economic forces, the same forces that produced Italian and Polish neighborhoods in the past and that yield Mexican and Korean areas today.

But black segregation is not comparable to the limited and transient segregation experienced by other racial and ethnic groups, now or in the past. No group in the history of the United States has ever experienced the sustained high level of residential segregation that has been imposed on blacks in large American cities for the past fifty years. This extreme racial isolation did not just happen; it was manufactured by whites through a series of self-conscious actions and purposeful institutional arrangements that continue today. Not only is the depth of black segregation unprecedented and utterly unique compared with that of other groups, but it shows little sign of change with the passage of time or improvements in socioeconomic status.

If policymakers, scholars, and the public have been reluctant to acknowledge segregation's persistence, they have likewise been blind to its consequences for American blacks. Residential segregation is not a neutral fact; it systematically undermines the social and economic well-being of blacks in the United States. Because of racial segregation, a significant share of black America is condemned to experience a social environment where poverty and joblessness are the norm, where a majority of children are born out of wedlock, where most families are on welfare, where educational failure prevails, and where social and physical deterioration abound. Through prolonged exposure to such an environment, black chances for social and economic success are drastically reduced.

Deleterious neighborhood conditions are built into the structure of the black community. They occur because segregation concentrates poverty to build a set of mutually reinforcing and self-feeding spirals of decline into black neighborhoods. When economic dislocations deprive a segregated group of employment and increase its rate of poverty, socioeconomic deprivation inevitably becomes more concentrated in neighborhoods where that group lives. The damaging social consequences that follow from increased poverty are spatially concentrated as well, creating uniquely disadvantaged environments that become progressively isolated—geographically, socially, and economically—from the rest of society.

The effect of segregation on black well-being is structural, not individual. Residential segregation lies beyond the ability of any individual to change; it constrains black life chances irrespective of personal traits, individual motivations, or private achievements. For the past twenty years this fundamental fact has been swept under the rug by policymakers, scholars, and theorists of the urban underclass. Segregation is the missing link in prior attempts to understand the plight of the urban poor. As long as blacks continue to be segregated in American cities, the United States cannot be called a race-blind society.

The Forgotten Factor

The present myopia regarding segregation is all the more startling because it once figured prominently in theories of racial inequality. Indeed, the ghetto was once seen as central to black subjugation in the United States. In 1944 Gunnar Myrdal wrote in *An American*

Dilemma that residential segregation "is basic in a mechanical sense. It exerts its influence in an indirect and impersonal way: because Negro people do not live near white people, they cannot ... associate with each other in the many activities founded on common neighborhood. Residential segregation ... becomes reflected in uni-racial schools, hospitals, and other institutions" and creates "an artificial city ... that permits any prejudice on the part of public officials to be freely vented on Negroes without hurting whites."

Kenneth B. Clark, who worked with Gunnar Myrdal as a student and later applied his research skills in the landmark *Brown v. Topeka* school integration case, placed residential segregation at the heart of the U.S. system of racial oppression. In *Dark Ghetto*, written in 1965, he argued that "the dark ghetto's invisible walls have been erected by the white society, by those who have power, both to confine those who have no power and to perpetuate their powerlessness. The dark ghettos are social, political, educational, and—above all—economic colonies. Their inhabitants are subject peoples, victims of the greed, cruelty, insensitivity, guilt, and fear of their masters."

Public recognition of segregation's role in perpetuating racial inequality was galvanized in the late 1960s by the riots that erupted in the nation's ghettos. In their aftermath, President Lyndon B. Johnson appointed a commission chaired by Governor Otto Kerner of Illinois to identify the causes of the violence and to propose policies to prevent its recurrence. The Kerner Commission released its report in March 1968 with the shocking admonition that the United States was "moving toward two societies, one black, one white—separate and unequal." Prominent among the causes that the commission identified for this growing racial inequality was residential segregation.

In stark, blunt language, the Kerner Commission informed white Americans that "discrimination and segregation have long permeated much of American life; they now threaten the future of every American." "Segregation and poverty have created in the racial ghetto a destructive environment totally unknown to most white Americans. What white Americans have never fully understood—but what the Negro can never forget—is that white society is deeply implicated in the ghetto. White institutions created it, white institutions maintain it, and white society condones it."

The report argued that to continue present policies was "to make permanent the division of our country into two societies; one, largely Negro and poor, located in the central cities; the other, predominantly white and affluent, located in the suburbs." Commission members rejected a strategy of ghetto enrichment coupled with abandonment of efforts to integrate, an approach they saw "as another way of choosing a permanently divided country." Rather, they insisted that the only reasonable choice for America was "a policy which combines ghetto enrichment with programs designed to encourage integration of substantial numbers of Negroes into the society outside the ghetto."

America chose differently. Following the passage of the Fair Housing Act in 1968, the problem of housing discrimination was declared solved, and residential segregation dropped off the national agenda. Civil rights leaders stopped pressing for the enforcement of open housing, political leaders increasingly debated employment and educational policies rather than housing integration, and academicians focused their theoretical scrutiny on everything from culture to family structure, to institutional racism, to federal welfare systems. Few people spoke of racial segregation as a problem or acknowledged its persisting consequences. By the end of the 1970s residential segregation became the forgotten factor in American race relations.

While public discourse on race and poverty became more acrimonious and more focused on divisive issues such as school busing, racial quotas, welfare, and affirmative action, conditions in the nation's ghettos steadily deteriorated. By the end of the 1970s, the image of poor minority families mired in an endless cycle of unemployment, unwed child-bearing, illiteracy, and dependency had coalesced into a compelling and powerful concept: the urban underclass. In the view of many middle-class whites, inner cities had come to house a large population of poorly educated single mothers and jobless men—mostly black and Puerto Rican—who were unlikely to exit poverty and become self-sufficient. In the ensuing national debate on the causes for this persistent poverty, four theoretical explanations gradually emerged: culture, racism, economics, and welfare.

Cultural explanations for the underclass can be traced to the work of Oscar Lewis, who identified a "culture of poverty" that he felt promoted patterns of behavior inconsistent with socioeconomic advancement. According to Lewis, this culture originated in endemic unemployment and chronic social immobility, and provided an ideology that allowed poor people to cope with feelings of hopelessness and despair that arose because their chances for socioeconomic success were remote. In individuals, this culture was typified by a lack of impulse control, a strong present-time orientation, and little ability to defer gratification. Among families, it yielded an absence of childhood, an early initiation into sex, a prevalence of free marital unions, and a high incidence of abandonment of mothers and children.

Although Lewis explicitly connected the emergence of these cultural patterns to structural conditions in society, he argued that once the culture of poverty was established, it became an independent cause of persistent poverty. This idea was further elaborated in 1965 by the Harvard sociologist and then Assistant Secretary of Labor Daniel Patrick Moynihan, who in a confidential report to the President focused on the relationship between male unemployment, family instability, and the inter-generational transmission of poverty, a process he labeled a "tangle of pathology." He warned that because of the structural absence of employment in the ghetto, the black family was disintegrating in a way that threatened the fabric of community life.

When these ideas were transmitted through the press, both popular and scholarly, the connection between culture and economic structure was somehow lost, and the argument was popularly perceived to be that "people were poor because they had a defective culture." This position was later explicitly adopted by the conservative theorist Edward Banfield, who argued that lower-class culture—with its limited time horizon, impulsive need for gratification, and psychological self-doubt—was primarily responsible for persistent urban poverty. He believed that these cultural traits were largely imported, arising primarily because cities attracted lower-class migrants.

The culture-of-poverty argument was strongly criticized by liberal theorists as a self-serving ideology that "blamed the victim." In the ensuing wave of reaction, black families were viewed not as weak but, on the contrary, as resilient and well adapted survivors in an oppressive and racially prejudiced society. Black disadvantages were attributed not to a defective culture but to the persistence of institutional racism in the United States. According to theorists of the underclass such as Douglas Glasgow and Alphonso Pinkney, the black urban underclass came about because deeply imbedded racist practices within American institutions—particularly schools and the economy—effectively kept blacks poor and dependent.

As the debate on culture versus racism ground to a halt during the late 1970s, conservative theorists increasingly captured public attention by focusing on a third possible cause of poverty: government welfare policy. According to Charles Murray, the creation of the underclass was rooted in the liberal welfare state. Federal antipoverty programs altered the incentives governing the behavior of poor men and women, reducing the desirability of marriage, increasing the benefits of unwed childbearing, lowering the attractiveness of menial labor, and ultimately resulting in greater poverty.

A slightly different attack on the welfare state was launched by Lawrence Mead, who argued that it was not the generosity but the permissiveness of the U.S. welfare system that was at fault. Jobless men and unwed mothers should be required to display "good citizenship" before being supported by the state. By not requiring anything of the poor, Mead argued, the welfare state undermined their independence and competence, thereby perpetuating their poverty.

This conservative reasoning was subsequently attacked by liberal social scientists, led principally by the sociologist William Julius Wilson, who had long been arguing for the increasing importance of class over race in understanding the social and economic problems facing blacks. In his 1987 book *The Truly Disadvantaged*, Wilson argued that persistent urban poverty stemmed primarily from the structural transformation of the inner-city economy. The decline of manufacturing, the suburbanization of employment, and the rise of a low-wage service sector dramatically reduced the number of city jobs that paid wages sufficient to support a family, which led to high rates of joblessness among minorities and a shrinking pool of "marriageable" men (those financially able to support a family). Marriage thus became less attractive to poor women, unwed childbearing increased, and female-headed families proliferated. Blacks suffered disproportionately from these trends because, owing to past discrimination, they were concentrated in location and occupations particularly affected by economic restructuring.

Wilson argued that these economic changes were accompanied by an increase in the spatial concentration of poverty within black neighborhoods. This new of poverty, he felt, was enabled by the civil rights revolution of the 1960s, which provided middle-class blacks with new opportunities outside the ghetto. The out-migration of middle-class families from ghetto areas left behind a destitute community lacking the institutions, resources, and values necessary for success in postindustrial society. The urban underclass thus arose from a complex interplay of civil rights policy, economic restructuring, and a historical legacy of discrimination.

Theoretical concepts such as the culture of poverty, institutional racism, welfare disincentives, and structural economic change have all been widely debated. None of these explanations, however, considers residential segregation to be an important contributing cause of urban poverty and the underclass. In their principal works, Murray and Mead do not mention segregation at all, and Wilson refers to racial segregation only as a historical legacy from the past, not as an outcome that is institutionally supported and actively created today. Although Lewis mentions segregation sporadically in his writings, it is not assigned a central role in the set of structural factors responsible for the culture of poverty, and Banfield ignores it entirely. Glasgow, Pinkney, and other theorists of institutional racism mention the ghetto frequently, but generally call not for residential desegregation but for race-specific policies to combat the effects of discrimination in the schools and labor markets. In general, then, contemporary theorists of urban poverty do not see high levels of black–white segregation as particularly relevant to understanding the underclass or alleviating urban poverty.

The purpose of this [argument] is to redirect the focus of public debate back to issues of race and racial segregation and to suggest that they should be fundamental to thinking about the status of black Americans and the origins of the urban underclass. Our quarrel is less with any of the prevailing theories of urban poverty than with their systematic failure to consider the important role that segregation has played in mediating, exacerbating, and ultimately amplifying the harmful social and economic processes they treat.

We join earlier scholars in rejecting the view that poor urban blacks have an autonomous "culture of poverty" that explains their failure to achieve socioeconomic success in American society. We argue instead that residential segregation has been instrumental in creating a structural niche within which a deleterious set of attitudes and behaviors—a culture of segregation—has arisen and flourished. Segregation created the structural conditions for the emergence of an oppositional culture that devalues work, schooling, and marriage and that stresses attitudes and behaviors that are antithetical and often hostile to success in the larger economy. Although poor black neighborhoods still contain many people who lead conventional, productive lives, their example has been overshadowed in recent years by a growing concentration of poor, welfare-dependent families that is an inevitable result of residential segregation.

We readily agree with Douglas, Pinkney, and others that racial discrimination is widespread and may even be institutionalized within large sectors of American society, including the labor market, the educational system, and the welfare bureaucracy. We argue, however, that this view of black subjugation is incomplete without understanding the special role that residential segregation plays in enabling all other forms of racial oppression. Residential segregation is the institutional apparatus that supports other racially discriminatory processes and binds them together into a coherent and uniquely effective system of racial subordination. Until the black ghetto is dismantled as a basic institution of American urban life, progress ameliorating racial inequality in other arenas will be slow, fitful, and incomplete.

We also agree with William Wilson's basic argument that the structural transformation of the urban economy undermined economic supports for the black community during the 1970s and 1980s. We argue, however, that in the absence of segregation, these structural changes would not have produced the disastrous social and economic outcomes observed in inner cities during these decades. Although rates of black poverty were driven up by the economic dislocations Wilson identifies, it was segregation that confined the increased deprivation to a small number of densely settled, tightly packed, and geographically isolated areas.

Wilson also argues that concentrated poverty arose because the civil rights revolution allowed middle-class blacks to move out of the ghetto. Although we remain open to the possibility that class-selective migration did occur, we argue that concentrated poverty would have happened during the 1970s with or without black middle-class migration. Our principal objection to Wilson's focus on middle-class out-migration is not that it did not occur, but that it is misdirected: focusing on the flight of the black middle class deflects attention from the real issue, which is the limitation of black residential options through segregation.

Middle-class households—whether they are black, Mexican, Italian, Jewish, or Polish—always try to escape the poor. But only blacks must attempt their escape within a highly segregated, racially segmented housing market. Because of segregation, middle-class blacks are less able to escape than other groups, and as a result are exposed to more poverty. At the same time, because of segregation no one will move into a poor black neighborhood except other poor blacks. Thus both middle-class blacks and poor blacks lose compared with the poor and middle class of other groups: poor blacks live under unrivaled concentrations of poverty, and affluent blacks live in neighborhoods that are far less advantageous than those experienced by the middle class of other groups.

Finally, we concede Murray's general point that federal welfare policies are linked to the rise of the urban underclass, but we disagree with his specific hypothesis that generous welfare payments, by themselves, discouraged employment, encouraged unwed childbearing, undermined the strength of the family, and thereby caused persistent poverty. We argue instead that welfare payments were only harmful to the socioeconomic well-being of groups that were residentially segregated. As poverty rates rose among blacks in response to the economic dislocations of the 1970s and 1980s, so did the use of welfare programs. Because of racial segregation, however, the higher levels of welfare receipt were confined to a small number of isolated, all-black neighborhoods. By promoting the spatial concentration of welfare use, therefore, segregation created a residential environment within which welfare dependency was the norm, leading to the intergenerational transmission and broader perpetuation of urban poverty....

Our fundamental argument is that racial segregation—and its characteristic institutional form, the black ghetto—are the key structural factors responsible for the perpetuation of black poverty in the United States. Residential segregation is the principal organizational feature of American society that is responsible for the creation of the urban underclass....

Article 26

The Long Shadow of Race

Michael D. Yates

I have always lived in the long shadow of race. Johnstown, Pittsburgh, Portland, Miami Beach, in every city racist remarks and racist actions were commonplace. You didn't have to look for them; they were hard to escape. And on our road trips, no matter where we went or for how few days, it was not at all unusual for a white person to offer a racist comment. It is almost as if there is an understanding among whites that they are all fellow conspirators in the race war.

In Johnstown, daily racism—in bars, at the college where I taught, even in union halls—was a fact of life. A colleague complained in the faculty dining room that he didn't know why his daughter had to pay for work done at the university's dental school clinic when all those "niggers" got it for free. In the college gym, students told me they cheered for the Boston Celtics because they were the "white team." A man in a bowling alley threatened to assault me because I said that Michael Jordan was a great basketball player. In a union class, I got a complaint on the student evaluation forms: too many blacks in the class. There was one.

Black people call the Steel City "Pittsburgh South." In our first home there, in an apartment building complex, the college kids got drunk on weekends and hurled racial epithets at passersby from their balconies. When we moved to another part of town, an old neighborhood woman warned us to keep our curtains closed. She said that black people looked in windows trying to spot something to steal.

I have already commented on the racism of Portland. In Miami Beach, during our six-week stay in 2002, while we were talking to the Cuban-American manager of a realty office, she began to berate the city's Haitian immigrants as dirty criminals. She automatically assumed that I would have no sympathy for these wretched souls who, desperately poor to start with, have been denied asylum, put in detention centers, forced to take the worst jobs, and subjected to vicious racial discrimination.

I got a haircut in a small shop in a mall along Santa Fe's Cerillos Road. I struck up a conversation with the white woman cutting my hair. She was a single mother with a teenage son, and beginning to plan for his college education. Out of the blue she said she was angry that the local schools were biased in favor of Hispanics and Indians. They got all the breaks. This astounded me. We had been reading about—and seen—the dismal conditions faced by the city's people of color. They were poor; they lived in substandard housing; they did the worst jobs; their neighborhoods were ravaged by drugs and alcohol. Many went hungry. The whole history of New Mexico and its capital city was awash in racism and violence against nonwhites. Yet here was a woman who had no hesitance to tell a stranger that the oppressors were really the victims.

In Flagstaff, Arizona, we went to a party organized by a progressive organization called the Friends of Flagstaff. Over its potluck dinner, we met a woman from Boston. She decried the lack of diversity in Flagstaff, saying without irony that she wished it was more like Boston, with its many ethnic restaurants. What was remarkable was her seeming unawareness that Flagstaff is a diverse city, with large Hispanic and Indian populations—Indians comprise nearly 20 percent of all residents. They must be invisible to her.

Again in Flagstaff, we were enjoying the exhibits in the Museum of Northern Arizona. We ended our visit with a stop at the museum's bookstore. We were admiring the Indian-made works of art for sale when an Indian artist came in and showed the manager some of his jewelry and asked if the museum was interested in buying his pieces. Apparently the craftsmanship was good, but the Indian had been drinking and was known to the manager. The manager and his assistant treated this man as if he were a pathetic drunk unworthy of their time. He kept lowering his price, giving up whatever pride he had to these white people with money. A few minutes later, he was dismissed. After he left, the two museum staffers mocked him. The assistant, not realizing her ignorance, said that perhaps it was time for the Indian to join AAA. We left the museum with heavy hearts. It was as if the history of white oppression of Indians had been reenacted in microcosm before our eyes.

In Estes Park, people smugly said about a group of shabby riverside shacks not far from our cabin, "Oh, that's where the Mexicans live." The local peace group didn't bother to solicit support from local Mexicans because "They probably wouldn't be interested. They have to work too hard and wouldn't have time." We were talking to a jewelry store owner who, after remarking on how much safer (often a code word for "whiter") Estes Park was than his former home in Memphis, Tennessee, said that the Estes Park crime report was pretty small and those arrested always had names you couldn't pronounce. (Those damned Mexicans again.) In the laundromat we met a woman from the Bayview section of Brooklyn, and she said that she had moved here because you couldn't recognize her Brooklyn neighborhood anymore. She told us, without I think realizing how racist she sounded, that there were so many Arabs there now that locals call it "Bay Root." "Get it?," she said, "Bay Root."

There are numerous inconvenient facts that racists are unwilling to confront. The following data compare mainly blacks and whites. This is because these are the most readily available and the ones I know best. Comparisons between whites and other minorities such as Hispanics or Indians would show the same trends.

More than one million black men and women are in our jails and prisons, about the same number as whites, though the black share of the population is less than one-sixth that of whites. It is more likely that a black person of college age is in prison than in college. There are no economic indicators showing a black (or Hispanic or American Indian) advantage. Black median income, whether for families or individuals, is less than for whites, as is wealth. Black wages are lower. Black poverty rates are higher, by wide margins. Black unemployment rates are typically double white rates. All of these indicators show differences between blacks and whites even after variables that might influence them are held constant. For example, on average, black workers with the same education, the same experience, working in the same industry, and living in the same region of the country as whites still earn less money.

These racial inequalities can be simply explained. A common argument made by whites is that, since more than 150 years have passed since the end of slavery, there has been more than enough time for blacks to catch up with whites economically. However, recent economic research shows the flaw in such arguments. Economists have shown that economic advantages carry over from generation to generation and disadvantages do the same. As economist Austan Goolsbee put it, "The recent evidence shows quite clearly that in today's economy starting at the bottom is a recipe for being underpaid for a long time to come" (*New York Times*, May 25, 2006). Across generations, we find:

Although Americans still think of their land as a place of exceptional opportunity—in contrast to class-bound Europe—the evidence suggests otherwise. And scholars have, over the past decade, come to see America as a less mobile society than they once believed. As recently as the later 1980s, economists argued that not much advantage passed from parent to child, perhaps as little as 20 percent. By that measure, a rich man's grandchild would have barely any edge over a poor man's grandchild…. But over the last 10 years, better data and more number crunching have led economists and sociologists to a new consensus: The escalators of mobility move much more slowly. A substantial body of research finds that at least 45 percent of parents' advantage in income is passed along to their children, and perhaps as much as 60 percent. With the higher estimate, it's not only how much money your parents have that matters—even your great-great-grandfather's wealth might give you a noticeable edge today. (*Wall Street Journal*, May 13, 2005)

Imagine my own great-great-grandfather and suppose he had been a black slave in Mississippi. He would have been denied education, had his family destroyed, been worked nearly to death, suffered severe privation during the Civil War, and been considered less than human. Then in 1865 he would have been "freed," to fend for himself and whatever family he had. No job, no land, no schools, no nothing. For twelve short years, he might have had some protection provided by the federal government against the murderous rage of white Southerners. But in 1877 even that ended, and afterward he would have been confronted with the full force of Jim Crow and the Ku Klux Klan. What chance would his children have had? How likely would they have been to catch up with their white overlords? Isn't zero the most likely probability? His grandchildren might have migrated north, but again with no wealth and not much schooling. His great-grandchildren would have lived through the Great Depression. How much property would they have been likely to accumulate? Finally, through the heroic struggle of my ancestors and my own generation, I would have seen the victories of the civil rights movement, the desegregation of the schools, the end of lynchings, and the opening up of a few decent jobs. I might have been an auto worker in Detroit for a dozen years, but then in the 1970s everything would have come crashing down again.

Too many whites, and a few blacks, cannot confront such facts and analysis. They'd rather comfort themselves with the notion that what lies behind these data is social pathology. When a local black minister wrote that black people in New Orleans were themselves responsible for the misery inflicted by Hurricane Katrina, Denver's talk show hosts had a field day. They said that he was heroic for having the courage to say such a thing, and they hoped for the day when a white politician like President Bush could say the same.

Article 27

Privileged Places: Race, Opportunity and Uneven Development in Urban America

Gregory D. Squires and Charis E. Kubrin

W hen 10-year-old Lafayette Rivers described his hopes in Alex Kotlowitz' award-winning book, There Are No Children Here, he began, "If I grow up, I'd like to be a bus driver." Rivers lived in a West Side Chicago public housing complex. Children growing up in more privileged neighborhoods often ponder what they will do when they grow up, but not if they will grow up. The fact that place and race exert such a profound impact on one's future, or whether there even will be a future, violates accepted notions of equal opportunity and fair play. The legitimacy of virtually all institutions is challenged when privilege is so unevenly distributed, and for reasons beyond the control of so many individuals. The costs are not borne by the Lafayette Rivers of the world alone. They are inflicted upon every community whose security and well being are threatened.

Real estate mantra tells us that three factors determine the market value of a home: location, location and location. The same could be said about the factors that determine the good life and people's access to it in metropolitan America. Place matters. Neighborhood counts. Access to decent housing, safe neighborhoods, good schools, useful contacts and other benefits is largely influenced by the community in which one is born, raised and resides. Individual initiative, intelligence, experience and all the elements of human capital are obviously important. But understanding the opportunity structure in the United States today requires complementing what we know about individual characteristics with what we are learning about place.

Privilege cannot be understood outside the context of place. A central feature of place that has confounded efforts to understand and, where appropriate, alter the opportunity structure of the nation's urban communities is the role of race. Racial composition of neighborhoods has long been at the center of public policy and private practice in the creation and destruction of communities and in determining access to the elements of the good life, however defined.

Place and race continue to be defining characteristics of the opportunity structure of metropolitan areas. Disentangling the impact of these two forces is difficult, if not impossible. But where one lives and one's racial background are both social constructs that significantly shape the privileges (or lack thereof) that people enjoy.

The linkages among place, race and privilege are shaped by dominant social forces that play out in response to public policy decisions and practices of powerful private institutional actors. This perspective emerges from what has been referred to as "the new urban sociology," or "urban political economy," which places class, race and relations of domination and subordination at the center of analysis. In general, this requires understanding how individual characteristics and choices (such as human capital and household neighborhood preferences) and voluntary exchanges that occur via competitive markets are both framed and complemented by structural constraints (such as exclusionary zoning and deindustrialization) in determining the distribution of valued goods and services. Specifically, this involves examining how land use practices, urban policy, the dynamics of race and class and other social forces determine who gets what and why.

Race and Uneven Development

Dominant features of metropolitan development in the post-World War II years are sprawl, concentrated poverty and segregation (if not hypersegregation). Clearly, these are not separate, mutually exclusive patterns and processes. Rather, they are three critical underpinnings of the uneven development of place and privilege.

Sprawl has crept into the vocabulary of metropolitan development in recent years. While there is no universal agreement on a definition of sprawl, there is at least a rough consensus that it is a pattern of development associated with outward expansion, low-density housing and commercial development, fragmentation of planning among multiple municipalities with large fiscal disparities among them, auto-dependent transport and segregated land use patterns.

Racial disparities between cities and suburbs, and racial segregation in general, persist as dominant features of metropolitan areas. Cities are disproportionately non-white, with over 52 percent of blacks and 21 percent of whites residing in central-city neighborhoods; while suburbs are disproportionately white, where 57 percent of whites but just 36 percent of blacks reside. Segregation, particularly between blacks and whites, persists at high levels, and Hispanic/white segregation has increased in recent years. The typical white resident of metropolitan areas resides in a neighborhood that is 80 percent white, 7 percent black,

8 percent Hispanic and 4 percent Asian. A typical black person lives in a neighborhood that is 33 percent white, 51 percent black, 11 percent Hispanic and 3 percent Asian. And a typical Hispanic resident lives in a community that is 36 percent white, 11 percent black, 45 percent Hispanic and 6 percent Asian.

Racial segregation, in conjunction with the concentration of poverty and growing economic inequality, results in growing isolation of poor minority households. If segregation is declining, albeit slightly, for blacks, it does not appear that this has translated into their being able to move into better neighborhoods. For example, in 1990, the typical black household with an income above $60,000 lived in a neighborhood where the median income was $31,585, compared with $46,760 for the typical white household in this income bracket. By 2000, these figures changed to $35,306 for blacks and $51,459 for whites. The same pattern holds for Hispanics. Further confounding the intersection of place and race is the fact that in 2000 poor blacks and Hispanics were far more likely than poor whites to live in poor neighborhoods. Whereas over 18 percent of poor blacks and almost 14 percent of poor Hispanics lived in such areas, less than 6 percent of poor whites did.

Wealth disparities are far greater. While blacks earn about 60 percent of what whites earn, their net wealth is approximately one-tenth that of whites. Substantial wealth disparities persist even between whites and non-whites who have equivalent educational backgrounds, comparable jobs and similar incomes.

These wealth disparities also reflect, at least in part, the fact that black middle-class neighborhoods are far more likely than white middle-class communities to be located in close proximity to poor neighborhoods, which residents frequently pass through while commuting to work, going to the grocery store and engaging in most normal daily activities. Proximity to problematic neighborhoods also affects the value of homes and, therefore, further contributes to these economic disparities.

Seventy percent of white families own their homes; approximately half of black families do so. For blacks, home equity accounts for two-thirds of their assets compared with two-fifths for whites. A study of the 100 largest metropolitan areas found that black homeowners received 18 percent less value for their investments in their homes than white homeowners. Biases, racial discrimination and segregation in the nation's housing and financial services markets have cost the current generation of blacks about $82 billion, with the disparity in home equity averaging $20,000 for those holding mortgages.

Spatial and Racial Inequality

Spatial and racial inequalities are directly associated with access to virtually all products and services associated with the good life—e.g., health, education, employment. Sprawl, concentrated poverty and racial segregation tend to concentrate a host of problems and privileges in different neighborhoods and among different racial groups. These "concentration effects" shape opportunities and lifestyles throughout the life cycle and across generations. Perhaps most problematic is the impact of uneven development on children like Lafayette Rivers, and how the proverbial vicious cycle recreates itself over time. Research has demonstrated links between neighborhood characteristics (like poverty and inequality) and teenage pregnancy, high school dropout rates and delinquent behavior. Patterns of privilege also emerge early in life, persist throughout the life cycle and recreate themselves in subsequent generations. Infant mortality rates, quality of schools, employment opportunities, life expectancy and more are affected by where one is born, lives, works and plays.

Access to clean air and water, exposure to lead paint, high rates of stress and obesity, poor diet, social isolation and proximity to hospitals and other medical facilities all vary by neighborhood and contribute to long-established disparities in health and wellness. The affluent and predominantly white D.C. suburb of Bethesda, Maryland, has one pediatrician for every 400 children, while the poor and predominantly black neighborhoods in the District's southeast side have one pediatrician for every 3,700 children. And while the hospital admission rate for asthma in the state of New York is 1.8 per 1000, it is three times higher in the Mott Haven area of the South Bronx.

If education is to be "the great equalizer of the conditions of men—the balance wheel of the social machinery" as the Massachusetts educator Horace Mann anticipated over 150 years ago, that day has yet to arrive. After two decades of progress in desegregating the nation's schools, it appears that progress may have come to a halt or perhaps may have even been reversed. In 2000, 40 percent of black students attended schools that were 90 to 100 percent black compared with 32 percent of black students who attended such schools in 1988. The share of Hispanic students attending schools that were 90 to 100 percent minority grew from 23 percent during the late 1960s to 37 percent in 2000. Continuing disparities result in fewer educational resources, less qualified teachers and higher teacher turnover and, ultimately, lower educational achievement in low-income and minority communities.

If there is one single factor that is most critical for determining access to the good life, it might be employment. This is particularly true in the United States where individuals and households are far more dependent on their jobs to secure basic goods and services than is the case with virtually all other industrialized nations. The importance of place and race have long been recognized by spatial mismatch theorists who posit that lower-income residents of poorer communities generally reside in or near central cities while job growth has been greater in outlying suburban communities. Those most in need of employment, therefore, find it not only more difficult to learn about available jobs but also more expensive to get to those jobs when they find one. As of 2000, no racial group was more physically isolated from jobs than blacks. The metropolitan areas with higher levels of black-white housing segregation were those that exhibited higher levels of spatial mismatch between the residential location of blacks and the location of jobs. Compounding these troubles are the "mental maps" many employers draw, in which they attribute various job-related characteristics (such as skills, experience, attitudes) to residents of certain neighborhoods. A job applicant's address often has an independent effect that makes it more difficult, particularly for racial minorities from urban areas, to secure employment. Moreover, recent research by Devah Pager, assistant professor of sociology at Princeton, has found that it is easier for a white person with a felony conviction to get a job than a black person with no felony convictions, even among applicants with otherwise comparable credentials or where blacks had slightly better employment histories. Such divergent employment experiences, of course, contribute directly to the income and wealth disparities.

In many cities, racial differences in poverty levels, employment opportunities, wages, education, housing and health care, among other things, are so strong that the worst urban conditions in which whites reside are considerably better than the average conditions of black communities. In "Toward a Theory of Race, Crime and Urban Inequality," from *Crime and Inequality*, Robert Sampson and William Julius Wilson assert that in not one U.S. city with a population over 100,000 do blacks live in ecological equality with whites when it comes to the basic features of economic and family organization. A depressing feature of these developments is that many of these differences reflect policy decisions which, if not designed expressly to create disparate outcomes, have contributed to them nevertheless.

Policy Matters

It has been argued that individuals or households make voluntary choices, based on their financial capacity, in selecting their communities when moving to those areas offering the bundle of services for which they are willing or able to pay. That is, they "vote with their feet." But many urban scholars have noted the role of public policies and institutionalized private practices (such as tax policy, transport patterns, land use planning) that serve as barriers to individual choice in housing markets and as contributors to spatial inequality in metropolitan areas.

Most households select their neighborhoods on the basis of the services, jobs, cultural facilities and other amenities that are available within the constraints of their budgets. Critical for many households is a dense network of families, friends and various social ties that bind them to particular locations. Even the most distressed neighborhoods, including some notorious public housing complexes, often have a culture, social organization and other attributes that residents want to retain. Community, defined in many different ways, attracts and retains residents of all types of neighborhoods.

But, again, these choices are made in a context shaped by a range of public policy decisions and private institutional practices over which most individuals have little control. Those decisions often have, by design, exclusionary implications that limit opportunities, particularly for low-income households and people of color. The conflict and hassles that racial minorities face outside their communities lead some to choose a segregated neighborhood for their home, even when they could afford to live elsewhere. Such decision making is framed and limited by a range of structural constraints. Individuals exercise choice, but those choices do not reflect what is normally understood as voluntary.

If suburbanization and sprawl reflect the housing choices of residents, they are constrained choices. Many factors contributed to the development of sprawling suburban communities: the long-term 30-year mortgage featuring low down payment requirements; availability of federal insurance to protect mortgage lenders; federal financing to support a secondary market in mortgage loans (Fannie Mae and Freddie Mac), which dramatically increases availability of mortgage money; tax deductibility of interest and property tax payments; and proliferation of federally funded highways.

The federal government's underwriting rules for Federal Housing Administration and other federal mortgage insurance products, and enforcement of racially restrictive covenants by the courts, along with overt redlining practices by mortgage lenders and racial steering by real estate agents, virtually guaranteed the patterns of racial segregation that were commonplace by the 1950s. Concentration of public housing in central-city high-rise complexes reinforced the patterns of economic and racial segregation that persist today. Exclusionary zoning ordinances of most suburban municipalities that created minimum lot size and maximum density requirements for housing developments (often prohibiting construction of multifamily housing) complemented federal policy.

Government policy has also encouraged the flight of businesses and jobs from cities to surrounding suburban communities and beyond. Financial incentives including infrastructure investments, tax abatements and depreciation allowances favoring new equipment over reinvestment in existing facilities all have contributed to the deindustrialization and disinvestment of urban communities. Often such investments subsidize development that would have occurred without that assistance. As one observer noted, "Subsidizing economic development in the suburbs is like paying teenagers to think about sex." The end result is often an unintended subsidy of private economic activity by jurisdictions that compete in a "race to the bottom" in efforts to attract footloose firms and mobile capital, starving traditional public services—like education—for resources in the process. A downward spiral is established that further undercuts the quality of life.

Place, Privilege and Policy

One of the more unfortunate debates in recent years has been over the question of whether race-specific or universal remedies are more appropriate for addressing the issues of race and urban poverty. (An even more unfortunate debate, of course, is with those who simply think we have done enough, or perhaps too much, and that neither race nor class remedies are needed.)

The primary attraction of the universal, or class-based, approaches, according to its proponents, is pragmatism. Recognizing the many common interests of poor and working households of any color, it is argued that the most significant barriers confronting these groups can be addressed with policy initiatives and other actions that do not ignite the hostility often associated with race-based discussions and proposals. Race-neutral policies that assist all of those who are working hard but not quite making it reinforce traditional values of individual initiative and the work ethic, thereby providing benefits to people who have earned them rather than to the so-called undeserving poor. Given the socioeconomic characteristics of racial minorities in general, it is further argued that such approaches will disproportionately benefit these communities, nurturing integration and greater opportunity in a far less rancorous environment than is created with debates over race-specific approaches. Given the "race fatigue" among many whites (and underlying prejudices that persist), class-based approaches are viewed as a much more feasible way to address the problems of urban poverty that affect many groups, but particularly racial minorities.

In response, it is argued that while the quality of life for racial minorities has improved over the years, such approaches simply do not recognize the extent to which race and racism continue to shape the opportunity structure in the United States. Colorblindness is often a euphemism for what amounts to a retreat on race and the preservation of white privilege in its many forms. In a world of scarce resources, class-based remedies dilute available support for combating racial discrimination and segregation. From this perspective, it is precisely the controversy over race that the class-based proponents fear, which demonstrates the persistence of racism and the need for explicitly anti-racist remedies, including far more aggressive enforcement of fair housing, equal employment and other civil rights laws. On the other hand, race-based remedies alone may not resolve all the problems associated with race and urban poverty given the many non-racial factors that contribute to racial disparity as indicated above.

In reality, both approaches are required. Class-based policies (such as increasing the minimum wage and earned income tax credit, implementing living wage requirements) and race-based initiatives (more comprehensive affirmative action and related diversity requirements), are essential if the underlying patterns of privilege are to be altered.

Uncommon Allies

Many constituencies that traditionally find themselves at odds with each other can find common ground on a range of policies designed to combat sprawl, concentrated poverty and segregation. Identifying and nurturing such political coalitions is perhaps the key political challenge. Coalitions that cut across interest groups and racial groups are essential. Many land use planning, housing and housing finance policy proposals, for example, are generally articulated in colorblind terms. Fair-share housing requirements, tax-based revenue sharing and inclusionary zoning are universal in character, although they often have clear racial implications.

Many suburban employers are unable to find the workers they need, in part because of the high cost of housing in their local communities. Often there are local developers who would like to build affordable housing and lenders who are willing to finance it, but local zoning prohibits such construction. These interests could join with anti-poverty groups and affordable housing advocates to challenge the traditional exclusionary suburban zoning ordinances. Developers, planners and affordable housing advocates came together in Wisconsin and secured passage of a state land use planning law that provided financial incentives to local municipalities who developed plans for increasing the supply of affordable housing units in their jurisdictions.

Similarly, school choice and fair housing groups—two groups that rarely ally – might recognize that severing the link between the neighborhood in which a family lives and the school that children must attend may well reduce homebuyers' concerns with neighborhood racial composition. This would reduce one barrier to both housing and school segregation while giving students more schooling options.

In many cities, developers, lenders, community development corporations, environmental groups, local governments and others are coming together to sponsor transit-oriented development. Such developments create new jobs for working families in locations that are accessible by public transportation, reducing traffic congestion, infrastructure costs and other disamenities. Growing such development would yield greater efficiencies in public investment, fewer environmental costs and more job opportunities.

This list is hardly meant to be exhaustive. The point is simply to show that there are some creative political alliances that can exercise a positive impact on some longstanding, and seemingly intractable, problems. Sprawl, concentrated poverty and segregation have many identifiable causes. The confluence of place, race and privilege becomes less mysterious over time. At least some approaches to reduce uneven development and its many costs are already available: land use planning tools like tax-based revenue sharing and the delineation of urban growth boundaries can be used more extensively to reduce sprawl and some of the associated costs; community reinvestment initiatives, housing mobility programs and inclusionary zoning ordinances can be expanded to diminish further the concentration of poverty; and fair housing law enforcement can be strengthened to reduce racial segregation. If policy is largely responsible for getting us where we are today, then policy can help us pursue a different path toward severing the links among race, place and privilege tomorrow.

References

The Geography of Opportunity: Race and Housing Choice in Metropolitan America, by Xavier de Souza Briggs, ed. Brookings Institution Press, 2005.

The Failures of Integration: How Race and Class are Undermining the American Dream, by Sheryll Cashin. New York: Public Affairs, 2004.

Place Matters: Metropolitics for the Twenty-first Century, by Peter Dreier, John Mollenkopf and Todd Swanstrom. 2nd ed. University Press of Kansas, 2004.

Urban Inequality: Evidence from Four Cities, by Alice O'Connor, Chris Tilly and Lawrence D. Bobo, eds. New York: Russell Sage Foundation, 2001.

American Metropolitics: The New Suburban Reality, by Myron Orfield. The Brookings Institution Press, 2002.

Waiting for Gautreaux: A Story of Segregation, Housing, and the Black Ghetto, by Alexander Polikoff. Northwestern University Press, 2006.

Part 8

Education

Article 28

The Overselling of Education

We Need a Better-Educated Citizenry, But the Cure for Increasing Inequality Lies Elsewhere.

Lawrence Mishel

In discussing rising inequality in the United States, Federal Reserve Board Chair Ben Bernanke recently said, "It's a very bad development.... It's creating two societies. And it's based very much, I think, on educational differences."

A better-educated workforce is widely touted as the panacea for every economic problem. Education is said to be the cure both for unemployment and income inequality. To hear leaders of the financial sector talk, the underlying problem with the economy has not been a runaway financial sector but an unqualified workforce. In a recent Reuters special report on the U.S. economy, Diane Swonk, an oft-quoted financial-sector economist, said, "The recession merely revealed a reality that has been with us for a long time. We faced a growing gap in education and skills that we tried to fill with debt and credit, which gave us the illusion of growth."

Or consider the statement of the Minneapolis Federal Reserve Bank president, Narayana Kocherlakota, which removes monetary policy as any part of the solution to current high unemployment:

This is very comfortable reasoning for the very comfortable class. It identifies "failing" schools and dumb workers for the economic calamity actually caused by a deregulated financial sector following a massive redistribution of income and wealth. This shift was driven by corporate political power that allowed the top 1 percent to capture some 56 percent of all the income growth over the two decades preceding the Great Recession.

Blaming inequality and joblessness on worker skill deficits is an old alibi. In 1987, the Reagan administration's Workforce 2000 report foretold future "skill mismatches." In 1990, George H.W. Bush's secretary of labor, Elizabeth Dole, said, "America faces a workforce crisis where there is a diminishing number of people eligible and qualified for the ever-increasing complexity of jobs in our economy." Many panels, such as the Commission on the Skills of the American Workforce, warned around that same time of the need to radically up-skill our workforce or face long-term income and productivity stagnation.

The Clinton administration echoed this theme, saying more education was needed for workers to adjust during a "transition" to a new economy. It must have been a surprise, therefore, that in the mid-1990s there was a sharp uptick in the economy's productivity that has lasted for 15 years and was accomplished with the very workforce that allegedly put our nation in danger. In the late 1990s, when labor markets were tight, the supposedly unqualified lower-skilled workforce enjoyed solid, real wage gains.

Are the Unemployed the "Unqualified"?

It is remarkable that anyone can claim that today's high unemployment is primarily due to a mismatch between the skills of the unemployed and the available jobs. After all, most of those who are unemployed today were productively employed just a year or two ago. The notion that production processes have radically changed is hard to square with the absence of a surge in productivity or investment. There have been roughly five unemployed people for every job opening, roughly twice the ratio at the worst moments of the last recession, which, recall, was considered a jobless recovery.

The shortfall in job openings relative to the last recovery is apparent in nearly every industry, indicating that the problem is across the economy rather than rooted in particular sectors. Nor do the unemployed appear "unqualified." Unemployment over the recession has doubled for every educational grouping, including college graduates whose unemployment is far higher than anytime since 1979 (the earliest year for monthly unemployment data).

Moreover, the percentage of unemployed who have been out of work for at least six months is the same across all education groups. In other words, unemployed college graduates bear the same risk of long-term unemployment as those with high school degrees. In sum, we do not have unemployment because of weak skills or poor schools: Rather, we have a serious shortfall in demand due to a loss of housing and stock wealth and recession-caused income losses compounded by the de-leveraging of our household and business sectors.

Is There a Looming Shortage of College Graduates?

There has been a drive to greatly increase college graduation rates, led by the Obama administration, the Gates Foundation, and others. A recent paper by Massachusetts Institute of Technology economist David Autor for the Hamilton Project and the Center for American

Progress contends that "rising demand for highly educated workers, combined with lagging supply, is contributing to higher levels of earnings inequality…. Workers that do not obtain postsecondary education face a contracting set of job opportunities." Autor's sole policy recommendations for rising inequality boil down to "an increased supply of college graduates should eventually help to drive down the college wage premium and limit the rise in inequality," and "the United States should foster improvements in K-12 education so that more people will be prepared to go on to higher education."

There is certainly a strong equity case for giving every student the opportunity to complete college and especially for assisting racial and ethnic minorities to achieve upward mobility. This would also assist long-term growth and provide a healthier, more informed citizenry. However, greatly boosting college graduation above its expected growth rate will not materially address either past or future inequalities. It will exacerbate the already deteriorating pay and benefits facing young college graduates and lead to falling wages among all college graduates, especially men.

Despite frequent claims, it is simply untrue that we have seen a three-decades-long radical increase in employers' demand for four-year college graduates. The widespread (even before the recession) utilization of college students and graduates working as unpaid (many unlawfully so) "interns" is evidence enough—if employers desperately needed these workers, they would pay them.

In fact, the trends of the last 10 years contradict this story. The wages and benefits received by young college graduates fell over the 2000-2007 business cycle and in this recession. Moreover, the wages of all college graduates have been flat over the last 10 years, with those for men having markedly declined. This should not be surprising as the relative demand for college graduates, according to Harvard's Claudia Goldin and Larry Katz, grew more slowly in the 2000s than in any postwar decade, following relatively slow growth in the 1990s. A major increase in the supply of college graduates would further erode the wages and benefits new college graduates obtain and drive down the wages of all college graduates, especially among men.

The college premium has barely budged in 10 years. Yet income inequality among households has soared since 2001, and the wage gap between high- and middle-wage workers has grown strongly as well. Something that's not growing—the college premium—cannot explain growing inequality. Having more college graduates will leave untouched the income inequality driven by the outsized income growth (from salaries and capital gains) claimed by the upper 1 percent and the upper 0.1 percent. Wage gaps are primarily driven by increased inequalities among workers with similar educations (among college graduates, for example) rather than by differences across education groups.

What is the Role of Education in Prosperity?

It's certainly true that America needs better-educated citizens beginning with pre-K and public education, stronger community colleges, more affordable paths to higher educa-tion, and comprehensive training policies that increase skills and lead to better-paid jobs. But none of these education policies are the primary cure either for the widening income inequality of the past three decades or the current crisis of joblessness. The income distribu-tion was much more equal during the postwar boom when most young workers had only a high school diploma—because we had strong institutions of worker representation and wage-setting as well as tax and regulatory policies that constrained the greed at the top.

More education and training are necessary to obtain the long-term growth we desire and to provide equal access to job opportunities for the entire population and workforce. Individuals deciding whether to pursue more education and training would be wise to enhance their human capital, as it will place them in a better position as wage earners and citizens.

That being said, the challenge we face with persistent unemployment exceeding 9 per-cent is not better education and training for those currently unemployed. Rather, we need more jobs.

The huge increase in wage and income inequality over the last 30 years was not caused by a skills deficit. Rather, workers face a "wage deficit." The key challenge is to provide good jobs and re-establish the basis for wages and compensation to grow in tandem with produc-tivity, as they did before 1979.

We do need more investment in education at all levels, so that the children of the work-ing class have a better opportunity to compete for good jobs. We also need what Europeans call an active labor-market policy, so that the money we invest in training is directly con-nected to re-employment at good wages, rather than operating in a vacuum.

The nation's productivity increased by 80 percent from 1979 to 2009, and good produc-tivity growth can be expected in the future. It is not education gaps that have caused nearly all of those gains to be captured by the top but rather economic policies that redistributed economic and political power.

Article 29

"Even the Best Schools Can't Close the Race Achievement Gap"

Richard Rothstein

The achievement gap between poor and middle-class, black and white children is an educational challenge, but we prevent ourselves from solving it because of a commonplace belief that poverty and race can't "cause" low achievement and that therefore schools must be failing to teach disadvantaged children adequately. After all, we see many highly successful students from lower-class backgrounds. Their success seems to prove that social class cannot be what impedes most disadvantaged students.

Yet the success of some lower-class students proves nothing about schools' power to close the achievement gap. There is a distribution of achievement in every social group. These distributions overlap. While average achievement of low-income students is below average achievement of middle-class students, there are always some middle-class students who achieve below typical low-income levels. Some low-income students achieve above typical middle-class levels. "Demography is not destiny," but students' family characteristics are a powerful influence on their relative average achievement, even in the best of schools.

Widely repeated accounts of schools that somehow elicit consistently high achievement from lower-class children almost always turn out, upon examination, to be flawed. In some cases, "schools that beat the odds" are highly selective, enrolling only the most able or most motivated lower-class children. Some are not truly lower-class schools—for example, schools enrolling children who qualify for subsidized lunches because their parents are poorly paid but highly educated. Some schools "succeed" with lower-class children by defining high achievement at such a low level that all students can reach it, despite big gaps that remain at higher levels. And some schools' successes are statistical flukes—their high test scores last for only one year, in only one grade and in only one subject.

While the idea that "if some children can defy the demographic odds, all can" seems plausible, it reflects a reasoning whose naiveté we easily recognize in other policy areas.

In human affairs, where multiple causation is typical, causes are not disproved by exceptions. Tobacco firms once claimed that smoking does not cause cancer because we all know people who smoked without getting cancer. We now consider such reasoning specious. We understand that because no single cause is rigidly deterministic, some people can smoke without harm, but we also understand that, on average, smoking is dangerous. Yet despite such understanding, quite sophisticated people often proclaim that success of some poor children proves that social disadvantage does not cause low achievement.

Social Class and Learning

Partly, our confusion stems from failing to examine the concrete ways that social class actually affects learning. Describing these may help to make their influence more obvious.

Overall, lower-income children are in poorer health, and poor health depresses student achievement, no matter how effective a school may be. Low-income children have poorer vision, partly because of prenatal conditions, partly because, even as toddlers, they watch too much television both at home and in low-quality daycare settings, so their eyes are more poorly trained. Trying to read, their eyes may wander or have difficulty tracking print or focusing. A good part of the over-identification of learning disabilities for lower-class children is probably attributable simply to undiagnosed vision problems for which therapy is available and for which special education placement should be unnecessary.

Lower-class children have poorer oral hygiene, more lead poisoning, more asthma, poorer nutrition, less adequate pediatric care, more exposure to smoke, and a host of other health problems—on average. Because, for example, lower-class children typically have less adequate dental care, they are more likely to have toothaches and resulting discomfort that affects concentration.

Because low-income children are more likely to live in communities where landlords use high-sulfur home heating oil, and where diesel trucks frequently pass en route to industrial and commercial sites, such children are more likely to suffer from asthma, leading to more absences from school and drowsiness (from lying awake wheezing at night) when present. Recent surveys of black children in Chicago and in New York City's Harlem community found one of every four children suffering from asthma, a rate six times as great as that for all children. Asthma is now the single biggest cause of chronic school absence.

Because primary care physicians are few in low-income communities (the physician to population ratio is less than a third the rate in middle-class communities), disadvantaged children (even those with health insurance) are also more likely to miss school for relatively minor problems, like common ear infections, for which middle-class children are treated promptly. If in attendance, children with earaches have more difficulty paying attention.

Each of these well-documented social class differences in health is likely to have a palpable effect on academic achievement. The influence of each may be small, but combined, the influence of all is probably huge.

The growing unaffordability of adequate housing for low-income families also affects achievement—children whose families have difficulty finding stable housing are more likely to be mobile, and student mobility is an important cause of failing student performance. [See "High Classroom Turnover: How Children Get Left Behind", Poverty & Race, May/June 2002.] A 1994 government report found that 30% of the poorest children had attended at least three different schools by third grade, while only 10% of middle-class children did so. Blacks were more than twice as likely as whites to change schools this much. It is hard to imagine how teachers, no matter how well trained, can be as effective for children who move in and out of their classrooms.

Differences in wealth are also likely to affect achievement, but these are usually overlooked because most analysts focus only on annual family income to indicate disadvantage. This makes it hard to understand why black students, on average, score lower than whites whose family incomes are the same. It is easier to understand this pattern when we recognize that children can have similar family incomes but be of different economic classes: black families with low income in any year are likely to have been poor for longer than white families with similar income in that year. White families are likely to own far more assets that support their children's achievement than are black families at the same income level, partly because black middle-class parents are more likely to be the first generation in their families to have middle-class status. Although median black family income is now nearly 2/3 of white income, black family assets are still only 12% of whites'. This difference means that, among white and black families with the same middle-class incomes, the whites are more likely to have savings for college. This makes white children's college aspirations more practical, and therefore more commonplace.

Child Rearing/Personality Traits

Social class differences however, amount to more than these quantifiable differences in health, housing, income and assets. There are powerful social class differences in child rearing habits and personality traits, and these too cause average differences in academic achievement by social class.

Consider how parents of different social classes tend to raise children. Young children of more educated parents are read to more consistently, and are encouraged to read more by themselves when they are older. Most children whose parents have college degrees are read to daily before they begin kindergarten; few children whose parents have only a high school diploma or less benefit from daily reading. White children are more likely than blacks to be read to in pre-kindergarten years.

A five-year-old who enters school recognizing some words and who has turned pages of many stories will be easier to teach than one who has rarely held a book. The latter can be taught, but the child with a stronger home literacy background will typically post higher scores on reading tests than one for whom book reading is unfamiliar—even if both children benefit from high expectations and effective teaching. So, the achievement gap begins.

If a society with such differences wants children, irrespective of social class, to have the same chance to achieve academic goals, it should find ways to help lower-class children enter school having the same familiarity with books as middle-class children have. This requires re-thinking the institutional settings in which we provide early childhood care, beginning in infancy.

Some people acknowledge the impact of such differences but find it hard to accept that good schools should have so difficult a time overcoming them. This would be easier to understand if Americans had a broader international perspective on education. Class backgrounds influence relative achievement everywhere. The inability of schools to overcome the disadvantage of less literate homes is not a peculiar American failure but a universal reality. Turkish immigrant students suffer from an achievement gap in Germany, as do Algerians in France, as do Caribbean, African, Pakistani and Bangladeshi pupils in Great Britain, and as do Okinawans and low-caste Buraku in Japan.

An international survey of 15-year-olds, conducted in 2000, found a strong relationship in almost every nation between parental occupation and student literacy. The gap between literacy of children of the highest status workers (like doctors, professors, lawyers) and the lowest status workers (like waiters and waitresses, taxi drivers, mechanics) was even greater in Germany and in the United Kingdom than it was in the United States. After reviewing these results, a U.S. Department of Education summary concluded that "most participating countries do not differ significantly from the United States in terms of the strength of the relationship between socioeconomic status and literacy in any subject." Remarkably, the Department published this conclusion at the very time it was guiding a bill through Congress—"No Child Left Behind"—that demanded every school in the nation abolish social class differences in achievement within 12 years.

Urging less educated parents to read to children can't fully compensate for differences in school readiness. If children see parents read to solve their own problems or for entertainment, children are more likely to want to read themselves. Parents who bring reading material home from work demonstrate by example to children that reading is not a segmented burden but a seamless activity that bridges work and leisure. Parents who read to children but don't read for themselves send a different message.

How parents read to children is as important as whether they do; more educated parents read aloud differently. When working-class parents read aloud, they are more likely to tell children to pay attention without interruptions or to sound out words or name letters. When they ask children about a story, questions are more likely to be factual, asking for names of objects or memory of events.

Parents who are more literate are more likely to ask questions that are creative, interpretive or connective, like "what do you think will happen next?," "does that remind you of what we did yesterday?" Middle-class parents are more likely to read aloud, to have fun, to start conversations, as an entree to the world outside. Their children learn that reading is enjoyable and are more motivated to read in school.

There are stark class differences not only in how parents read but in how they converse. Explaining events in the broader world to children, in dinner talk, for example, may have as much of an influence on test scores as early reading itself. Through such conversations, children develop vocabularies and become familiar with contexts for reading in school. Educated parents are more likely to engage in such talk and to begin it with infants and toddlers, conducting pretend conversations long before infants can understand the language. Typically, middle-class parents "ask" infants about their needs, then provide answers for the children ("Are you ready for a nap, now? Yes, you are, aren't you?"). Instructions are more likely to be given indirectly ("You don't want to make so much noise, do you?"). Such instruction is really an invitation for a child to work through the reasoning behind an order and to internalize it. Middle-class parents implicitly begin academic instruction for infants with such indirect guidance.

Yet such instruction is quite different from what policymakers nowadays consider "academic" for young children: explicit training in letter and number recognition, letter-sound correspondence, and so on. Such drill in basic skills can be helpful but is unlikely to close the social class gap in learning.

Soon after middle-class children become verbal, parents typically draw them into adult conversations so children can practice expressing their own opinions. Lower-class children are more likely to be expected to be seen and not heard. Inclusion this early in adult conversations develops a sense of entitlement in middle-class children; they feel comfortable addressing adults as equals and without deference. Children who want reasons rather than being willing to accept assertions on adult authority develop intellectual skills upon which later academic success in school will rely. Certainly, some lower-class children have such skills and some middle-class children lack them. But, on average, a sense of entitlement is social class-based.

Parents whose professional occupations entail authority and responsibility typically believe more strongly that they can affect their environments and solve problems. At work, they explore alternatives and negotiate compromises. They naturally express these personality traits at home when they design activities where children figure out solutions for themselves. Even the youngest middle-class children practice traits that make academic success more likely when they negotiate what to wear or to eat. When middle-class parents give orders, they are more likely to explain why the rules are reasonable.

But parents whose jobs entail following orders or doing routine tasks exude a lesser sense of efficacy. Their children are less likely to be encouraged to negotiate clothing or food. Lower-class parents are more likely to instruct children by giving directions without extended discussion. Following orders, after all, is how they themselves behave at work. So their children are also more likely to be fatalistic about obstacles they face, in and out of school.

Middle-class children's self-assurance is enhanced in after-school activities that sometimes require large fees for enrollment and almost always require parents to have enough free time and resources to provide transportation. Organized sports, music, drama and dance programs build self-confidence (with both trophies and admiring adult spectators) and discipline in middle-class children. Lower-class parents find the fees for such activities more daunting, and transportation may also be more of a problem. In many cases, such organized athletic and artistic activities are not available anywhere in lower-class neighborhoods. So lower-class children's sports are more informal and less confidence-building, with less opportunity to learn teamwork and self-discipline. For children with greater self-confidence, unfamiliar school challenges can be exciting; such children, who are more likely to be from middle-class homes, are more likely to succeed than those who are less self-confident.

Homework exacerbates academic differences between middle- and working-class children because middle-class parents are more likely to assist with homework. Yet homework would increase the achievement gap even if all parents were able to assist. Parents from different social classes supervise homework differently. Consistent with overall patterns of language use, middle-class parents—particularly those whose own occupational habits require problem solving—are more likely to assist by posing questions that decompose problems and that help children figure out correct answers. Lower-class parents are more likely to guide children with direct instructions. Children from both strata may go to school with completed homework, but middle-class children gain more in intellectual power from the exercise than do lower-class children.

Twenty years ago, Betty Hart and Todd Risley, researchers from the University of Kansas, visited families from different social classes to monitor the conversations between parents and toddlers. Hart and Risley found that, on average, professional parents spoke over 2,000 words per hour to their children, working-class parents spoke about 1,300, and welfare mothers spoke about 600. So, by age three, children of professionals had vocabularies that were nearly 50% greater than those of working-class children and twice as large as those of welfare children.

Deficits like these cannot be made up by schools alone, no matter how high the teachers' expectations. For all children to achieve the same goals, the less advantaged would have to enter school with verbal fluency similar to the fluency of middle-class children.

The Kansas researchers also tracked how often parents verbally encouraged children's behavior, and how often parents reprimanded their children. Toddlers of professionals got an average of six encouragements per reprimand. Working-class children had two. For welfare children, the ratio was reversed, an average of one encouragement for two reprimands. Children whose initiative was encouraged from a very early age are probably more likely, on average, to take responsibility for their own learning.

Social class differences in role modeling also make an achievement gap almost inevitable. Not surprisingly, middle-class professional parents tend to associate with, and be friends with, similarly educated professionals. Working-class parents have fewer professional friends. If parents and their friends perform jobs requiring little academic skill, their children's images of their own futures are influenced. On average, these children must struggle harder to motivate themselves to achieve than children who assume that, as in their parents' social circle, the only roles are doctor, lawyer, teacher, social worker, manager, administrator or businessperson.

Even disadvantaged children now usually say they plan to attend college. College has become such a broad rhetorical goal that black eighth graders tell surveyors they expect to earn college degrees as often as white eighth graders respond in this way. But despite these intentions to pursue education, fewer black than white eighth graders actually graduate from high school four years later, fewer eventually enroll in college the year after high school graduation, and even fewer persist to get bachelor's degrees.

A bigger reason than affordability is that while disadvantaged students say they plan on college, they don't feel as much parental, community or peer pressure to take the courses or to get the grades to qualify and to study hard to become more attractive to college admission officers. Lower-class parents say they expect children to perform well, but are less likely to enforce these expectations, for example with rewards or punishments for report card grades. Teachers and counselors can stress doing well in school to lower-class children, but such lessons compete with children's own self-images, formed early in life and reinforced daily at home.

Culture and Expectations

Partly, there may be a black community culture of underachievement that helps to explain why even middle-class black children often don't do as well in school as white children from seemingly similar socioeconomic backgrounds. Middle-class black students don't study as hard as white middle-class students, and blacks are more disruptive in class than whites from similar income strata. This culture of underachievement is easier to understand than to cure. Throughout American history, many black students who excelled in school were not rewarded in the labor market for that effort. Many black college graduates could only find work as servants, as Pullman car porters or, in white-collar fields, as assistants to less qualified whites. Many Americans believe that these practices have disappeared and that blacks and whites with similar test scores now have similar earnings and occupational status. But labor market discrimination, even for blacks whose test scores are comparable to whites, continues to play an important role. Especially for black males with high school educations, discrimination continues to be a big factor.

Evidence for this comes from the continued success of employment discrimination cases—for example, a prominent 1996 case in which Texaco settled for a payment of $176 million to black employees after taped conversations of executives revealed pervasive racist attitudes, presumably not restricted to executives of this corporation. Other evidence comes from studies finding that black workers with darker complexions have less labor market success than those with lighter complexions but identical education, age and criminal records. Still more evidence comes from studies in which blacks and whites with similar qualifications are sent to apply for job vacancies; the whites are typically more successful than the blacks. One recent study trained young, well-groomed and articulate black and white college graduates to pose as high school graduates with otherwise identical qualifications except that some reported convictions for drug possession. When these youths submitted applications for entry level jobs, the applications of whites with criminal records got positive responses more often than the applications of blacks with no criminal records.

So the expectation of black students that their academic efforts will be less rewarded than efforts of their white peers is rational for the majority of black students who do not expect to complete college. Some will reduce their academic effort as a result. We can say that they should not do so and, instead, should redouble their efforts in response to the greater obstacles they face. But as long as racial discrimination persists, the average achievement of black students will be lower than the average achievement of whites, simply because many blacks (especially males) who see that academic effort has less of a payoff will respond rationally by reducing their effort.

Helpful Policies

If we properly identify the actual social class characteristics that produce differences in average achievement, we should be able to design policies that narrow the achievement gap. Certainly, improvement of instructional practices is among these, but alone, a focus on school reform is bound to be frustrating and ultimately unsuccessful. To work, school improvement must combine with policies that narrow the social and economic differences among children. Where these differences cannot easily be narrowed, school should be redefined to cover more of the early childhood, after-school and summer times when the disparate influences of families and communities are most powerful.

Because the gap is already huge at age three, the most important new investment should probably be in early childhood programs. Pre-kindergarten classes for four-year-olds are needed, but barely begin to address the problem. The quality of early childhood programs is as important as the existence of programs themselves. Too many low-income children are parked before television sets in low-quality daycare settings. To narrow the gap, care for infants and toddlers should be provided by adults who can create the kind of intellectual environment that is typically experienced by middle-class infants and toddlers. This requires professional care-givers and low child:adult ratios.

After-school and summer experiences for lower-class children, similar to programs middle-class children take for granted, would also likely be needed to narrow the gap. This does not mean remedial programs where lower-class children get added drill in math and reading. Certainly, remediation should be part of an adequate after-school and summer program, but only a part. The advantage that middle-class children gain after school and in summer likely comes from self-confidence they acquire and awareness they develop of the world outside, from organized athletics, dance, drama, museum visits, recreational reading and other activities that develop inquisitiveness, creativity, self-discipline and organizational skills. After-school and summer programs can be expected to have a chance to narrow the achievement gap only by attempting to duplicate such experiences.

Provision of health care services to lower-class children and their families is also required to narrow the achievement gap. Some health care services are relatively inexpensive, like school vision and dental clinics that cost less than schools typically spend on many less effective reforms. A full array of health services will cost more, but likely can't be avoided if there is a true intent to raise the achievement of lower-class children.

Policies to make stable housing affordable to low-income working families with children and policies to support the earnings of such families should also be thought of as educational policies—they can have a big impact on student achievement, irrespective of school quality.

The association of social and economic disadvantage with an achievement gap has long been well known to educators. Most, however, have avoided the obvious implication: To improve lower-class children's learning, amelioration of the social and economic conditions of their lives is also needed. Calling attention to this link is not to make excuses for poor school performance. It is, rather, to be honest about the social support schools require if they are to fulfill the public's expectation that the achievement gap disappear. Only if school improvement proceeds simultaneously with social and economic reform can this expectation be fulfilled.

Article 30

Money, Schools, and Justice

Stan Karp

For the past 30 years, battles over school funding have been clogging the nation's courts. Ever since the U.S. Supreme Court declared in 1973 (San Antonio v. Rodriguez) that education was not a fundamental right protected by the U.S. Constitution, equity advocates have fought a state-by-state battle against the "savage inequalities" of school finance systems that provide sharply different levels of education to students from different class, race, and community backgrounds.

Typically, inequities have been traced to wide gaps in per-pupil spending and to finance systems that rely heavily on unequal property tax bases to fund schools. More recently, "adequacy" cases have focused on the gap between what school funding systems provide and what state and federal education standards (including the No Child Left Behind law) demand of schools. In many ways school funding systems simply mirror—and reproduce—the inequality we see all around us.

Although the details are complicated, the heart of the matter is simple: Our schools don't get enough money, and the money they do get is not distributed fairly. Beneath the legal briefs, the legislative jargon, and the complex formulas that dominate debate over school finance, lie two central questions: Will we provide schools with the resources they need to make high-quality education possible, and will we provide those resources to all children, or only some children? The answers we give will go a long way toward determining whether our society's future will be one of democratic promise or deepening division.

Since the early 1970s, more than 40 state high courts have issued decisions in school finance cases. About half have declared existing funding systems illegal or inadequate and mandated a variety of corrective measures.

But as New Jersey's Education Law Center has pointed out, "Law books are filled with wonderful paper victories which have never been implemented." While glaring disparities in school funding may persuade judges to order reform, it's been difficult to prevent governors and state legislators from limiting the impact of court orders. Restrained by separation-of-powers concerns and a conservative political climate, most courts have given states wide latitude to proceed with half measures and evasive action.

In some states, tentative steps toward equity taken under court pressure have been thwarted by the rising tide of antitax populism. California is a prime example. The state's 1972 Serrano decision was one of the first rulings that required a state to correct massive inequities among districts in educational services. Some efforts were made to equalize spending by revising aid formulas and transferring some property tax revenues from wealthier to poorer districts. But these efforts were derailed by Proposition 13, a 1978 ballot initiative that capped property taxes in one of the opening rounds in the "tax revolt" that came to shape local, state, and federal tax policy in the '80s and '90s (and which, despite promises of relief to hard-pressed taxpayers, has succeeded primarily in swelling government budget deficits, starving public services, and redirecting wealth upward). As a result, California was forced to assume a greater share of local school spending, which did lead to a degree of greater "equity" among districts. But there was also a dramatic decline in spending on schools in California relative to other states. In the '60s, California was fifth in per-pupil spending; by the end of the '90s it was 30th, well below the national average. Class size in California grew to among the highest in the nation. Because of Proposition 13 and its offspring, support for California schools tended toward "equalization" at a level that kept them in a state of perpetual budgetary crisis.

The property tax issue is both a root problem and, in some ways, a distraction from the core issues of adequacy and equity. Local property taxes still supply about 43 percent of all school funds. State support varies, but on average provides about 49 percent. The federal government's share of education spending, despite the huge impact of federal policies like NCLB, is still only about 8 percent.

Since the distribution of property in the United States has never been more unequal, and since many communities have never been more segregated by race and class, it's inevitable that schools heavily dependent on property taxes will be unequal. In fact, with more than 16,000 separate school districts, the reliance on property taxes functions as a sorting mechanism for class and race privilege, and allows pockets of "elite schooling" to exist within the public system. Any real chance of increasing and redistributing education resources requires fundamentally changing the connection between school spending and local property taxes.

In some ways, relying on local property taxes serves the agenda of the conservative forces that dominate state and local governments. When local communities must assume growing fiscal burdens for schools by more heavily taxing local residential and commercial property, it creates a strong budgetary pressure for austerity. When school budgets are presented like sacrificial lambs to hard-pressed local taxpayers, (who never get to vote on tax abatements for real estate developers or whether the Defense Department should build another aircraft carrier), the budget process is driven not by what schools and children need, but by how to keep the tax rate flat. When only a fraction of the local population has children in the schools, and an even smaller fraction usually votes on budget referendums, you have a system that works well to undercut quality education and keep communities divided. The reliance on property tax funding for schools, then, works at one level to protect privilege and at another as a vise to squeeze local budgets.

Nevertheless, there are growing efforts to find alternatives sparked by court orders, heavy local tax burdens, and the ongoing national debate about education reform. One set of fiscal reforms is geared to redistributing property tax revenues from richer districts to poorer ones. Another seeks to replace property taxes with other taxes—often sales taxes—and have the state assume a larger fraction of overall school spending. Still another set of proposals involves redefining state aid formulas so that fewer funds go to districts as "flat grants" and more through "foundation formulas," which guarantee a base level of funding for each student and are calculated in ways that promote greater equalization.

The problem is that no particular financial mechanism, in itself, guarantees either equity or quality in education. It's true that relying on some taxes, like property and sales taxes, tends to be regressive, while progressive income and corporate taxes are fairer ways to raise revenues. But choosing a particular funding mechanism does not assure that adequate funds will be available. A number of states have adopted new formulas promising better funding, only to see them cut once the higher costs became clear. If the underlying motivation is a desire to cut taxes or hold down educational spending, rather than to promote quality and equity, it may not matter what fiscal mechanism is chosen to do the job.

Another response has been to try to define what an "adequate" education means, and then peg funding formulas to the cost of providing it. Here again, debate persists over what level of educational services the state is obligated to provide for all.

This tension is reflected in New Jersey's Abbott decisions, which are arguably the most progressive rulings for poor urban schools in the history of school finance cases. The case takes its name from an alphabetical list of families who sued the state on behalf of their children, and initially it covered familiar territory. The New Jersey Supreme Court ruled that the state's system of school funding, which relies heavily on unequal property tax bases in nearly 600 separate districts, denied children in urban areas equal access to the "thorough and efficient" education guaranteed by the state's constitution. The Education Law Center documented gross inequality and pressing need in urban districts, and the court established unequivocally that it was the state's obligation to redress this inequality.

Where Abbott really blazed new ground was in the standard it set for this equity mandate. Throughout long years of litigation, the court repeatedly pressed the state to define the essential elements of a "thorough and efficient" education. Repeatedly, successive state administrations avoided this request, fearing that a generous definition would obligate them to provide such resources to poor districts, while a low estimate would require explaining why the state's most successful districts were spending much more (a gap that would call attention to the very inequality the court was seeking to address.)

The state tried changing the subject from "money" to "standards." It adopted "core curriculum content standards" and argued that if all districts implemented these standards, all students would receive an equally adequate education. Essentially, the Court responded: nice try, but no sale. Standards may be helpful in defining educational expectations and outcomes, it argued, but they are not a substitute for the programs, staff, and resources needed to reach them. When the court looked closely at the funding formula passed by the state legislature to support the new standards, the numbers looked suspiciously like political calculations designed to keep state school aid at or near existing levels without redressing the record of inequality the court had before it.

Frustrated by the state's evasions, the New Jersey high court ultimately devised its own formula. It took as its equity standard the level of spending in the state's richest and most successful school districts. Arguing, plausibly, that these districts obviously knew what it took for kids to succeed educationally, the court ordered the state to raise per pupil spending in the poorest urban districts to the average level of the 130 richest. And citing deeper social problems and the cumulative effects of concentrated poverty, the court ordered "supplemental funding" in poor districts for programs like full-day pre-K, summer school and tutoring, above and beyond parity for regular educational programs.

Abbott remains, "the first decision in the history of school finance reform to establish an equality standard for the allocation of education resources to poor urban children." Moreover, the court's decision was phrased in striking language that made clear the implications of the social problems it was addressing. "The fact is that a large part of our society is disintegrating, so large a part that it cannot help but affect the rest. Everyone's future is at stake, and not just the poor's," it wrote.

This extraordinary decision opened up a new era of reform in New Jersey's urban districts. While unending battles over implementation and budgetary issues continue, there has also been significant progress since Abbott funding started to flow in the late 1990s. Over 40,000 3- and 4-year-olds now attend high-quality, full-day pre-K and kindergarten programs. The math and language test score gap between urban and suburban 4th graders has been cut in half. New Jersey boasts the highest high school graduation rates in the country, including the highest rates for African American and Hispanic students, though significant gaps among groups and communities remain.

But while Abbott brought long overdue equity to the 31 poor urban districts that were parties to the case, it did not fix the state's overall school finance system. More than 400 "middle districts" remain squeezed by property tax formulas and perpetual state budget crisis. Poor rural districts and surrounding "Abbott rim" districts have had little success gaining access to the same levels of funding.

In fact, New Jersey's experience underscores the contradiction between equity goals and school funding systems based on local property taxes. The state is among the highest spenders on education and has the best funding levels for poor schools. But it ranks 41st out of 50 states in the total share of local school costs picked up at the state level: about 40 percent. Because the Abbott mandates directed a larger portion of this state aid to the poorest districts, suburban and rural districts were pitted in competition for an increasingly inadequate pool of state funds. State aid to non-Abbott districts has remained flat for five years, making them more dependent than ever on raising local property taxes, which are now the highest in the nation. Unless New Jersey adopts a new school funding formula that significantly increases state share and reduces reliance on local property taxes, sustaining both the Abbott commitments and the state's status as a leader in educational achievement will be increasingly difficult.

Almost monthly, a prominent academic or government agency issues a report claiming that public education is vitally important to some aspect of our nation's future from global competitiveness to national security to multicultural harmony. But the main prerequisite for improving this critical social institution is a funding system that provides excellent schooling for all kids through sustainable and fair tax policies. This means moving away from systems that rely on local property taxes and toward regional, state, and federal funding sources.

To really make good on promises of educational equity and excellence will take tens of billions of dollars over many years, the kind of sums that have been poured into the military for decades. In 2005-06, total K-12 education spending in the U.S. was about $500 billion. The most recently proposed military budget for FY 2008 is $622 billion. Public and private reports have documented a need for more than $300 billion in construction and renovation of K-12 facilities (costs that are generally not included in the per-pupil expenditures that are the focus of most equalization efforts). And putting aside for the moment the many dubious aspects of the No Child Left Behind act, studies indicate that to even approach NCLB's fanciful goal of 100 percent proficiency for all students on state tests by 2014 would require an annual increase in school spending of about $130 billion above current levels, about ten times the current size of Title I, the largest federal education program.

Only a national effort to reform social spending and tax policies can generate such resources. That means public campaigns to put new state and federal tax policies behind the nation's lofty educational rhetoric. It also means broader public efforts to reorder the nation's social priorities. That, after all, is what excellence and equity in school funding is ultimately all about.

Article 31

Getting the Lead Out

Erik Ness

Colleen Moore is tapping her finger. It's her right index finger, and it travels up and down with the precision of a metronome.

She's not nervous, impatient, or compulsive. She's demonstrating the finger-tapping test, which illuminates the loss of function that occurs when someone has been poisoned by lead, mercury, or organophosphate pesticides.

"You look at the frequency at which people can tap for given periods of time," explains Moore. "If you are toxified, you won't be able to do that for very long."

Moore is a developmental psychologist at the University of Wisconsin-Madison. Her new book, *Silent Scourge: Children, Pollution and Why Scientists Disagree*, catalogs a disturbing body of evidence showing that environmental pollution puts an increasing and measurable burden on the education of American children. The book focuses on how six pollutants-lead, mercury, PCBs, pesticides, noise, and radioactive and chemical wastes-hamper children's ability to develop and learn.

Children exposed to these pollutants experience consequences both subtle and profound. "These types of pollution are usually silent and insidious," she writes. "The effects … are revealed by carefully constructed psychological assessments of memory, attention, learning, motor skills, intelligence, personality, emotion, and other characteristics."

Yet society does not control these substances with kids in mind. Many of today's environmental regulations are based largely on studies involving adult biology and adult maladies. Existing research is overlooked and marginalized by the political climate of environmental science, while many critical questions go unanswered for lack of requisite funding and clout.

This raises another important societal question: How can politicians- including the Bush administration, which claims to care enough about the structure and performance of public education to dramatically rewrite education policy-ignore so much science that speaks to the very question of why some children can't learn? Coal miners used to bring

"Getting the Lead Out" by Erik Ness, Reprinted with permission from *Rehinking Schools*, Winter 2003. www.rethinkingschools.org.

canaries into the mines because they were more sensitive than humans to the deadly methane gases found in coal seams. When the canaries died, it was time to get out of the mine.

"We're looking at the wrong thing," Moore admonishes. "Children are like canaries."

Leaden

Proving any connection between the wide range of potential pollutants and a wide range of educational difficulties is a nightmare for scientists, educators, and parents alike.

Lead poisoning provides perhaps the clearest evidence of individual harm. No reputable physician can dispute that even small amounts of lead can reduce intellectual functioning and diminish the capacity of a child to learn. Much of this damage is permanent. And while lead poisoning is in decline, the Centers for Disease Control estimates that some 300,000 children in the United States are poisoned by lead every year, mostly poor children of color.

Lead has long been known as a hazard. Between 1909 and 1934, 11 European nations and Cuba recognized lead's danger and banned or restricted its use in interior paint. But in the United States, paint companies fought regulation, even touting the value of lead in advertising targeted at children.

Lead use became more widespread with its addition to gasoline. In 1925, even after public health doctors sounded the alarm and the surgeon general convened a commission to examine the public-health implications of leaded gasoline, the commission ruled in favor of industry on the dubious strength of a few poorly done studies showing no ill-effects. (The commission also recommended that Congress fund further study, but that never happened.) The case laid the basis for modern environmental policy, in which the burden of proof rests most heavily on the polluted, not the polluter. It took another five decades to amass the data necessary to change the status quo. Lead in gasoline was not phased out until the 1970s and 1980s; it remained in paint until 1978.

Lead was not a trivial additive to paint. Until the 1950s, as much as half, by weight, of a can of paint was lead. Coat by coat, room by room, house by house, America's housing stock became increasingly toxic. As the housing stock has aged, outright decay and renovation keep the lead in circulation, through paint chips and lead-laden dust. It takes only a grain or two of lead a day to poison a child. Those aged six months to five years are most at risk, either by directly ingesting peeling paint, or through putting hands tainted with lead dust in their mouths.

There are no clear-cut symptoms for lead poisoning; only a blood test can unmask the demon. Lead inhibits a child's body from absorbing iron, a basic building block of development in the bones and nervous system, including the brain. It also mimics calcium, and can be incorporated at critical junctions in neural transmitters that affect both brain function and sensory perception such as hearing or sight. A lead-damaged nervous system can lead to a variety of other problems including learning disabilities, ADHD, increased aggression, drug use, even a greater likelihood of criminal behavior. This may sound like a stereotypical rap sheet, but in fact all of these symptoms are linked to lead poisoning by a significant and growing body of science. [For more on the science of lead, follow the link at www. rethinking schools.org.]

A great deal of the research on the effects of lead has focused on children's scores on IQ tests. Moore says the tests can provide important data, but it's possible to make the case against lead without them. For example, an important paper by University of Pittsburgh researcher Herbert Needleman relies on a variety of other tests: symbol-digit substitution, hand-eye coordination, finger tapping, pattern memory and comparison, vocabulary, serial-digit learning, mood scales, and more. Still, in the world of lead poisoning research, the IQ test remains important: It allows scientists to evaluate impacts on a larger scale, and it's part of the regulatory and policy framework of local, state, and federal governments. For example, though a reduction of 4-5 IQ points is not disastrous in a single poisoned child, that IQ reduction in a population will increase by 50 percent the number of children who qualify for special education.

"If you have a toxin that creates a difference in IQ scores, then it's done something," says Moore. "Exactly what, and what the biological processes are is another question, but it has done something. Everyone agrees on that."

Failing Schools

Under the cover of these individual tragedies lies a more disturbing idea: Lead poisoning in enough children can lead to the symptoms of a failing school. "[A] host of social problems, including 'failing schools,' represent symptoms of lead ingestion by children during their first three years of life," argues Mike Martin of the Arizona School Boards Association. Martin spent a year and a half digging through the public health and education literature trying to examine the question in more detail. He found that the idea that lead poisoning could be an important component of educational dysfunction has been floating around for some time. More than 10 years ago, Newsweek put lead on its cover and quoted Bailus Walker, dean of public health at the University of Oklahoma and former commissioner of public health in Massachusetts: "The education community has not really understood the dimensions of this because we don't see kids falling over and dying of lead poisoning in the classroom. But there's a very large number of kids who find it difficult to do analytical work or [even] line up in the cafeteria because their brains are laden with lead."

Eight years later, in 1999, Jacquelyne Faye Jackson, a research associate at the Institute of Human Development at the University of California, Berkeley was compelled to ask:

"Where are the voices of educators in this policy debate? After all, it is educators who will face the formidable challenge of trying to prepare future generations of African-American and other minority children for productive life in the 21st century after society has allowed those children to suffer ongoing lead exposure at levels known to undermine their educational potential."

Patti Peplinski, a special education teacher at the Broad Street Academy in Milwaukee, recalls her earlier ignorance when it comes to lead. As a young teacher, she would pass out pamphlets to parents about lead poisoning and consider her job done. "I started teaching around the same time that the lead poisoning laws were changing," she says. Like many people, she thought the problem had been solved. "I didn't realize there was anything that I could personally do about it."

Then one day a child came to her who had been diagnosed with a pervasive developmental disorder. The case didn't make sense to her: He had a lot of skills, including knowing his ABCs, but at age two he had changed. She began to do some research, then ordered a lead test. The next day, the boy was admitted to the hospital with blood lead levels six times the current standard.

"The dots began to connect themselves," says Peplinski, as she realized that a whole lot more of her students were probably suffering the effects of lead poisoning on one level or another. If that wasn't enough, another five year old showed up one day, also lead poisoned. What hurt the most was that she had met the boy when he was an infant, on a home visit for the boy's brother, who also showed some symptoms of lead poisoning. She had talked to the mother, but that clearly had not been sufficient. "Things could have been different for that child," she laments.

Peplinski has become a hard-core lead activist, working with parents, public health professionals, and even writing a K-12 curriculum on lead poisoning prevention. She keeps one folder filled with news clippings about failing schools and falling test scores.

"I don't blame everything on lead, but if you take lead in combination with other factors, lead is the one thing we can control," she says. "We can't control the poverty. We can't control if there are drugs and alcohol. We can't control a lot of the other environmental issues. Lead poisoning is something we can control."

While knowledgeable professionals feel certain that lead poisoning is a factor in many failing schools, the proof is, as yet, inconclusive. Lyke Thompson, Director of the Center for Urban Studies at Wayne State University in Detroit, is working to make the connection. Using health department data from the state of Michigan, he was able to match known cases of lead poisoning with school districts. Then he found an association between the number of lead poisoned kids and a school district's scores on state achievement tests.

He then focused on elementary schools in Grand Rapids, Mich., and matched the afflicted kids to their schools. Again there was an association. "There is a tendency for those places where there are large quantities of lead poisoned kids to also be places where schools are being found deficient," says Thompson.

"There can't be any question from the medical literature anymore," argues Thompson. "Whichever variable you want to look at, lead leads to a decline. It leads to a decline in intelligence, it leads to a decline in achievement, [and] it leads to an increase in misbehavior. Does that then surface at an aggregate level? Does it affect overall school district performance? Is it part and parcel of the failing schools phenomenon? What I'm finding in preliminary statistical work is that it is." Preliminary, he stresses-more research on a wider scale is needed.

Environmental Racism

Rhonda Anderson, an environmental justice organizer for the Sierra Club in Detroit is graphic about the burden on the children of her community. "It's standing over us like a pit bull chomped down on us, and we are just having to drag it along with us."

Detroit is particularly hard hit. Its lead problem catapulted to a higher level of scrutiny last winter when the Detroit Free Press rolled out the results of a seven-month investigation. While the lead paint problem was significant, with remediation largely ineffective, the newspaper unearthed another source of lead. The paper commissioned its own soil tests around a defunct lead smelter and found 10 locations with lead levels exceeding the Environmental Protec-tion Agency's danger level of 400 parts per million. The EPA knew about the soil contamination but did nothing. The paper concluded that the "nation's lead strategy is often snarled in bureaucracy and too limited in its scope."

According to a report from Environmental Health Perspectives:

Detroit's citizens are heavily hit with the consequences of pollution and poor environmental policies. For example, one out of three Detroit children under age five who are tested have lead poisoning (defined by Centers for Disease Control guidelines as 10 micrograms/deciliter). This rate is four times the national average-and only an estimated 10 percent of children in the area have been tested. Rates of asthma in Detroit are among the highest of affected urban areas in the country: A 1996 study published in Pediatrics found that, of 380 children in two Detroit schools, 14 percent had active, diagnosed asthma.

Lead poisoning can afflict anybody, but lead exposure varies dramatically along income, racial, and ethnic divides.

"In the 1980s African Americans under the age of five had seven times the chance of high lead exposure as middle-class or upper-income whites. Now that number is 16 times," reports Moore. "Everybody's exposure is lower on average, but where we haven't cleaned it up is in the inner-city and sub-standard housing." Chicago, Providence, St. Louis, Philadelphia, Baltimore, New York-any area with housing stock built before 1978-is susceptible to lead poisoning.

It's environmental racism, pure and simple, says Anderson. "The problems that we're presently experiencing in the city of Detroit in regards to test scores, dropout rates, and even violence, I believe have a lot to do with the degree of not only lead poisoning, but other environmental issues as well," she says. "Our children are up against so much it's unbelievable. It's unfair. It's a crime. We should all be very, very embarrassed."

Donele Wilkins, executive director of Detroiters Working for Environ-mental Justice, works full time just to put these inequities on the table. She believes lead poisoning is one of the biggest problems in the Detroit School system. "For a long time, special education teachers have known there's been a problem. When we interface, the light bulbs come on, and they begin to think, 'I'll bet our kids are lead poisoned. They have these behavioral problems, they can't sit still in the classroom, and their attention spans are really short. They just can't learn. It has to be more than not getting the proper support in their homes. There has to be something else going on.' Because they see it in the classroom, they're on the front lines."

"If you do not bring in this question of exposure to certain contaminants like lead when you're talking about school reform, you'll never resolve the problem," she says. "You've got to remove the hazard. This is a preventable disease."

Dr. Sandra Screen, director of psychological assessment for the Detroit Public School system, is more equivocal about the larger impacts of lead. Her co-workers are very aware of the problem, she says. "We do have an increase in children that have significant cognitive deficits, as opposed to the past 15 years. We have more children that need specialized attention. We need more teachers, when there is already a shortage of teachers." But where those deficits come from is hard to say. "There are a myriad of problems that children encounter before entering school," she says, and even if there is lead poisoning, a simple test does not address the problem.

Nationwide from 1988 to 1999 special education enrollments grew 33 percent while general enrollments climbed 15 percent. The increasing role and cost of special education should give an incentive to policy makers to find out why special education is growing so quickly and why minority students are over-represented. Many factors are involved, from racial stereotyping, to language barriers, to standardized testing. But a National Academy of Sciences committee charged with investigating why more minorities end up in special education pointed to lead as part of the problem. "We know that minority children are disproportionately poor, and poverty is associated with higher rates of exposure to harmful toxins, including lead, alcohol, and tobacco in early stages of development."

"Environmental pollution is a double-edged issue," says Claire Barnett of the Healthy Schools Network. "On one side of the edge, they've got skyrocketing enrollments of kids who are already adversely impacted. They're arriving in pre-K programs, special education, or in regular kindergarten with learning disabilities, autism, behavioral disorders, asthma-all of which are linked to environmental pollutants, some of them actually caused by environmental pollutants."

"At the same time," Barnett continues, "all of those pollutants which are known causes or triggers are also present in schools. Schools have plenty of lead to go around. They also have plenty of asthma triggers to go around."

What Can Be Done?

Sometime in 2004 a scientific advisory panel will consider a proposal to further lower exposure limits to lead. The ruling should be controversial, in part because the Bush Administration insisted on adding a doctor who has provided expert testimony on behalf of paint companies fighting a lead poisoning lawsuit in Connecticut.

Colleen Moore argues the real decision is not scientific but moral: "Protecting children from pollution is plainly an ethical choice," she says. "Officials talk as if science will give us an exact answer to problems. But science always entails some uncertainty, and it's very important to realize that in environmental areas because it impacts the policy," she explains. "Science doesn't make policy. Science can't make policy. The best science should be a part of policy. But the question of how much exposure to any pollutant or negative environmental influence is too much is plainly an ethical question."

Milwaukee teacher Patti Peplinski believes teachers can make a difference by using the same approach that they use for fire prevention: talk about it in the classroom. [See "Teaching About Toxins," page 22.] "It's common knowledge now to stop, drop, and roll. I want lead poisoning prevention to be the same way." And she has written a K-12 curriculum to do just that. (See sidebar, page 20.) "Teach younger kids to stay away from peeling paint, and wash your hands before you eat. Teach older kids why it's dangerous, what to look out for." She proudly relates the story of seeing a former student who told her that he still remembered her lesson about staying away from peeling paint.

Martin, of the Arizona School Boards Association, acknowledges that public schools-especially so-called failing schools-are fighting for their lives. "Politicians have indulged in a frenzy of school bashing over the past few years," he says. "I fear that the current social and educational climates are too preoccupied with intimidating individual students and teachers to give much attention to something that implicates societal responsibility for failing schools." He hopes the new science of lead's effect on the brain will force policy makers to "re-examine some social issues through a new prism."

"The upshot is that we may be able to make more impact on improving school performance through improving housing than through any of these administrative reorganizations that are supposed to make schools better," says Lyke Thompson. "We don't know whether those things work. But I can say, tentatively, there is an association between lead poisoning and school performance."

"We know enough about lead poisoning from the medical literature alone that we should be taking action to deal with lead poisoning so that all the children in our country have the full chance to succeed," says Thompson. "In Michigan, estimates are that it would take $10 billion to deal with the old lead paint in our housing. We're spending $87 billion in Iraq instead. The priorities need to be reconsidered, substantially."

Article 32

At Many Colleges, the Rich Kids Get Affirmative Action

Daniel Golden

Despite her boarding-school education and a personal tutor, Maude Bunn's SAT scores weren't high enough for a typical student to earn admission to Duke University.

But Ms. Bunn had something else going for her—coffeemakers. Her Bunn forebears built a fortune on them and, with Duke hoping to woo her wealthy parents as donors, she was admitted.

Afterward, her parents promptly became co-chairmen of a Duke fund-raising effort aimed at other Duke parents. "My child was given a gift, she got in, and now I'm giving back," says Maude's mother, Cissy Bunn, who declines to say how much the family has contributed to the university.

Most universities acknowledge favoring children of alumni who support their alma mater. But to attract prospective donors, colleges are also bending admissions standards to make space for children from rich or influential families that lack longstanding ties to the institutions. Through referrals and word-of-mouth, schools identify applicants from well-to-do families. Then, as soon as these students enroll, universities start soliciting gifts from their parents.

Duke says it has never traded an admission for a donation. "There's no quid pro quo, no bargains have been struck," says Peter Vaughn, director of development communications. While it won't comment on individual cases, the university notes that financial gifts from parents are used to update facilities and provide financial aid, among other things.

The formal practice of giving preference to students whose parents are wealthy—sometimes called "development admits"—has implications for the legal challenge to affirmative action, which the U.S. Supreme Court will hear April 1 [2003]. Special admissions treatment for the affluent has racial overtones, at least indirectly. Reflecting the distribution

235

of wealth in America, the vast majority of major donors to higher education are white. Defenders of minority preference say such advantages for white applicants are precisely why affirmative action is still needed.

Top schools ranging from Stanford University to Emory University say they occasionally consider parental wealth in admission decisions. Other elite schools, such as Massachusetts Institute of Technology, say parental means don't influence them. "I understand why universities leverage parent contacts to enrich themselves," says Marilee Jones, dean of admissions at MIT. "If somebody's offering them a check, why not take it? But I honestly think it's out of control."

While children of the wealthy have long had advantages getting into colleges, a look at how "development" admissions works at Duke shows how institutionalized the process has become at some major universities.

Under-endowed compared with rivals such as Harvard, Princeton and Stanford, Duke has been particularly aggressive in snaring donors through admissions breaks. Widely considered one of the nation's top ten universities, Duke accepts 23% of its applicants and turns down more than 600 high-school valedictorians a year. Three-fourths of its students score above 1320 out of a perfect 1600 on the SATs.

Yet in recent years, Duke says it has relaxed these standards to admit 100 to 125 students annually as a result of family wealth or connections, up from about 20 a decade ago. These students aren't alumni children and were tentatively rejected, or wait-listed, in the regular admissions review. More than half of them enroll, constituting an estimated 3% to 5% of Duke's student body of 6,200.

The strategy appears to be paying off. For the last six years, Duke says it has led all universities nationwide in unrestricted gifts to its annual fund from non-alumni parents: about $3.1 million in 2001–2002. A university fund-raising campaign recently met its $2 billion goal. While 35% of alumni donate to Duke, 52% of parents of last year's freshman class contributed to the university—besides paying $35,000 in tuition and room and board.

Students admitted for development reasons graduate at a higher rate than the overall student body, Duke says, although their grades are slightly lower. These applicants are held to the same lesser standard as some top athletes; not whether they can excel, but whether they can graduate. "There's never been a case where I think the student can't be successful at Duke, and the student is admitted," says admissions director Christoph Guttentag.

Caroline Diemar, a Duke senior, says she favors maintaining minority preference for college admissions because she knows from experience that well-connected white students get a boost too. The daughter of an investment banker, she applied early to Duke despite an 1190 SAT score. Her candidacy was deferred to the spring.

She then buttressed her application with recommendations from two family friends who were Duke donors, and she was accepted. "I needed something to make me stand out," says Ms. Diemar, a sociology major with a 3.2 grade point average, below the 3.4 average of the senior class. "Everybody at Duke has something that got them in." The lesson she learned: "Networking is how you go about everything."

After she enrolled, Duke recruited Ms. Diemar's parents to serve as co-chairmen of a fund-raising effort. Her father, Robert Diemar, declined to say how much he has given to Duke. "We support all of our five children's schools," said Mr. Diemar, a Princeton alumnus. He said Duke accepted his daughter on merit.

The practice of giving preference to the children of potential donors has caused fissures on Duke's campus, with some worrying that it dilutes the student body's intellectual vitality and undermines racial and economic diversity. In November 2000, a report to the trustees by a university committee on admissions called for a one-third cut in applicants accepted for development reasons. Mr. Guttentag says he plans to reduce such admissions to about 65 this year to achieve "greater flexibility" in shaping next fall's freshman class.

Duke President Nannerl O. Keohane thinks the Supreme Court should uphold affirmative action because preferences for children of potential donors is "disproportionately favorable to white students.... The two are definitely linked, and it seems odd to me to allow one sort of preference, but not the other."

The University of Michigan, defendant in the affirmative action case before the Supreme Court, wants to continue to allow preferential treatment for minorities. It also gives preferential admissions treatment to children of potential donors—but only if they're white or Asian.

Discretionary Points

Under the 150-point "Selection Index" Michigan uses for undergraduate admissions, a review committee may award 20 "discretionary" points to children of donors, legislators, faculty members and other key supporters. Minorities under-represented in higher education—Hispanics, African-Americans and Native Americans—qualify for an automatic 20 points, but they are ineligible for the discretionary points. The university says less than 1% of admitted students receive this edge.

The late Terry Sanford, Duke president from 1969 to 1985, practiced donor preference on a large scale. Mr. Sanford, a gregarious former North Carolina governor, used his wide circle of contacts in business, politics and the media to elevate Duke from a regional to a national university. According to Keith Brodie, Duke's president emeritus, Mr. Sanford would personally meet each year with the admissions and development directors to ensure special attention for 200 of his friends' children applying to Duke. More than 100 would ultimately enroll.

As president from 1985 to 1993, Dr. Brodie says, he removed himself from the admissions process, resisted lobbying by some trustees, and trimmed the number of underqualified students admitted due to donor preference to 20 a year. "A Duke education is too valuable an asset to squander," says Dr. Brodie, a professor of psychiatry, who was criticized as president for a lack of fund-raising zeal. "University presidents are under greater pressure than ever to raise money," he adds. "I suspect many of them have turned to admissions to help that process."

Harold Wingood, who was senior associate director of admissions under Dr. Brodie, recalls that 30 to 40 students per year were upgraded from "rejected" to "wait-list," or from "wait-list" to "admit" due to their family ties. "We'd take students in some cases with SAT scores 100 points below the mean, or just outside the top 15% of their class," says Mr. Wingood, now dean of admissions at Clark University in Worcester, Mass. "They weren't slugs, but they weren't strong enough to get in on their own."

The numbers have increased under Ms. Keohane, Duke's current president. Duke says it admitted about 125 non-alumni children in 1998, and again in 1999, who had been tentatively rejected or wait-listed prior to considering family connections. It accepted 99 such students in 2000. Similar data aren't available for 2001 or 2002, the school says.

Ms. Keohane says she didn't intentionally increase the number of wealthy applicants given a leg up. She says "it is possible that the numbers drifted upward" during the recent $2 billion-fund-raising campaign because "more people in development expressed interest in candidates. But this was certainly not a policy directive even a conscious choice."

The system at Duke works this way: Through its own network and names supplied by trustees, alumni, donors and others, the development office identifies about 500 likely applicants with rich or powerful parents who are not alumni. (Children of major alumni donors are given similar preference in a separate process.) It cultivates them with campus tours and basic admissions advice; for instance, applying early increases their chances. It also relays the names to the admissions office, which returns word if any of the students forget to apply—so development can remind them.

The development office then winnows the initial 500 into at least 160 high-priority applicants. Although these names are flagged in the admissions-office computer, admissions readers evaluate them on merit, without regard to family means. About 30 to 40 are accepted, the others tentatively rejected or wait-listed. During an all-day meeting in March, Mr. Guttentag and John Piva Jr., senior vice president for development, debate these 120 cases, weighing their family's likely contribution against their academic shortcomings.

In her 2001 book, *Admissions Confidential*, former Duke admissions officer Rachel Toor recalled that most admissions officers "hated to see these kids get in" because they were "the weakest part of our applicant pool." Nevertheless, most of the 120 students are admitted.

Once these children of privilege enroll, the development office enlists their parents as donors and fund raisers. According to Dr. Brodie, Duke's parent program originated as a forum for parent concerns about safety issues, but it has evolved into a fund-raising vehicle.

A committee of more than 200 non-alumni parents provides its volunteer army for the four classes currently at Duke. Committee members usually give at least $1,000 to Duke, and the eight co-chairmen and the national chairman much more—including at least two seven-figure gifts endowing faculty chairs.

Membership in the parents' committee is by invitation only and is overwhelmingly white. Lately, one affluent Chicago suburb—Lake Forest—has dominated its higher echelons. Lake Forest luminaries on the committee have included department-store heir Marshall Field V, who has given at least $100,000 to Duke; Paul Clark, chief executive of Icos Corp., a biotech firm; Robert DePree, chairman of corn-meal maker House-Autry Mills Inc.; and investment banker Willard Bunn III, Maude's father.

The Lake Forest couples are social friends, serve on many of the same Chicago-area boards and several sent their children to the same private elementary school, Lake Forest Country Day. They write recommendations to Duke for each other's children.

'Pretty Intimate Group'

Susan DePree, Robert's wife, describes the Duke parents committee as a "pretty intimate group" but not "clubby." She declined to say how much she and her husband have contributed to Duke, but says they solicited at least one six-figure gift from a parent-committee member.

Maude Bunn, whose family lives in Lake Forest, attended an elite boarding school in Lawrenceville, N.J., where the Bunn Library opened in 1996. She says other Lake Forest parents recommended her to Duke.

Cissy Bunn acknowledges her daughter didn't fit the academic profile of a Duke student. "She's bright, she had good grades, but she doesn't meet the superstar status," Mrs. Bunn says. "Did my normal child take the place of somebody who could really make a difference in the world? Sure, yes, to an extent. But there are so many things you can lose sleep over. I'm happy for me and my child."

Maude Bunn says she initially felt very awkward at Duke because her admission "wasn't necessarily on my own merits." But these days, the sophomore says she is thriving. "The more time I've spent here, I feel more and more confident—they didn't have to take me if they didn't think I was equal to all the other students they are admitting," she says. "I'm doing just as well as everybody I know if not better." She is studying art history and wants a career in fashion.

Now her younger sister Meg, a high-school senior, is applying to Duke. Maude says the family likes Meg's chances. "The people my mother works with for fund raising told her, 'It's really hard to get the first child in,'" she says. "After that, sisters and brothers are easier." Duke says it, like many universities, gives some preference to siblings.

Mrs. Bunn says she's not twisting anyone's arm. "I told them, 'If she's qualified at all, that would be lovely,'" she says. "If she gets in, I'd be happy to stay on the parents' committee.'"

As college admission becomes increasingly competitive, parents try to help their children's chances in any way they can. Duke accepted Jane Hetherington in 2000, despite SAT scores in the mid-1200s and what she calls "average" grades in high school. She attributes her acceptance to a "wonderful recommendation" by Norman Christensen Jr., then dean of Duke's Nicholas School of the Environment and Earth Sciences, a graduate program. She got the recommendation after one meeting with him.

At the time, her father, John Hetherington, was vice president of Westvaco Corp., a paper-products firm that had donated to the school, sponsored research there and hired some of its graduates. Mr. Hetherington asked a family friend on the school's advisory board to have the dean interview Ms. Hetherington.

Mr. Christensen, a Duke professor, says he was impressed by Ms. Hetherington's devotion to environmental studies. The student's father later reciprocated by arranging a meeting between the school's new dean and Westvaco's chief executive officer, hoping the company would increase support for the school. Nothing came of it, says Mr. Hetherington. (Westvaco merged with Mead Corp. last year.)

"I don't feel we benefited from anything you would describe as the traditional white power structure network," says Mr. Hetherington, who is now a Republican state representative in Connecticut and favors a "sunset law" for affirmative action. He doesn't think his position affected his daughter's acceptance into college. "It worked out for some reason," he says. "In all candor, we got lucky."

Part 9

Environment

Article 33

A Small Price for a Large Benefit

Robert H. Frank

Forecasts involving climate change are highly uncertain, denialists assert—a point that climate researchers themselves readily concede. The denialists view the uncertainty as strengthening their case for inaction, yet a careful weighing of the relevant costs and benefits supports taking exactly the opposite course.

Organizers of the recent climate conference in Copenhagen sought, unsuccessfully, to forge agreements to limit global warming to 3.6 degrees Fahrenheit by the end of the century. But even an increase that small would cause deadly harm. And far greater damage is likely if we do nothing.

The numbers—and there are many to choose from—paint a grim picture. According to recent estimates from the Integrated Global Systems Model at the Massachusetts Institute of Technology, the median forecast is for a climb of 9 degrees Fahrenheit by century's end, in the absence of effective countermeasures.

That forecast, however, may underestimate the increase. According to the same M.I.T. model, there is a 10 percent chance that the average global temperature will rise more than 12.4 degrees by 2100, and a 3 percent chance it will climb more than 14.4 degrees. Warming on that scale would be truly catastrophic.

Scientists say that even the 3.6-degree increase would spell widespread loss of life, so it's hardly alarmist to view the risk of inaction as frightening.

In contrast, the risk of taking action should frighten no one. Essentially, the risk is that if current estimates turn out to be wildly pessimistic, the money spent to curb greenhouse gases wouldn't have been needed to save the planet. And yet that money would still have prevented substantial damage. (The M.I.T. model estimates a zero probability of the temperature rising by less than 3.6 degrees by 2100.)

Moreover, taking action won't cost much. According to estimates by the Intergovernmental Panel on Climate Change, a tax of $80 a metric ton on carbon dioxide—or a cap-and-trade system with similar charges—would stabilize temperatures by midcentury.

243

This figure was determined, however, before the arrival of more pessimistic estimates on the pace of global warming. So let's assume a tax of $300 a ton, just to be safe.

Under such a tax, the prices of goods would rise in proportion to their carbon footprints—in the case of gasoline, for example, by roughly $2.60 a gallon.

A sudden price increase of that magnitude could indeed be painful. But if phased in, it would cause much less harm. Facing steadily increasing fuel prices, for example, manufacturers would scramble to develop more efficient vehicles.

Even from the existing menu of vehicles, a family could trade in its Ford Explorer, getting 15 miles per gallon, for a 32-m.p.g. Ford Focus wagon, thereby escaping the effect of higher gasoline prices. Europeans, many of whom already pay $4 a gallon more than Americans do for gasoline, have adapted to their higher prices with little difficulty.

In short, the cost of preventing catastrophic climate change is astonishingly small, and it involves just a few simple changes in behavior.

The real problem with the estimates is that the outcome may be worse than expected. And that's the strongest possible argument for taking action. In a rational world, that should be an easy choice, but in this case we appear to be headed in the wrong direction.

This strange state of affairs may be rooted in human psychology. As the Harvard psychologist Daniel Gilbert put it in a 2006 op-ed article in The Los Angeles Times, "Global warming is bad, but it doesn't make us feel nauseated or angry or disgraced, and thus we don't feel compelled to rail against it as we do against other momentous threats to our species, such as flag burning."

People tend to have strong emotions about topics like food and sex, and to create their own moral rules around these emotions, he says. "Moral emotions are the brain's call to action," he wrote. "If climate change were caused by gay sex, or by the practice of eating kittens, millions of protesters would be massing in the streets."

But the human brain is remarkably flexible. Emotions matter, but so does logic. Even though we did not evolve under conditions that predisposed us to become indignant about climate change, we can learn to take such risks more seriously. But that won't happen without better political leadership.

Senator James Inhofe, a Republican from Oklahoma, has said that "the claim that global warming is caused by man-made emissions is simply untrue and not based on sound science." On compelling evidence, he's wrong. Yet he and his colleagues have the power to block legislation on greenhouse gases.

WE don't know how much hotter the planet will become by 2100. But the fact that we face "only" a 10 percent chance of a catastrophic 12-degree climb surely does not argue for inaction. It calls for immediate, decisive steps.

Most people would pay a substantial share of their wealth—much more, certainly, than the modest cost of a carbon tax—to avoid having someone pull the trigger on a gun pointed at their head with one bullet and nine empty chambers. Yet that's the kind of risk that some people think we should take.

Robert H. Frank is an economist at the Johnson Graduate School of Management at Cornell University.

Article 34

Is There a Scientific Consensus on Global Warming?

www.skepticalscience.com

Scientists need to back up their opinions with research and data that survive the peer-review process. A survey of all peer-reviewed abstracts on the subject 'global climate change' published between 1993 and 2003 shows that not a single paper rejected the consensus position that global warming is man caused (Oreskes 2004). 75% of the papers agreed with the consensus position while 25% made no comment either way (focused on methods or paleoclimate analysis).

Subsequent research has confirmed this result. A survey of 3,146 earth scientists asked the question *"Do you think human activity is a significant contributing factor in changing*

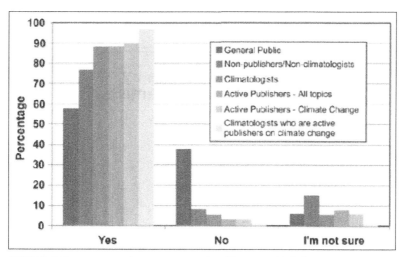

FIGURE 1 Response to the survey question "Do you think human activity is a significant contributing factor in changing mean global temperatures?" (Doran 2009) General public data come from a 2008 Gallup poll.

mean global temperatures?" (Doran 2009). More than 90% of participants had Ph.D.s, and 7% had master's degrees. Overall, 82% of the scientists answered yes. However, what are most interesting are responses compared to the level of expertise in climate science. Of scientists who were non-climatologists and didn't publish research, 77% answered yes. In contrast, 97.5% of climatologists who actively publish research on climate change responded yes. As the level of active research and specialization in climate science increases, so does agreement that humans are significantly changing global temperatures.

Most striking is the divide between expert climate scientists (97.4%) and the general public (58%). The paper concludes:

> *"It seems that the debate on the authenticity of global warming and the role played by human activity is largely nonexistent among those who understand the nuances and scientific basis of long-term climate processes. The challenge, rather, appears to be how to effectively communicate this fact to policy makers and to a public that continues to mistakenly perceive debate among scientists."*

This overwhelming consensus among climate experts is confirmed by an independent study that surveys all climate scientists who have publicly signed declarations supporting or rejecting the consensus. They find between 97% to 98% of climate experts support the consensus. Moreover, they examine the number of publications by each scientist as a measure of

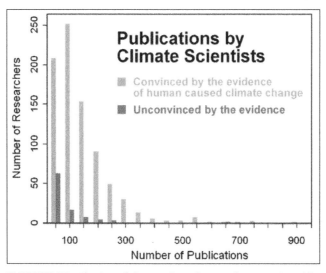

FIGURE 2 Distribution of the number of researchers convinced by the evidence of anthropogenic climate change and unconvinced by the evidence with a given number of total climate publications.

expertise in climate science. They find the average number of publications by unconvinced scientists (eg—skeptics) is around half the number by scientists convinced by the evidence. Not only is there a vast difference in the number of convinced versus unconvinced scientists, there is also a considerable gap in expertise between the two groups.

Scientific Organizations Endorsing the Consensus

The following scientific organizations endorse the consensus position that "most of the global warming in recent decades can be attributed to human activities":

- American Association for the Advancement of Science
- American Astronomical Society
- American Chemical Society
- American Geophysical Union
- American Institute of Physics
- American Meteorological Society
- American Physical Society
- Australian Coral Reef Society
- Australian Meteorological and Oceanographic Society
- Australian Bureau of Meteorology and the CSIRO
- British Antarctic Survey
- Canadian Foundation for Climate and Atmospheric Sciences
- Canadian Meteorological and Oceanographic Society
- Environmental Protection Agency
- European Federation of Geologists
- European Geosciences Union
- European Physical Society
- Federation of American Scientists
- Federation of Australian Scientific and Technological Societies

- Geological Society of America

- Geological Society of Australia

- International Union for Quaternary Research (INQUA)

- International Union of Geodesy and Geophysics

- National Center for Atmospheric Research

- National Oceanic and Atmospheric Administration

- Royal Meteorological Society

- Royal Society of the UK

The Academies of Science from 19 different countries all endorse the consensus. 11 countries have signed a joint statement endorsing the consensus position:

- Academia Brasiliera de Ciencias (Brazil)

- Royal Society of Canada

- Chinese Academy of Sciences

- Academie des Sciences (France)

- Deutsche Akademie der Naturforscher Leopoldina (Germany)

- Indian National Science Academy

- Accademia dei Lincei (Italy)

- Science Council of Japan

- Russian Academy of Sciences

- Royal Society (United Kingdom)

- National Academy of Sciences (USA) (12 Mar 2009 news release)

A letter from 18 scientific organizations to US Congress states:

"Observations throughout the world make it clear that climate change is occurring, and rigorous scientific research demonstrates that the greenhouse gases emitted by human activities are the primary driver. These conclusions are based on multiple

independent lines of evidence, and contrary assertions are inconsistent with an objective assessment of the vast body of peer-reviewed science."

The consensus is also endorsed by a Joint statement by the Network of African Science Academies (NASAC), including the following bodies:

- African Academy of Sciences
- Cameroon Academy of Sciences
- Ghana Academy of Arts and Sciences
- Kenya National Academy of Sciences
- Madagascar's National Academy of Arts, Letters and Sciences
- Nigerian Academy of Sciences
- l'Académie des Sciences et Techniques du Sénégal
- Uganda National Academy of Sciences
- Academy of Science of South Africa
- Tanzania Academy of Sciences
- Zimbabwe Academy of Sciences
- Zambia Academy of Sciences
- Sudan Academy of Sciences

Two other Academies of Sciences that endorse the consensus:

- Royal Society of New Zealand
- Polish Academy of Sciences

Article 35

Smoke, Mirrors, and Hot Air

The Union of Concerned Scientists

I n an effort to deceive the public about the reality of global warming, ExxonMobil has underwritten the most sophisticated and most successful disinformation campaign since the tobacco industry misled the public about the scientific evidence linking smoking to lung cancer and heart disease. As this report documents, the two disinformation campaigns are strikingly similar. ExxonMobil has drawn upon the tactics and even some of the organizations and actors involved in the callous disinformation campaign the tobacco industry waged for 40 years. Like the tobacco industry, ExxonMobil has:

- *Manufactured uncertainty* by raising doubts about even the most indisputable scientific evidence.

- Adopted a strategy of *information laundering* by using seemingly independent front organizations to publicly further its desired message and thereby confuse the public.

- *Promoted scientific spokespeople* who misrepresent peer-reviewed scientific findings or cherry-pick facts in their attempts to persuade the media and the public that there is still serious debate among scientists that burning fossil fuels has contributed to global warming and that human-caused warming will have serious consequences.

- *Attempted to shift the focus* away from meaningful action on global warming with misleading charges about the need for "sound science."

- *Used its extrdordinary access to the Bush administration* to block federal policies and shape government communications on global warming.

The report documents that, despite the scientific consensus about the fundamental under standing that global warming is caused by carbon dioxide and other heat-trapping emissions, ExxonMobil has funneled about $16 million between 1998 and 2005 to a network of ideological and advocacy organizations that manufacture uncertainty on the issue. Many of these organizations have an overlapping—sometimes identical—collection of

From *Smoke, Mirrors and Hot Air*, from the Union of Concerned Scientists. Reprinted by permission.

spokespeople serving as staff, board members, and scientific advisors. By publishing and republishing the non-peer-reviewed works of a small group of scientific spokespeople, ExxonMobil-funded organizations have propped up and amplified work that has been discredited by reputable climate scientists.

ExxonMobil's funding of established research institutions that seek to better understand science, policies, and technologies to address global warming has given the corporation "cover," while its funding of ideological and advocacy organizations to conduct a disinformation campaign works to confuse that understanding. This seemingly inconsistent activity makes sense when looked at through a broader lens. Like the tobacco companies in previous decades, this strategy provides a positive "pro-science" public stance for ExxonMobil that masks their activity to delay meaningful action on global warming and helps keep the public debate stalled on the science rather than focused on policy options to address the problem.

In addition, like Big Tobacco before it, ExxonMobil has been enormously successful at influencing the current administration and key members of Congress. Documents highlighted in this report, coupled with subsequent events, provide evidence of ExxonMobil's cozy relationship with government officials, which enables the corporation to work behind the scenes to gain access to key decision makers. In some cases, the company's proxies have directly shaped the global warming message put forth by federal agencies. Finally, this report provides a set of steps elected officials, investors, and citizens can take to neutralize ExxonMobil's disinformation campaign and remove this roadblock to sensible action for reducing global warming emissions.

Part 10

Health and Health Care

Article 36

A False Promise of Reform

Physicians for a National Health Program

As much as we would like to join the celebration of the House's passage of the health bill last night, in good conscience we cannot. We take no comfort in seeing aspirin dispensed for the treatment of cancer.

Instead of eliminating the root of the problem—the profit-driven, private health insurance industry—this costly new legislation will enrich and further entrench these firms. The bill would require millions of Americans to buy private insurers' defective products, and turn over to them vast amounts of public money.

The hype surrounding the new health bill is belied by the facts:

- About 23 million people will remain uninsured nine years out. That figure translates into an estimated 23,000 unnecessary deaths annually and an incalculable toll of suffering.

- Millions of middle-income people will be pressured to buy commercial health insurance policies costing up to 9.5 percent of their income but covering an average of only 70 percent of their medical expenses, potentially leaving them vulnerable to financial ruin if they become seriously ill. Many will find such policies too expensive to afford or, if they do buy them, too expensive to use because of the high co-pays and deductibles.

- Insurance firms will be handed at least $447 billion in taxpayer money to subsidize the purchase of their shoddy products. This money will enhance their financial and political power, and with it their ability to block future reform.

- The bill will drain about $40 billion from Medicare payments to safety-net hospitals, threatening the care of the tens of millions who will remain uninsured.

- People with employer-based coverage will be locked into their plan's limited network of providers, face ever-rising costs and erosion of their health benefits.

Statement "A false promise of reform" by Oliver Fein, S. Woolhandler, D. Himmelstein, M. Flowers, and Mark Almberg, March 22, 2010 from Physicians for a National Health Program, www.pnhp.org. Reprinted by permission.

Many, even most, will eventually face steep taxes on their benefits as the cost of insurance grows.

- Health care costs will continue to skyrocket, as the experience with the Massachusetts plan (after which this bill is patterned) amply demonstrates.

- The much-vaunted insurance regulations—e.g. ending denials on the basis of pre-existing conditions—are riddled with loopholes, thanks to the central role that insurers played in crafting the legislation. Older people can be charged up to three times more than their younger counterparts, and large companies with a predominantly female workforce can be charged higher gender-based rates at least until 2017.

- Women's reproductive rights will be further eroded, thanks to the burdensome segregation of insurance funds for abortion and for all other medical services.

It didn't have to be like this. Whatever salutary measures are contained in this bill, e.g. additional funding for community health centers, could have been enacted on a stand-alone basis.

Similarly, the expansion of Medicaid—a woefully underfunded program that provides substandard care for the poor—could have been done separately, along with an increase in federal appropriations to upgrade its quality.

But instead the Congress and the Obama administration have saddled Americans with an expensive package of onerous individual mandates, new taxes on workers' health plans, countless sweetheart deals with the insurers and Big Pharma, and a perpetuation of the fragmented, dysfunctional, and unsustainable system that is taking such a heavy toll on our health and economy today.

This bill's passage reflects political considerations, not sound health policy. As physicians, we cannot accept this inversion of priorities. We seek evidence-based remedies that will truly help our patients, not placebos.

A genuine remedy is in plain sight. Sooner rather than later, our nation will have to adopt a single-payer national health insurance program, an improved Medicare for all. Only a single-payer plan can assure truly universal, comprehensive and affordable care to all.

By replacing the private insurers with a streamlined system of public financing, our nation could save $400 billion annually in unnecessary, wasteful administrative costs. That's enough to cover all the uninsured and to upgrade everyone else's coverage without having to increase overall U.S. health spending by one penny.

Moreover, only a single-payer system offers effective tools for cost control like bulk purchasing, negotiated fees, global hospital budgeting and capital planning.

Polls show nearly two-thirds of the public supports such an approach, and a recent survey shows 59 percent of U.S. physicians support government action to establish national health insurance. All that is required to achieve it is the political will.

The major provisions of the present bill do not go into effect until 2014. Although we will be counseled to "wait and see" how this reform plays out, we cannot wait, nor can our patients. The stakes are too high.

We pledge to continue our work for the only equitable, financially responsible and humane remedy for our health care mess: single-payer national health insurance, an expanded and improved Medicare for All.

Oliver Fein, M.D.
President

Garrett Adams, M.D.
President-elect

Claudia Fegan, M.D.
Past President

Margaret Flowers, M.D.
Congressional Fellow

David Himmelstein, M.D.
Co-founder

Steffie Woolhandler, M.D.
Co-founder

Quentin Young, M.D.
National Coordinator

Don McCanne, M.D.
Senior Health Policy Fellow

******

Part 11

Global Perspective
and Global Issues

Article 37

Sharing the Benefits of a Productive Economy and Promoting Family-Friendly Employment Policies

Jerry Kloby

Remedies from Around the World

Many nations have employment insurance programs similar to the United States, though the details vary (e.g., length of coverage and larger payments if the unemployed worker has dependents). But overall the United States lacks a comprehensive system for coping with the economic system's tendency to discard workers. Paul Swain, a senior economist at the Organization for Economic Cooperation and Development (OECD) points out that "a number of countries have found ways to make their labor markets more flexible, without sacrificing their greater commitment to a government role in equalizing incomes" (Uchitelle 2007). In other words, according to Swain, rather than governments trying to stop creative destruction they can do more to assist the workers who are displaced or left behind. The expectations of what private employers should do can change as well. For example, in Japan, when companies are looking to relocate or to add automation that may cut jobs, they perform a type of triage—first dividends are cut, then salaries starting with the highest first. If expenses need to be cut further then the company will pursue layoffs. The expectations in Japan are such that in turn for loyalty to the company, the company is expected to be loyal to the worker by providing job security and other benefits, such as health care coverage.

In Denmark, employers are relatively free to lay off workers but workers are protected by the government, which pays them 70 percent of their lost income for up to four years. Denmark, as is the case in many OECD nations, also finances retraining and education. The Danish government spends three percent of the nation's GDP on retraining, compared with less than one percent in the United States. In the United States, the responsibility for retraining and education generally falls on the individual but the cost of higher education and/or technical schools is often prohibitive for someone who has just lost his or her job. Consequently, many people who lose their jobs are only able to undergo superficial training for a new occupation and they are unlikely to end up with a job that matches their former pay.

Many countries go much further than merely providing unemployment benefits. Well-established policies maintain a high social wage and redistribute income. Paid vacations, paid sick days, full health insurance, subsidized housing, and paid parental leave are very common among the wealthiest democratic nations. In the United States, many workers are not covered by health insurance, they may not have sick days, and some do not qualify for paid vacation time. For the most part, whether one has these benefits is simple the luck of the draw—some employers provide them, some don't. But in most other highly developed nations these are considered citizen rights and all citizens (and often alien residents) are eligible for such benefits.

The United States is the only economically advanced nation that does not guarantee its workers a yearly paid vacation. Although some American workers may get three or four weeks of paid vacation, such benefits are often the reserve of workers who have been at the same job for a long period of time, and are usually only provided by large employers. Access to paid vacation is available to an estimated 78 percent of private sector workers in the United States but the rate is much lower for low-wage workers (69 percent) than high-wage workers (88 percent). And low-wage workers receive less time off—10 days compared to 14 for high-wage workers. Only a minority of part-time workers receive any paid vacation time.

Outside the U.S., Canada and Japan have the least generous paid vacation policy, with each of those nations mandating a minimum of 10 days off. Australia and New Zealand both require employers to provide at least 20 paid vacation days. In the European Union, the Working Time Directive agreed in 1993 to set a minimum of 20 paid vacation days. Some EU countries go much further. France requires 30 days, Finland, Sweden, Norway, and Denmark require 25 and Germany 24. In addition, many unions have negotiated vacation time well above the federally mandated minimum. In Germany and Denmark, for example, the collectively negotiated average is 30 days of paid vacation. In Sweden it is 33 days, and in Italy and Luxembourg it's 28 days. Three countries go so far as to require employers to provide workers with a cash payment above their regular pay to help cover vacation expenses. Russell Shorto, an American citizen living in Holland writing in the *New York Times* tells of an unexpected deposit of $4,265 vacation money into his bank account:

> *This money materializes in the bank accounts of virtually everyone in the country just before the summer holidays; you get from your employer an amount totaling 8 percent of your annual salary, which is meant to cover plane tickets, surfing lessons, tapas: vacations. And we aren't talking about a mere*

"paid vacation"—this is on top of the salary you continue to receive during the weeks you're off skydiving or snorkeling ... even if you are unemployed you still receive a base amount of [vacation pay] from the government ...

Many countries also mandate a minimum number of paid holidays. Austria, Portugal, and Italy require employers to provide 13 paid holidays. In the United States, there is no legal minimum for paid holidays, though many workers receive them. The Bureau of Labor Statistics estimates that the average number of paid holidays for a full-time worker is seven and for a part-time worker it is just two. Again higher-wage workers and workers in large firms are more likely to benefit.

In the United States, where there is a great deal of rhetoric about family values and about how important children are, there is, paradoxically, often a "caring penalty" on those who take their family responsibilities seriously. Often this penalty falls most heavily on women. Consider, for starters, the fact that for many American women there is no paid maternity leave available to them. Although some workers employed by more generous companies are able to get some paid leave, our national law on this matter is very weak. The Family and Medical Leave Act, enacted in 1993, requires employers to grant 12 weeks of unpaid leave to eligible employees for the birth of a child or to care for an immediate family member with a serious health condition. However, the law only requires this of companies that employ at least 50 workers, which means about half of all workers are not covered by the law. One of the result of such a lax national policy is a loss of income for many workers, especially women, when they must take time off from work. In fact, the caring penalty means that many workers end up losing their jobs to take care of children and other family members. Three out of every four married mothers of school-aged children are in the workforce and an estimated 44 million Americans care for adult relatives. Yet U.S. social policy has been painfully slow in adjusting to this reality of the modern economy. One result is that forty percent of all job loss in the United States can be attributed to the need for workers to take time off to care for a sick family member.

In terms of parental leave, the United States is one of very few nations without a national paid leave policy. The International Labor Organization convention on maternity leave stipulates a minimum of 14 weeks leave. A total of 163 nations provide their citizens with paid maternity leave. As expected, the OECD nations (with the exception of the United States) lead the way in providing family support. Bulgaria permits women workers to take up to 63 weeks of paid leave to have a child. The first six weeks are at 82% of regular pay and the remainder are at 75% of full pay. Estonia provides 28 weeks of paid maternity leave, while Lithuania, Italy and Romania each provide 21 weeks. Poland, Denmark and Finland each provide 18 weeks and Germany and Japan provide 14 weeks of paid maternity leave.

However, "maternity leave" is not the only leave available for parents to take care of young children. Several countries offer "paternity leave" specifically for fathers, and many countries offer a broader "parental leave" that provides paid leave to cover a broader range of circumstances. For example, in Australia, Germany, Iceland, Norway, and Sweden, there is no separate requirement of "maternity leave." Instead, the mother's rights are integrated into a more comprehensive "parental leave" policy. Furthermore, in the interest of gender equity, several countries have "paternity leave" designed to encourage fathers to play an active role in child rearing (referred to as a "father quota"). Iceland, for example, provides up to 3 months paid leave for fathers on a "use it or lose it" basis. Finland has a similar policy.

In many cases, the most generous and comprehensive family-friendly employment policies are the parental leave policies, most of which go a long way toward not only eliminating any "caring penalty" but also toward promoting gender equity. Sweden's parental leave policy provides up to 480 days of parental leave (including a father quota of 60 days). Most of the leave is covered at 80 percent of regular pay. The leave can be used for many purposes including reducing the work day in order to care for one's children after school. Swedish parents are eligible for parental leave coverage up until their youngest child turns eight and parents of adoptive children have the same benefits. Sweden also provides additional leave entitlements that include temporary leave to care for sick children up to age 15. Parents can take up to 120 days off at 80 percent of full pay per child per year (OECD Family Database).

In the United States, some states have enacted paid family leave policies that provide a little bit of help for workers who need time off. In 2004, California was the first to do so. The state provides a six week leave at 55 percent of salary. New Jersey and the state of Washington followed with similar laws. However, implementing such a policy on a state by state basis may never succeed in providing coverage for all working Americans and the differences in the policy from state to state will mean inequitable treatment for the nation's citizens.

The family-friendly employment policies enacted by so many nations are important legislation tailored to today's economy and the modern workforce. The policies help take financial stress off married couples, provide economic support that keeps children out of poverty, and create a society where working people are valued. Likewise, economic inequality is reduced and social solidarity is strengthened. In addition, there are other hard to measure benefits that are derived from social policies that help keep all families and individuals on more secure economic footing.

Relatively low levels of anxiety about economic security may be one reason that people in Denmark were found to be the most satisfied with their lives. Research has clearly demonstrated that a prosperous economy and authentic democracy are associated with high levels of well-being. Denmark offers its citizens a broad range of social benefits from generous unemployment compensation, to inexpensive health care, to free tuition at colleges and universities. In fact, many Danes who pursue a higher education are paid a salary for their efforts. Denmark also has the lowest degree of income inequality of all nation's measured. The University of Leicester "World Map of Happiness, which ranked Denmark number 1," used a variety of criteria to rate life satisfaction in 178 countries. The United States ranked 23rd.

A similar study examined the well-being of children in 21 wealthy nations. The UN children's organization, Unicef, examined relative poverty, educational and health standards, sexual behavior, and children's relationships with friends and parents. The Netherlands ranked highest on the child well-being scale, followed by Sweden, Denmark and Finland. Children in the Netherlands also scored the highest on the subjective well-being scale. The last ranked nation in terms of overall child well-being was the United Kingdom, just slightly behind the United States. Both the U.K. and the U.S. scored in the bottom third in five of the six dimensions studied.

Article 38

More than Welcome: Families Come First in Sweden

Brittany Shahmehri

Recently, my husband's laptop needed repair, and he called technical support to arrange for service. When he explained the problem, the phone representative at the multinational computer company said, "I'm going to recommend level-two support, but the technician will have to call you tomorrow to schedule an appointment. Today he's home with his sick kid."

When we still lived in the US, my husband might have wondered what a sick child had to do with his laptop. But last year we moved to Sweden, where parents not only are legally entitled to stay home with their sick children, but also get paid for doing so. Most amazing is that there's no shame in it. For fathers as well as mothers, it's assumed that when your child is sick, you are going to take care of him or her. That's more important than fixing someone's laptop on the spot. The computer company knows it and my husband's employer knows it. In almost every circumstance, the laptop can wait a day.

Even visiting tourists can see that Sweden has a child-friendly culture. A stroller logo is as common as the wheelchair logo in public restrooms and elevators. Buses accommodate strollers, and trains have places for children to play. (By the way, the children ride free.) Gas stations often have tiny working toilets as well as the standard toilets, as do zoos and other places that cater to children. Amazing, I thought, the first time I visited.

But on closer examination, all of this is just window dressing. Sweden has one of the most generous parental leave policies in the world. Parents of each newborn or newly adopted child share 450 paid days to care for that child. The childcare system is of extremely high quality, offers a wide range of options, and is subsidized for all families. Parents are legally entitled to work reduced hours at their current jobs until their children reach the age of eight (when they formally enter school), and can take up to 60 paid days to care for sick children. Toss in protected time to nurse a baby on the job and tuition-free universities, and to an American working parent, it sounds like utopia!

Why Such Widespread Support?

According to Dr. Irene Wennemo, a Swedish family policy expert, the question of support-ing families in Sweden is generally framed in terms of how the state should implement policies and what level of resources should be invested. "It's very accepted here that the state should be responsible for the living standard of children," Wennemo told me. "Children aren't a private thing; society has a responsibility for part of the cost."

Most of the reasons for this are self-evident. Children are members of society. It's not good for people, especially children, to live in poverty. Children should have equal oppor-tunities. It's necessary for society that people have children so it should be easy to combine working and having children. It's good for men and women to have equal access to both work and family.

"If you want a society in which it is accepted that both partners go out and work, then you have to take people's needs seriously," says Gunnar Andersson, a sociologist at Lund University. "Both school and child care must be really good, and there must be much more flexibility for all."[1]

"This is what our parents worked for," explains Anneli Elfwén, a Swedish midwife with two young sons. In the 1950s most Swedish women stayed home with the children. When women began to enter the workforce in the late 1960s, the need for stronger family policy became clear. The modern versions of parental leave policy and subsidized child care were implemented in the early 1970s and met with wide popular support. When I asked Elfwén why support for family policy was so widespread, she laughed, "Maybe we get it in the breastmilk. It's very natural for us."

How It Works

When Elfwén's first son, Simon, was born in 1995, Elfwén was entitled to the same paren-tal leave benefits that are offered to all Swedish families. She and her husband could share the 450 days of leave as they pleased, though one month was reserved for her, and one for her husband; and if either of them chose not to take their individual time, they would forfeit it.

One of the most unique aspects of Swedish parental leave is that it can be taken part time. Elfwén and her husband used the flexibility in their schedules to extend the time Simon spent at home with one of his parents. Between paid leave, flexible jobs, and the help of grandparents, the Elfwéns juggled a two-career, two-parent family. When their second son, Olle, was born in 1998, he too was entitled to 450 days of his parents' time. This made it possible for Elfwén to maintain the career that she loves, while keeping her children home until they were about three. The parental leave made all the difference.

Parents can continue to work reduced hours until their children reach the age of eight. This option was chosen by a couple I know, both schoolteachers. The mother took one day a week off, the father one day, and they staggered their hours on remaining days, so that their children spent less time in child care. Both parents were able to maintain professional lives while sharing the responsibility for raising their children.

Choices in Child Care

When it was time for the Elfwéns to choose a preschool for Simon, they selected a Waldorf school with low student-teacher ratios and organic vegetarian meals. There are also traditional preschools, Montessori schools, cooperative schools, Christian schools, and even day-care centers that focus on gender equality. Families pay the county rather than the childcare center, and the amount depends on each family's household income. This means that, with few exceptions, parents can send their child to any childcare center without consideration to finances. So a single mother studying at university might pay $30.00 a month for her child to attend a school, while a family with three children and a household income of $40,000 would pay around $240 a month to have their three children in the same school. As of 2002, there will be a cap of $115 a month for the first child, ramping down according to income.

Of course, things are not perfect. It can be difficult to find a spot in the middle of the year, so it's necessary to plan ahead. The school we chose for my four year old did not suit him, so we kept him home while waiting for a place in a new school. In looking at the options, however, we were impressed with the low student-teacher ratios at all the preschools we visited, and the consistently high quality of care.

Separate Taxation and Child Allowances

A few other odds and ends round out the package. People are taxed individually in Sweden, so a woman's income won't fall into a high tax bracket just because the household income is high. In addition, cash payments take the place of tax deductions for children. Each month, about $95.00 per child is deposited into the account of every family with a child, from the unemployed to the royal family. Families with more than two children receive a small bonus, so for my three children, we get a cash payment of $300 a month. Many families turn the amount over to their children when they reach the age of 15 so they can learn to handle a checking account and manage their clothing and leisure purchases.

The Employer's Role

In Sweden, creating balance between work and family life is not left solely to the government and individual families. Section five of the Swedish Equal Opportunity Act reads,

"An employer shall facilitate the combination of gainful employment and parenthood with respect to both female and male employees." Employers, in other words, are legally obligated to help employees combine parenthood and work. Employees who believe that an employer has directly violated this principle can take their case to the office of the Equal Opportunity Ombudsman (JämO).

Claes Lundkvist filed one of the eight cases registered with JämO last year regarding parenthood and employment. A broadcast journalist for Swedish Radio, Lundkvist generally took his children to daycare each morning, and his wife, a physiotherapist with her own business, picked them up at the end of the day. But a new contract required Lundkvist to transfer to a branch more than an hour away. And his working hours were inflexible. "My wife was very stressed taking all the responsibility," Lundkvist says. "It didn't work." After he read JämO's web page, he decided to pursue the issue.

Fathers' involvement as parents should be encouraged, according to JämO: "Employers may have an old-fashioned view of parenthood, or think that 'your wife can take care of that,' when the husband wants to be free to care for sick children or asks for more flexible working hours in order to combine work and family."[2] Changing the attitude of such employers is one of JämO's goals. JämO accepted Lundkvist's case, recognizing that without some adjustment in his new situation, his ability to combine work and family would be seriously impaired. The case initially met with resistance from Lundkvist's employers, and as he was a contract worker, JämO's power was limited. Lundkvist has since, however, negotiated a solution that offers some flexibility.

With each case filed, the resulting publicity strengthens public debate about men's rights and responsibilities as fathers. "It's hard to change gender roles," says Tommy Ferrarini, a PhD student at the Institute of Social Research in Stockholm who is currently doing research on family policy. But Ferrarini believes measures such as parental leave time allotted for the father shift social expectations. "It puts pressure on the employers when something becomes a right. It's all very individualized &[This means] increased individual autonomy for the mother, the father, and the children. You give both parents the possibility of self-fulfillment."

What Family Policy Means for Women

Swedish mothers don't think they're doing it all, and they don't think the system is perfect. Some women have jobs that are more flexible than others; some are happier with their child care than others. While men are doing a larger share of the housework than in the past, couples still fight about who does the laundry. You'd be hard pressed to find a Swedish mom who would call herself a superwoman. Observing the situation, however, I see women who come pretty close to fulfilling the American "superwoman" myth. The vast majority of women have careers. With the help of their partners, they juggle children and work and birthday parties and still manage to make it to aerobics every week.

In the US, in contrast, the superwoman myth operates in a male-dominated corporate culture, and society views accepting help as a weakness. If you are given a day off, you should be grateful. If your husband takes two unpaid weeks at the birth of a child, he should be grateful. If his company calls after a week and asks him to return early (as my husband's company did), you should apologize when you say no, and then thank them for understanding.

In Sweden, you can certainly say "thank you" if you like, but no one has done you any favors. Among CEOs and entrepreneurs, you may see a more male-dominated culture, but even there, people are still likely to take a good portion of the five to eight weeks vacation they receive annually.

Swedish women face many of the same problems as their American counterparts. Career advancement slows while children are young. Juggling everything can be challenging. But women in Sweden don't have to do it alone. Families are supported by society, both financially and culturally. This means that women also give back to society, and not just in tax dollars—though even there, their contribution is substantial. Having women in the workplace changes the culture. Today, 43 percent of representatives in the Swedish Parliament and half of all State Ministers are women. In the long run, that will have an effect on the tone of the government and the laws that are passed.

Children Are People, Too

Children in Sweden are not considered merely a lifestyle choice. They are members of society in their own right. Flexibility and support for families means that parents are better able to meet the needs of their children, something the children deserve. This approach offers myriad benefits to children, both emotionally and physically. Recent studies have suggested that "parental leave has favorable and possibly cost-effective impacts on pediatric health."[3] The same studies also indicate that with longer parental leaves, child and infant mortality rates go down.[4]

Respect for children is an important aspect of Swedish culture. Sweden has a Children's Ombudsman who represents children and young people in public debates, the ultimate goal being that young people can make their voices heard and gain respect for their views. In line with this, corporal punishment of any kind is illegal. Though controversial when first proposed, a Parliamentary Minister put the issue into context. "In a free democracy like our own, we use words as arguments, not blows & If we can't convince our children with words, we will never convince them with violence."[5]

Children in Sweden are people, not property. Family policy is very much about creating a better situation for men and women who choose to have families, but at its core, family policy is all about children. A society that cherishes and respects children must make it possible for every child to be raised with certain minimal standards. Ensuring healthcare coverage, making sure that children have enough to eat, and keeping children free of the risks that inevitably accompany poverty are a few modest goals. In Sweden, every child is entitled to be home with his or her parents for the first year of life. That's the minimum standard the society has chosen.

What that means is that any child you see on the street had access to her parents for the most important time in her development, and has access to free, high-quality medical and dental care. You know that she has enough food to eat, and that she likely attends a well-run preschool. That child has advocates in government and the support of society. Who will that child become? Right now it doesn't matter. The bottom line is that she lives in a society that values her just the way she is.

Notes

1. Kristina Hultman, "A Step Away from a Childless Society?" New Life: A Gender Equality Magazine for New Parents (Stockholm: Swedish Government Division for Gender Equality, 2001): 10.
2. "What is JämO?," a brochure published by the Equal Opportunity Ombudsman's office; see www.jamombud.se [1].
3. C. J. Ruhm, "Parental Leave and Child Health," NBER Working Paper No. W6554 (Cambridge, MA: National Bureau of Economic Research, 1998): 27.
4. Sheila Kamerman, "Parental Leave Policies: An Essential Ingredient in Early Childhood Education and Care Policies," Social Policy Report 14, no. 2 (2000): 10.
5. Louise Sylwander, "The Swedish Corporal Punishment Ban-More than Twenty Years of Experience," Barnombudsmannen website, www.bo.se [2] (choose the British flag for English).

CPSIA information can be obtained at www.ICGtesting.com
Printed in the USA
LVOW03s0330211114

414778LV00004B/5/P